Women & Social Change in America

D1296420

Women & Social Change in America

JOAN D. MANDLE

THE PENNSYLVANIA STATE UNIVERSITY
DELAWARE COUNTY CAMPUS

PRINCETON BOOK COMPANY, Publishers
Princeton, New Jersey

Copyright © 1979 by Princeton Book Company, Publishers
Library of Congress Catalog Card Number 78-84301
ISBN 0-916622-11-8
Printed in the United States of America

Design by AHIA
Typesetting by Backes Graphics

For J. and J.

Preface

My motivation for writing this book lies in my commitment to the goal of women's liberation. Particularly important to me is the role of the women's movement in fostering the development of human freedom and potential. I have been involved in movements for social change since the early 1960s, and I believe that such struggles are essential for the achievement of a just and truly democratic American society. This book examines the process of social change and clarifies the role of the women's movement in the recent changes in women's and men's lives.

Women's changing position in American society has become the focus of discussion for scholars from many disciplines, and this volume contributes to the dialogue by analyzing the changes that have occurred since 1960. Rather than merely chronicling these changes, however, I hope to use the example of women's lives to cast light on the more general issue of social change. My intention is twofold: to illuminate the sources and consequences of the changes that women have experienced in recent years, and, in so doing, to contribute to an understanding of how society alters over time.

I begin by exploring theoretical issues relevant to the general problem of social change; these issues in turn will be the prism through which I examine women's position in society and the changes it has experienced. Following a brief survey of the status and roles of women in American society prior to 1960, I investigate the changes in women's involvement in society—in their roles as daughters, wives, mothers, workers, homemakers, and political actors—that have occurred since 1960. Specifically, I try to determine how such basic aspects of women's social life as their personality development, their position in the economy, and their roles in the family have changed, and what the sources, interrelations, and future implications of these changes are. Finally, I give special attention to the emergence of the women's movement in the mid-1960s, tracing its sources, its new ideology, and its role in reinforcing change in all aspects of women's lives.

Many friends and colleagues contributed support, criticism, and suggestions at various stages of the writing. Especially helpful were Jessie Bernard, Stephen Cimbala, Joan Huber, Carole Joffe, Dorothy Kurz, Jay Mandle, and Sandra Rigby. My colleagues at the Delaware County Campus of The Pennsylvania State University offered intellectual support, and the University generously provided a Phase III grant, which facilitated the completion of this volume.

Contents

Tables

Figures

Women & Social Change in America

Chapter 1
The Theoretical Framework

PHILOSOPHY AND SOCIAL CHANGE

Sociologists' concern with the process of social change and the forces that promote or retard change is neither new nor unique to their discipline. Sociology itself is a relatively modern discipline, whose origins are usually traced to the work of the early nineteenth-century French scholar Auguste Comte.[1] But sociologists' focus on the process of change has its roots in the concerns of philosophers and social thinkers of earlier centuries. The history of social thought reveals an interest in change among the earliest philosophers, who puzzled over what constitutes reality and whether that reality is characterized by change or stability.

Concern with social change is as old as concern with society itself. One of the earliest pre-Platonic philosophers, Heraclitus (500 B.C.), built a philosophic system around the argument that the stuff of reality is fire, which is characterized by constant flux and universal change. "Nothing ever is; everything is becoming," he wrote, signifying that the nature of the world is constant change and that stability is merely illusion.[2] Nevertheless, the belief in impermanence and change was unusual among the early philosophers. Rather, as Bertrand Russell argues, "the search for something permanent is perhaps one of the deepest of the instincts leading to philosophy."[3] The ideas of the philosopher Parmenides (450 B.C.), for example, are more typical of this search. In contrast to Heraclitus, he focused on the unity and permanence of all reality, arguing that everything that exists has always existed and will continue to exist infinitely—"nothing ever changes."[4] In different ways, both Plato and Aristotle also concerned themselves with denying the existence of change, arguing instead that reality is eternal and timeless. According to Harry Elmer Barnes's discussion of the roots of sociological thought, both Plato and Aristotle reflected "the notion that social stability is the end most to be sought in the institutions of society."[5]   Plato, for example, wrote that "the best state will be one which most nearly copies the heavenly model by having a minimum of change and a maximum of static perfection."[6]

Modern philosophers have also grappled with the issues of change and stability, although the growth of such interests as linguistic analysis and the rise of scientific knowledge have displaced them as central concerns. Nonetheless, modern philosophers, including Spinoza and Hegel reiterated in new forms the old assertion that reality is stable and permanent.[7] Spinoza's assertion that God provides unity and stability to the world and Hegel's belief in "Absolute Idea" as a unitary reality reflect their emphases on permanence. Belief in stability and permanence, however, was increasingly challenged in the nineteenth century by new theories that stressed change, reform, conflict, and even revolution. The famous theories of evolutionary change popularized by Charles Darwin's discoveries constituted important sources for newly developing social theory and for an emerging perspective that emphasized the changing nature of reality.[8] Finally, the increasing number and popularity of utopian schemes for the reorganization and reform of society implied not only the possibility but also the desirability of change.[9]

Thus, this debate over change and the nature of reality—the attempt to understand and explain whether reality is changing or permanent— is a thread that binds social thinkers in diverse societies and times. Although, as suggested above, the question of the existence of change is an important preoccupation of modern social thinkers, a second significant area of disagreement should be noted. This second debate centers on the question of whether reality, in its essence, is a physical substance or whether it is an idea or attitude of the mind. When applied to the issue of change this ongoing debate between empiricists such as John Locke or David Hume and idealists such as René Descartes, Immanuel Kant, or Hegel raises the important question, simply put, of what it is that changes—physical reality or ideas in our minds?[10]

The idealists, among whom the most important is Descartes (1596- 1650), emphasized in a variety of ways the importance of the mind as that which is real. Descartes' famous formulation, "Cogito ergo sum" ("I think therefore I am"), as well as Kant's assertion that mind alone really exists, attempt to establish that the world exists only in, and is not real outside of, our ideas about it.[11] The mind, then, in its consciousness and ideas creates reality, and reality has no existence outside of that process. The empiricists, on the other hand, argue that reality has its existence in material objects and substances, which exist whether or not we think about them. Locke's famous assertion, for example, that the mind is a tabula rasa, an empty slate that is filled and formed by experiences in the material world, emphasizes the reality of material substance apart from our thinking about it.[12] In fact, for Locke the condition of our being able to think at all is the experience with physical reality; the mind exists only because material substance has reality independent of our ideas of it. This debate, then, is a central feature of modern philosophy and reflects the concern of philosophers not only with the stable or changing nature of reality, but also, assuming that change exists, with the question of whether it is characterized by changes in ideas or by changes in material factors.

SOCIOLOGICAL THEORIES OF CHANGE

Even such a cursory examination of the history of social thought as the above reveals philosophers' concerns with both the existence and nature of change. These concerns became the central focuses for much of sociological theory after its separation from philosophy. Again our discussion can only hope to summarize briefly some of the major trends in sociological theory in the areas that concern us. But even with these limits, the parallels to earlier philosophic thought are apparent, for the history of sociological thought includes as a central component a debate between those sociologists who emphasize the stability of society and those who focus on the questions of conflict and change.[13] Sociologists such as Comte, Emile Durkheim, and, most important for modern American sociology, Talcott Parsons, can be broadly characterized as emphasizing the importance of order, cohesion, and stability in society.[14] The theoretical work of these scholars seeks to account for the stability of society and to identify the factors that are crucial for its cohesion. Their work either largely neglects the issue of change and the existence of conflict or points to the dire consequences of change.[15] In contrast, the work of such social theorists such as Karl Marx, Max Weber, and Herbert Spencer emphasizes the importance and ubiquity of social change. Although all of these theorists are interested primarily in understanding and explaining conflict and social change, they differ greatly in their view of how change occurs. Spencer, for example, stresses evolution and Social Darwinism, while Marx focuses on revolutionary change. What is common to them, however, is their belief that reality is most accurately understood by explaining its changing nature and the forces that account for that change.[16]

A second area of debate among social theorists encompasses, in a slightly different form, the age-old philosophic problem of whether ideas and attitudes are the most important components and/or sources of change (an idealist position) or whether physical or material factors such as institutions and organizations are most important (an empirical or materialist position).[17] The greatest sociological contributions to the idealist position have been made by Weber, and to a lesser extent by Parsons and Neil Smelser, who argue that change involves and is primarily produced by changes in the ideas people have of themselves and their world. Weber, for example, in his classic work, *The Protestant Ethic and the Spirit of Capitalism*, argues that a new set of ideas, norms, and values—the Protestant ethic—existed prior to and was the major source of the physical and economic changes embodied in the Industrial Revolution and the rise of capitalism.[18] It is society's norms and values, ideas of right and wrong, proper and improper behavior that are the major components and sources of social change.[19]

In contrast, Marx, theoreticians working in the Marxist tradition, and, to a lesser extent, recent American sociologists such as William Ogburn have made major contributions to the other side of the debate, emphasizing the importance of structural or material factors in social change.[20] They argue that change is produced by and significantly composed of structural changes in the way a society is organized and in the behavioral patterns generated by that institutional organization. Ogburn's work, for example, stresses the importance of technological advances, which generate changes in the economic organization and social institutions of society. Marx himself argued that the rise of capitalism was generated primarily by alterations in the way goods and services were produced and by the conflict between classes in society that were catalyzed by those changes. Unlike Weber, Marx suggests that the norms and values consistent with capitalism did not exist prior to the structural changes in economic institutions that ultimately resulted in the construction of a new capitalist mode of production. Because of their role in social change, the organization of society, and especially the structure of its economic institutions, assume particular importance in the work of these scholars.

The differing views of the social thinkers we have examined—the analysts of change and those of stability, the materialists as well as the idealists—share a common outlook and system of analysis that treats the social system, its institutions and culture, as a whole, that is, on the "macro" level. In the history of social thought, however, another area of divergence emerged with the development of social analysis based on concern for the behavior, motivation, and personality of individual members of the society. These concerns tended to refocus emphasis away from a macro analysis of the social system. Proponents of this alternative model of analysis, the "micro" theorists, argue that only by understanding the individual dimension can one fully comprehend the sources and effects of social change or the resistance to its demands. The emergence of theories of social psychology, and in particular the seminal work of Sigmund Freud, shifted the focus of much social analysis to concern with the individual personality, its sources, shape, and effects.

These three theoretical relationships—materialism versus idealism, change versus stability, and societal (macro) as opposed to individual (micro) focuses of analysis—are the threads that interconnect discussions of all major social problems. For each problem addressed, these dialectical relationships will differ in degree of emphasis. Nonetheless, in discussing any serious social problem, consideration of these three fundamental concerns is useful. Thus, in attempting to understand the changing position of women in American society, I shall investigate the relative importance of ideological as opposed to institutional factors in causing change, the opposition between the dynamic of change and the forces of stability, and the competing claims of micro and macro levels of analysis in understanding women's position in American society.

EARLY FEMINIST WRITINGS ON WOMEN

Any overview of the history of social thought on the subject of women and social change runs into difficulty because few of the theorists mentioned above ever discussed women in their work. Moreover scholars who have seriously considered the problem of women's position in society typically have neglected broader issues of the nature of reality and social change.[21] Nevertheless, a brief examination of the most important of the early contributions to the thinking about women and society will inform our later discussion of modern American women.[22]

The first modern contribution to an analysis of the position of women is Mary Wollstonecraft's *A Vindication of the Rights of Women*, published in London in 1790, in which she called for equality of education for men and women. However the most famous and influential of the early writings on women is John Stuart Mill's *The Subjection of Women*.[23] Published in 1869, this call for the equality of the sexes offers insights into the sources and forms of women's subjection in the mid-nineteenth century. Mill rejected the idea that women are biologically determined to be inferior to men and argued that both men and women must unite to change the laws and customs that he believed to be the major sources of inequality. His plea for equality was made on the grounds of rationality and morality, for as Alice Rossi notes:

> His stand throughout the essay poses an implicit question: what "reasonable" man or woman could fail to abandon a narrow view of women's potential, who could resist encouraging women to cultivate a wider sphere of options and skills, once they had finished reading his logical analysis of the position of women?[24]

However logical the analysis or impassioned the plea for a new morality of justice and equality between the sexes, Mill's work nevertheless lacks a framework couched in terms of a broad theoretical understanding of the processes of social change and the factors important in that process.

The next major contribution to a discussion of women's position in society, and the only early contribution by an American woman, is Charlotte Perkins Gilman's *Women and Economics,* written in 1898.[25] Although Gilman far more than Mill was concerned with broader issues of social change, her belief in the inevitability of progress through the process of evolution (that is, Social Darwinism) strikes the modern reader as naive and simplistic. Gilman asserts that in the evolution of the human species, a period of subjection of women was necessary for the social development of humanity, that this period has passed, and that increase in equality between the sexes is therefore inevitable. Despite her failure to provide any substantive evidence to support her claim, Gilman's work as a whole provides many important insights into the nature of female inequality. She suggests that the economic dependence of women on men is an important issue in understanding women's inferiority, and she provides a strikingly sophisticated discussion of the socialization process that produces adult females who conform to expectations of inferiority. Nonetheless, her overall contribution is compromised by the lack of a rigorous analysis of the process of social change as applied to the position of women in society.

Much of the writing on women in the twentieth century takes the form not of scholarly analysis but rather of polemic arguments focused on the struggle for voting rights for women. Although the men and women who produced pamphlets, newspapers, and speeches in favor of female suffrage and equality were committed to social change and aware of their involvement in the process, their practical attempts toward stimulating change seem to have precluded the time or desire to reflect on the topic on a more abstract level.[26] Rossi's collection of feminist writings provides a sampling of these contributions, but one searches in vain for material related to broad theoretical issues of women and social change. Rossi herself notes the lack of such contributions, arguing that only the works of Mill, Gilman, and Simone de Beauvoir begin to fill that gap by providing "the rare quality of rigorous intellectual analysis combined with passionate commitment to the goal of sex equality."[27]

Thus we are confronted with a paradox. In the history of social thought, those whose theoretical concerns centered on social change for the most part neglected the position of women, while writers whose attention has been turned to the position of women lacked a sophisticated perspective on the process of social change in general.

WOMEN AND SOCIAL CHANGE

The principal hypothesis of this book is that women's lives have been profoundly affected by the long-term process of economic development. I argue that major technological change in American society has produced changes in women's lives on the macro level—in terms of women's role in the economy and their level of political participation, for example—and also on the micro level—in terms of personality development and the nature of family relationships. Moreover, the process of economic growth and expansion in American society is the taproot of the modern women's liberation movement.

To assign centrality to the process of economic development implies giving primary importance to material as opposed to ideological change. While this may be true, it is important to note that as eminent a student of the development experience as Simon Kuznets has emphasized the importance of ideological change in the long-term process of development.[28] Thus changes in social ideas and attitudes will be explored along with changes in society's institutional structure. Similarly, although economic development is profoundly a macro phenomenon, the pressures that result are experienced, and must be analyzed, on the individual, micro, level as well. Finally, by pointing to development as central, we focus attention on change rather than on social forces of stability. Yet it is essential to examine the tendencies in society that impede and deflect the forces of change that are set in motion by the process of development. Thus, while positing long-term economic development as the predominant source of changes in women's lives examined in this book, I must also deal with all of the dimensions of the three basic theoretical issues explored above.

My discussion of the origins of the women's movement in the mid-1960s and its development in the following decade and a half requires a similar examination. I hypothesize that the origins of the movement can be found in both the micro and macro changes that have occurred in women's personality and in their economic, social, and family roles and that are associated with long-term economic development. With its emergence, however, the women's movement became a force for change in its own right as it developed a vision of changes in all aspects of women's lives. This vision—which we can perhaps define as an embryonic ideological hegemony—embraced new ideas concerning women on both the individual and societal levels and emphasized the importance of alternative ideas and norms as well as material structures in seeking women's "liberation." While the development and impact of the women's movement are clearly phenomena characterized by change, a full understanding of this social movement requires an examination of tendencies toward stability as well. The unwillingness of some women to support the movement, the hostility with which its emergence was greeted by certain sectors of society, and its own failure to fully realize its goals bespeak the importance of understanding the forces of stability and resistance to change as social factors affecting women's position.

The presence of change and stability, material and ideological influences, and social and individual considerations thus must be recognized, even as I argue that the causal process studied here originated in economic development. Indeed, a full formulation of the flow of causality suggested in this study would be: long-term economic development triggered changes in women's personality development and in their social, economic, and family roles; these changes in turn influenced the development of a new social movement; the movement's pressure for social change and its alternative ideology encompasses and further affects all aspects of women's lives in American society.

In constructing this theoretical perspective, I have been influenced by, and in the following chapters shall explicitly employ, the diverse contributions of many scholars, including Weber, Erik Erikson, and de Beauvoir. However, the theoretical models of Karl Marx and Sigmund Freud dominate my thinking on the subject of women and social change—and thus the perspective embodied in this book. I turn now to brief introductory discussions of the way in which the tools contained in the theories of Marx and Freud can be applied to an understanding of the position of modern American women and the phenomenon of social change.

Marxist Theory

Karl Marx, (1818-1883) never addressed himself in depth to the oppression of women or to their role in social change. Rather, his greatest contribution was a macro theoretical model of social change and his development of a variety of tools for the analysis of social change.[29] He emphasized the importance of the organizational structure of society and particularly of its economic institutions for an analysis of society and for an assessment of the possible extent and direction of social changes. In terms of the three theoretical problems discussed earlier, the thrust of Marx's work clearly falls on the side of macro rather than micro analysis, emphasizes the centrality of material rather than normative changes, and reflects a belief in the ubiquity of change.

Although women's position in society is not a major theme of Marx's writings, he was not totally insensitive to this issue. In his early writings on the development of human potential he argued that human development could not be complete as long as inequality existed between men and women. In his *Economic and Philosophic Manuscript* he stated that

> the relation of man to woman is the most natural relation of human
> being to human being. It therefore reveals the extent to which man's
> natural behavior has become human. . . . From this relationship one can
> therefore judge man's whole level of development.[30]

Society's progress toward full humanity could then be judged by the development of egalitarian relationships between men and women. In his later work, in which his focus shifted to an analysis of class relations in a capitalist society, Marx expressed concern for the exploitation of women workers. In one section of *Capital* he discusses the death of a twenty-year-old woman milliner who "had worked without intermission for twenty-six and a half hours with sixty other girls, thirty in one room that only afforded one-third of the cubic feet of air required for them."[31] And in the most famous of his works, *The Communist Manifesto,* he denounces the exploitation of women in the capitalist family, where they are regarded as "a mere instrument of production."[32] Finally, in *The Origins of the Family, Private Property and the State,* Marx's long-time collaborator, Frederick Engels, discussed at length women's position in society and proposed a scheme for the emancipation of women.[33]

Despite these direct concerns with women, Marx's contribution to an understanding of women and social change is best examined in terms of his broader model of social organization and social change. Rather than his own writings on women, it is his methods and model, as applied to women primarily by contemporary Marxist scholars, that I shall examine here and use in analyzing the changing position of women in American society.

As noted above, Marxist theory focuses on the structure and organization of social institutions, and on the productive or economic system in particular, as an important influence on a social group's position in society. The way in which societies organize themselves to produce and distribute goods is the key to understanding other aspects of social behavior and existence. Thus in order to understand the position of women in society, Marxists have traditionally begun with an examination of their place in the productive process. In an industrialized, capitalist society—a society with a machine technology, private ownership of the means of production, and a labor force free to enter into and out of contractual relationships with employers—the most striking feature of women's economic position is their isolation in home and family roles that historically have excluded them from paid work. This exclusion from the labor force and the process of production in a capitalist society means that women lack direct access to income, power, prestige, and status in the society, and it is thus a major cause for their inferior position in society.[34] Women's claim to income, and to the power and status that accompany it in a capitalist society, remains indirect, that is, through their dependence upon and attachment to males, whether fathers or husbands.[35]

A second source of oppression, closely related to the above, is found in the work performed in the home by women in their roles as wives and mothers. Although such work is economically valuable,[36] society neither regards it as "productive" activity nor considers it as "real work" for which women should be rewarded with income, status, or power.[37] Such "products" as clean laundry, regular meals, well-cared-for children, and pleasant homes are all the results of women's labor, but the "value" of this labor is not recognized in direct wages. Rather, women as a group must depend on what their husbands decide to give them.

A source of general oppression noted by Marxists is rooted in the class position of the majority of both men and women in a capitalist society. According to Marx, capitalist societies can be analytically divided into two major classes, the capitalists and the proletariat. Capitalists are the minority who own and control the property and wealth of society, while the bulk of the population, the proletariat or working class, obtains most of its income through wages or salaries paid for actual labor.[38] Although the proletariat produce the wealth of the society, they are exploited by the capitalists, who, through ownership of the means of production, reap the benefits of workers' labor through profits. Thus, both male and female members of the proletariat are exploited by capitalism and are in an inferior position with regard to income, power, and prestige compared to the small group of capitalists which owns and controls society's wealth.[39] In addition, although all members of the proletariat are paid wages lower than the value of what they produce, when women do engage in labor for wages—"real work"—they are often further exploited as a sex by their concentration in sex-segregated occupations and by the denial of access to more prestigious and better paying jobs.

Thus in Marxist theory the sources of women's oppression in society are closely linked to their role in the productive process. That is, within capitalist societies women are oppressed and exploited through their exclusion from paid work, through their unpaid contribution to production in their roles as wives and mothers, and finally, through their special exploitation when they are permitted to engage in wage labor. Although Marxist theory generally devotes less attention to noneconomic institutions, there is the assumption that exploitation and oppression are also generated by other institutions within a capitalist society, such as schools, religious and political institutions, and even the family. Finally, since in Marxian theory the ideological or cultural sphere is influenced by the structure of production, it is assumed that the oppression characteristic of the productive institutions will be reflected in the ideology of the society. Women's inferior position, much like that of the proletariat as a whole, can be expected to be reflected in and reinforced by the noneconomic institutions of society as well as by its cultural or ideological sphere.

Marxist theory not only provides tools that are useful in explaining the system of stratification in society, but it also contains insights into the dynamics of social change. Since from a Marxist perspective the sources of women's oppression are multiple, social changes to liberate women must themselves be complex. One source of oppression would be eliminated by ending women's exclusion from the labor force and ensuring their equality with men in economic institutions.[40] A second source of exploitation could be abolished by reducing or eliminating the special responsibilities of women for unpaid household labor and home-related activities.[41] Finally, a Marxist theory of social change suggests that the oppression shared by male and female members of the proletariat could be eliminated by the liquidation of private ownership and control of the productive economic institutions of society. Thus the establishment of socialism and the elimination of capitalism would be the third requirement for eliminating the oppression of women in American society.

Because change is the central focus of Marx's analysis, his work does not provide a detailed statement of the forces of stability in society. However, in his discussion of the history of class conflict he suggests that powerful groups will resist the decline or overthrow of their power on the part of less powerful or oppressed social groups. In the case of women, resistance to change might be predicted from groups of individuals—men or women—whose position is threatened by the increased status, equality, or power of women. Marxist theory of course stresses the importance of political movements that may serve as catalysts for social change.[42] The development of group solidarity and self-consciousness is viewed as necessary for the waging of political struggle. Obstacles to the creation of such solidarity are many, however. In the case of the development of a social movement dedicated to changing women's position, these might include the fear of society's rejection or ridicule, the threat of losing the security and support of home and family life, or the tendency of women to view one another as competitors rather than as members of a collective group. In sum, Marxist insights into the structural sources of oppression, the dynamics of change embodied in the overall social organization of society, and the role of social and political movements' struggles will be important tools for my analysis of women and social change.

Freudian Theory

In some ways Freud's work contrasts sharply with that of Marx. While Marx analyzed the macro organization and dynamics of society, Freud (1856-1939) concentrated on the development of the individual personality and its interaction with the social environment. The emphasis that Marx placed on material forces is reflected somewhat in Freud's focus on innate instincts and drives, but the latter ascribed great influence to the culture and idea system of society, which shapes the process of socialization and the content of repression. Finally, Freud believed, as did Marx, in the potential for social and personality change. However he more explicitly elucidated the conservative forces inherent in the human psyche and was significantly more pessimistic about the nature of change and the possibility of liberation.

My choice of Freudian theory as part of an overall framework in a book concerned with women may strike some as peculiar, particularly if they are familiar with his reputation as a scholar whose theories were used to justify and often develop female inferiority, submissiveness, and passive acceptance of the feminine roles of wife and mother.[43] Freud himself seems to have admitted a negative attitude toward women in his essay on femininity, which he closes with, "That is all I have to say to you about femininity. It is certainly incomplete and fragmentary and does not always sound friendly."[44] Recently, however, Juliet Mitchell and other feminist scholars have argued that Freud's general insights into human personality development and psyche are useful, perhaps even essential, to an understanding of women today. Thus many of Freud's specific statements on women are less important here than is his overall model of psychic development and change within the intellectual framework of psychoanalysis. As was true for Marx, it is the general theory of the nature of human reality and social change with which I am largely concerned. It is Freud's model, and its applications to women, as developed by modern Freudians, that I shall elucidate here and use in the discussion of women and social change.

One of Freud's most crucial insights is that one must examine early childhood experiences in order to understand adult personality development and behavior.[45] The core experiences that mold the adult personality occur at relatively young ages and are primarily influenced through the child's interaction with its adult socializers—namely its parents. For Freud, the development of that personality rests on the early repression of certain desires, needs, and goals of the child and their location in the unconscious, a layer of our psyche of which we are not aware but which nonetheless influences our behavior and personality for the rest of our lives.

Freud's theory of psychic development postulates the universal desire among humans for gratification of instinctual desires.[46] These desires, which Freud collectively refers to as the id, are controlled during the process of early childhood development and socialization. At this time the id is partly repressed and partly channeled and redirected to culturally and socially acceptable goals. During this process, children pass through a series of conflicts emanating from the contradiction between the pleasure-seeking id on the one hand, and the society's acceptable behavioral patterns and values on the other. These conflicts, of course, take a variety of forms, depending on the stage of sexuality that the child has reached.

From their earliest years, children are involved in conflicts generated by their society through their parents' repressing and/or channeling of their most basic desires. As children develop, however, they are increasingly expected to control their own desires by mechanisms developed within their psyches. The successful development of the ego and superego, according to Freudian theory, make such self-control possible as children learn what the society considers to be acceptable outlets for sexual energy and acceptable ways of obtaining pleasure and gratification. By internalizing these cultural precepts so that they become part of his or her own personality, each child is able to repress his or her id and to channel or sublimate that energy toward culturally acceptable ends. This sublimation, according to Freud, is the fount of creative energy, which helps to build and advance civilization. On the other hand, failure to successfully resolve developmental conflicts can lead to neurotic behavior in adults or more severe forms of mental illness.

In classical Freudian theory, one of the most important and influential points of crisis and conflict in this developmental pattern occurs at about the age of five and is referred to as the Oedipal conflict. Successful resolution of this conflict enables boys to repress their id desires for their mothers and to sublimate and transfer these desires to hard work and to the women whom the society and parents view as acceptable sexual and marital partners. The primary mechanism of this process is the fear of castration, which leads the boy to develop a strong superego by internalizing parental norms of acceptable behavior. It is the superego in turn, that gives him the ability to sublimate and repress even more effectively his socially unacceptable id desires. Thus the fear of castration is the crucial mechanism in the development of the male ability to internalize the culture, repress the id, sublimate unacceptable desires, and successfully resolve the most difficult of all psychic crises.[47]

But what of the development of the female psyche? Freud argues that the development of girls is "more difficult and more complicated" than that of boys.[48] According to Freud, because females do not possess penises and therefore do not fear castration, women's adult personality is different from that which men develop. On the one hand, according to Freud, women's less developed superegos do not allow them as much capacity for sublimation as men have. On the other hand, compared with men, they are not as able to become independent by transferring their ties from their parents to other goals and individuals.[49] In addition, the lack of a penis, according to Freud, leaves women with great anxiety and deep feelings of envy and inferiority. Freud argues however, that these factors ensure the development of the "normal" adult female personality characterized by passivity, masochism, and dependence. In addition, women's frustrated desire for a penis, the symbol of male superiority, is resolved by their achievement of motherhood and by the symbolic substitution of a baby for the desired penis.[50]

Of course, Freud's theories and observations have been revised, challenged, and gleaned for their most useful insights by other scholars. Most recently, scholars have reassessed and applied Freudian theory to the position of modern women and to theories of change in women's role in society. Juliet Mitchell's *Psychoanalysis and Feminism* is especially significant in that regard. She argues that Freud's characterization of women with respect to their passivity, masochism, lack of contribution to cultural development, penis envy, and inferiority to men are better explained as reactions not to the anatomical but rather to the social inferiority of women in society. As Eli Zaretsky succinctly put it in a review of Mitchell's book, "What the little girl learns is not the superiority of the penis, but the inferiority of women."[51] Freud's model of psychic development makes sense when viewed as the process

that produces culturally defined femininity by means of repression. A
girl, if she is "normal," internalizes a culture that inculcates her inferiority and enforces the development of a passive, submissive, narcissistic feminine role. The repression of characteristics considered unfeminine is thus rooted not in women's physiology, but in the social
and cultural structure of society. Women's oppression, according to
this revision of Freudian theory, is rooted in the early childhood interaction with male and female parents in the family, and in the repression
of drives, goals, desires, abilities, and needs not consistent with the
culture's idea of the "proper" feminine personality.

Freud's theoretical work also provides insights into social sources of
change and stability applicable to the investigation of women's position. Since, according to Freud, the major source of oppression lies
in personality, so too the locus of change must be in the development
of the psyche and personality in childhood. One step in the elimination
of the oppression of women would be to change the cultural ideas of
femininity, thus altering the personality characteristics repressed and
encouraged in female children. Second, changes in the structure of
child-rearing and particularly in the intense dependence upon and relationships between mothers and children of both sexes would presumably make the Oedipus complex less difficult to resolve.[52] According to Freudian theory then, changes in cultural norms, in early childhood socialization experiences, and also in the nature of interaction
with parents are essential in the effort to overcome the deep-seated
psychological roots of female inferiority and male superiority.[53]

Freud's analysis, however, is fundamentally pessimistic about the
ease with which change can be accomplished. His major work of social
analysis, *Civilization and Its Discontents,* is pervaded with the senti-
ment that human beings can do little about the major sources of what
he refers to as their "unhappiness."[54] Furthermore, his insistence on
the formative nature of early childhood experiences implies that major
alterations in that basic personality in adulthood are both difficult and
painful. Change for adults is not altogether ruled out in the Freudian
model, however, because of the possibility of understanding the unconscious memories of repressed drives through psychoanalysis. In sum,
Freudian analysis of the micro process of individual personality development, his emphasis on the importance of cultural ideas in shaping instinctual drives, and his discussion of the possibilities and problems for
change will inform my subsequent analysis of women and social change.

CONCLUSION

In this chapter we have briefly explored several issues relating to social change that have perplexed scholars from earliest times to the present day, including the philosophical questions of whether reality is mind or matter and whether it is static or constantly changing. More recently, social theory has developed through debates between those who emphasize the importance of change and those who give preeminence to order and stability, between those who believe that the material aspects of society are primarily responsible for social change and those who view attitudes, norms, or consciousness as the prime movers, and between those who advocate macro analysis and those who emphasize micro analysis. Turning to early feminist writing, we found that the most important contributions to the subject generally failed to provide useful insights into these theoretical questions. While the theories of Marx and Freud will serve as the models for my discussion of women and social change in the following chapters, they will do so in the context of the three philosophic problems that I have outlined above.

NOTES

1. Don Martindale, *The Nature and Types of Sociological Theory* (Boston: Houghton Mifflin, 1960), pp. 16-17.
2. Bertrand Russell, *A History of Western Philosophy* (New York: Simon & Schuster, 1945), p. 45; see also Martindale, *Sociological Theory*, pp. 147-148.
3. Russell, *Western Philosophy*, p. 45.
4. *Ibid.*, p. 48.
5. Henry Elmer Barnes, *An Introduction to the History of Sociology* (Chicago: University of Chicago Press, 1948), pp. 8-9.
6. Russell, *Western Philosophy*, p. 106.
7. *Ibid.*, p. 725.
8. Martindale, *Sociological Theory*, pp. 150-176.
9. Barnes, *History of Sociology*, pp. 39-45.
10. Russell, *Western Philosophy*, pp. 604-745.
11. *Ibid.*, p. 564.
12. *Ibid.*, p. 610.
13. See Martindale, *Sociological Theory*, and Barnes, *History of Sociology*. I would like to emphasize that no sociologists declare, as did the early Greeks, that change is illusory or that reality or society is completely unstable. Rather, the debate among sociologists is one of emphasis, on the question of the importance, the centrality, and the desirability of social change. For an interesting discussion of this topic see Alvin Gouldner, *The Coming Crisis of Western Sociology* (New York: Basic Books, 1970).
14. For a critique of functionalism that centers on its belief in stability see R. Dahrendorf, "Out of Utopia: Toward a Reorientation of Sociological Analysis," *American Journal of*

Sociology, 64 (1958):115-127. For a discussion of Comte's "social conservatism" see Robert A. Nisbet, *The Sociological Tradition* (New York: Basic Books, 1966), p. 15.

15. Gouldner, *Coming Crisis*, p. 332. In its analysis of society's institutions, Gouldner believes, Parsons's functionalism "treats these institutions as given and unchangeable in essentials." See also Emile Durkheim, *Suicide* (Glencoe: Free Press, 1951). Durkheim's work emphasizes negative aspects of social change.

16. Martindale, *Sociological Theory*, Chap. 7 ("Conflict Theories"); Charles H. Anderson, *Toward a New Sociology* (Homewood: Dorsey Press, 1974). Anderson's exposition of Marxist sociology is excellent.

17. Again it must be emphasized that the debate rests primarily on questions of emphasis. Neither idealism nor materialism completely denies the existence of institutions or ideas in the process of social change.

18. Max Weber, *The Protestant Ethic and the Spirit of Capitalism*, ed. Talcott Parsons (New York: Charles Scribner's Sons, 1958).

19. Talcott Parsons, *Societies: Evolutionary and Comparative Perspectives* (Englewood Cliffs: Prentice-Hall, 1966), p. 113. Parsons believes that "within the social system, the normative elements are more important for social change than the 'material interests' of constitutive units." See also Neil Smelser, *Social Change in the Industrial Revolution: An Application of Theory to the British Cotton Industry* (Chicago: University of Chicago Press, 1959).

20. See, for example, Karl Marx, *Capital: A Critique of Political Economy*, (New York: International Publishers, 1973), and William F. Ogburn, *Social Change with Respect to Culture and Original Nature* (New York: Viking Press, 1950).

21. For an interesting summary of famous early scholars whose work included some attention to the subject of women see Mary Cohart (ed.), *Unsung Champions of Women* (Albuquerque: University of New Mexico Press, 1975).

22. The best collection of feminist writings is Alice Rossi (ed.), *The Feminist Papers from Adams to de Beauvoir* (New York: Bantam Books, 1974).

23. Mary Wollstonecraft, *A Vindication of the Rights of Women* (New York: W. W. Norton, 1967); Alice Rossi (ed.), *Essays on Sex Equality: John Stuart Mill and Harriet Taylor Mill* (Chicago: University of Chicago Press, 1970), pp. 123-242.

24. Rossi (ed.), *Feminist Papers*, pp. 194-195. Rossi also notes that Mill's work is appealing in part because it is polemic and free of theoretical overviews of social change.

25. Charlotte Perkins Gilman, *Women and Economics: A Study of the Economic Relation between Men and Women as a Factor in Social Evolution* (Boston: Maynard Press, 1900).

26. Rossi (ed.), *Feminist Papers*.

27. *Ibid.*, p. 4.

28. Simon Kuznets, "Modern Economic Growth: Findings and Reflections," in Kuznets, *Population, Capital, and Growth: Selected Essays* (New York: W. W. Norton, 1973), pp. 165-166.

29. Tom Bottomore, *Marxist Sociology* (London: Macmillan, 1975).

30. Robert C. Tucker (ed.), *The Marx-Engels Reader* (New York: W. W. Norton, 1972), p. 69.

31. Marx, *Capital*, 1:239-240.

32. Karl Marx and Frederick Engels, *The Communist Manifesto* (New York: International Publishers, 1948), pp. 26-28.

33. Frederick Engels, *The Origin of the Family, Private Property and the State* (New York: International Publishers, 1973).

34. Engels, *Origin of the Family*.

35. Of course Marxists argue that society's highest rewards do not derive from wage labor, but from returns on the ownership of capital or the means of production.

36. Margaret Benston, "The Political Economy of Women's Liberation," *Monthly Review*, 21 (1969):13-27; Juliet Mitchell, *Woman's Estate* (New York: Pantheon, 1971).

37. For discussion of the development of women's household roles see Ann Oakley, *Woman's Work: The Housewife, Past and Present*, (New York: Random House, 1976).

38. For excellent discussions of Marxian theory, see Bottomore, *Marxist Sociology* and Anderson, *Toward a New Sociology*.

39. For evidence of a ruling class in American society, see G. William Domhoff, *Who Rules America?* (Englewood Cliffs: Prentice-Hall, 1967).

40. In *Origin of the Family*, Engels explicitly calls for female labor force participation as a means of changing women's inferior status.

41. Benston, "Political Economy of Women's Liberation."

42. C. Wright Mills, *The Marxists* (New York: Dell, 1972), pp. 87-88.

43. Juliet Mitchell begins her seminal book by stating, "The greater part of the feminist movement has identified Freud as the enemy." Mitchell, *Psychoanalysis and Feminism* (New York: Pantheon, 1974), p. xv. For critiques of Freud's position on women see: Betty Friedan, *The Feminine Mystique* (New York: W. W. Norton, 1963); Kate Millet, *Sexual Politics* (New York: Doubleday, 1970); Judd Marmor, "Changing Patterns of Femininity and Masculinity," in Nona Glazer Malbin and Helen Youngelson Wachaer (eds.), *Woman in a Man Made World* (New York: Rand McNally, 1973), pp. 68-73.

44. Sigmund Freud, Lecture XXIII, in *New Introductory Lectures on Psychoanalysis* (New York: W. W. Norton, 1965), p. 135.

45. Mitchell, *Psychoanalysis and Feminism*. See also Eli Zaretsky, "Male Supremacy and the Unconscious," *Socialist Revolution*, 4 (1975):7-55.

46. Sigmund Freud, *Civilization and its Discontents* (New York: W. W. Norton, 1961).

47. Freud does not suggest that all conflicts are adequately resolved but explicates the ideal form of successful resolution. Again, the failure to resolve crises produces faulty development and mental illness of one form or another.

48. Freud, *New Introductory Lectures*, p. 117.

49. *Ibid.*, p. 134; Freud, *Civilization and its Discontents*, p. 50.

50. Mitchell, *Psychoanalysis and Feminism*, ("The Castration Complex and Penis Envy"); Sigmund Freud, "Some Psychical Consequences of the Anatomical Distinction between the Sexes," in *Standard Edition of the Complete Psychological Works of Sigmund Freud*, 19 (London: Hogarth Press, 1964):253.

51. Zaretsky, "Male Supremacy," p. 22.

52. Bruno Bettleheim, *Children of the Dream* (New York: Macmillan, 1969). Freud's work suggests that the Oedipal conflict can never be eliminated completely. Bettleheim discusses evidence on the success of child rearing outside of the nuclear family.

53. Phillip Slater, *The Pursuit of Loneliness* (Boston: Beacon Press, 1970).

54. Sigmund Freud, *Civilization and its Discontents*, p. 33.

Chapter 2
American Women
and Historical Change

In order to carry out the major task of this work, that is, an analysis of the changing position of women in American society since 1960, I shall first explore historical changes experienced by women and the society of which they were a part. As C. Wright Mills has written, the present is never fully understandable without such an historical perspective,[1] and this is particularly true with respect to the dynamics with which this study is concerned. By briefly outlining the major trends that have affected women in the past, I shall be better able to isolate those factors that are important in the period after 1960. The discussion in this chapter will be divided into two parts: the first will explore the macro structural changes that affected women between 1850 and 1960, while the second will focus primarily on changes in ideas or attitudes relevant to women during that period. An analysis of the micro psychological aspects of the changes in women's position will be omitted here because the available data do not allow firm judgments with regard to changes in psychic phenomena.

STRUCTURAL CHANGE

My starting date of 1850 is dictated by the lack of sufficient data to allow other than speculative discussion about women's lives in the United States prior to the mid-nineteenth century. On the other hand, the end date of 1960 is somewhat arbitrary, but I believe that the new dynamics affecting women's place in American society, which began to emerge in the early 1960s and have continued to the present time, deserve separate treatment.

It is generally acknowledged that the century after 1850 was a period of rapid social change and economic development. According to a lead-

ing student of economic development, this process was associated with
"a more sweeping change in the way of life than occurred in any previous century of human history."[2] Those accompanying changes that
have been best documented and most studied are the structural transformations in the income, residence, education, mortality, and fertility
of people living in societies undergoing economic development. Less
easily documented are changes in social, cultural, and attitudinal factors.[3] In the following sections I shall discuss the impact of both of
these types of changes on women's lives in the United States.

Industrialization and Urbanization

Concomitant with the process of economic growth and its associated
shift toward increasing industrialization and mechanization of production is the increasing concentration of production and workers. The
demographic implication of these trends is the dramatic population
movement from rural to urban areas, along with a comparable shift
from farming to nonagricultural occupations. Both of these changes
occurred in the United States during our period. Between 1800 and
1850 the proportion of the American population residing in rural areas
declined slightly, from 94 to 85 percent; by 1960, however, only 37
percent of the American people were still living in rural areas (see Table
2.1).[4]

The shift in occupations is even more dramatic: in 1850, two out of
three workers were classified as engaging in farm occupations, while
in 1960 less than one out of ten were so classified (see Table 2.2).
Thus, during this period the United States was transformed from a
rural, agriculturally dominated society to an industrialized and urbanized society. And, along with men, women flooded into the cities and
were dramatically affected by the industrialization of society.

One of the most important aspects of these developments for women
can be seen by examining the changes that occurred in the locus of
production. Typically, most production of needed goods had been
carried out in the home, with all members of the family participating.
Relatively few of the family's needs were obtained from the society as
a whole. The role of women in this process was extremely important
because they, along with all other members of the family, participated
in farming, canning, clothes making, animal care, doctoring, and other
duties necessary to the family's survival.[5] In the words of Robert
Smuts, "the work of women, in short, provided almost all that was

necessary for keeping house, feeding, clothing, and otherwise sustaining the family."[6] A similar pattern appeared in Great Britain. There women were often responsible for the management of large-scale agricultural enterprises, such as dairies, and also for the family's production of textile items that it put up for sale.[7]

With the shift to an urban and industrialized society there emerged a new conception and definition of work: labor done in return for a money wage. Increasingly more "jobs" that paid wages were performed at locations other than the home, and increasingly fewer family members engaged in this newly defined work.[8] The process of economic development, then, is associated with a new definition of work and the need to leave home in order to engage in work, not as a family unit, but as individuals. Although in the early period of industrialization women and children were found in the "working" labor force, as time went on this new form of economic organization increasingly excluded children and married women from wage labor. The effect on women, then, was increasingly to exclude them from what the society defined as "productive" work. And since economic growth meant that a smaller proportion of products was produced in the home, fulfillment of the family's needs became more and more dependent on money or wages.[9] Women, themselves excluded from wage earning, became dependent on the money wages of their husbands or fathers, wages that they themselves did not earn.

The Family and Demographic Changes

The changes associated with economic development and industrialization had important implications for the structure and functions of the family as well. The productive role of the family declined with industrialization, as one family member, the adult male, worked outside of the home to earn the wages on which the rest of the family depended.[10] Responsibility for many other functions previously fulfilled by the family was transferred from the private to the social sphere. We have already noted the impact of the change in location of work, but the growth of educational, recreational, religious, and social service institutions should also be mentioned.[11] Women's involvement in economic production, and their responsibility as the primary providers of education, religious and social services within the family declined during this period.

The shift of functions away from the family and from women in particular could be interpreted as having precipitated a decline in the status of women relative to men.[12] Some have argued, however, that the loss of functions in the family denotes not a decline in the status of women or in the importance of the family, but rather a shift toward family members' specialization in the performance of a particular function or functions. In the case of women, it is argued, their major task became the emotional and psychological well-being of family members. With such specialization, these functions are presumably fulfilled more efficiently.[13] Nonetheless, it is generally acknowledged that the separation of the "private" life of the family not only from what was considered "productive" work, but also from other aspects of "public" life, such as political, recreational, and religious institutions, was a characteristic trend early in this period. To the extent that there was such a separation of "spheres," women were constrained to the family or private sphere, and their links with the increasingly important public and social world remained undeveloped.[14]

The role of marriage also may have altered at this time, although we have less evidence in this regard. While in the earlier period the union between man and wife may have been motivated by the need to establish a new economic unit in which both contributed to production, women could survive economically even outside of marriage. As Alice Clark puts it, "Men did not at this time regard marriage as necessarily involving the assumption of a serious economic burden but, on the contrary, often considered it to be a step which was likely to strengthen them in life's economic battles. . . ."[15] With economic development and the associated separation of married women from the wage labor force, however, women were less able to support themselves outside of the marital unit. In light of their economic dependence on men, it might be suggested that there was an increased motivation for women to marry and to do so at younger ages. Table 2.5 shows a downward trend in the average age of marriage and an upward trend in the proportions of both males and females who were married. While almost 33 percent of the male population was single in 1890, by 1960 the proportion had dropped to under 25 percent. A similar decline for women shows a shift from 24 to 18 percent single. The movement away from a view of marriage as a mutually necessary economic arrangement and the emphasis on the emotional feelings between a man and a woman as the motivation for marriage will be discussed in a later section.[16] It should be noted here, however, that the increased importance of emotional ties and the fading of the role of marriage as a productive partnership may have contributed to the increasing instability of marriages in our period, as reflected in a rising divorce rate (see Table 2.5).

Other important demographic changes are also associated with the process of economic development.[17] The "demographic transition" that typically occurs embodies a dramatic shift in both the birth and death rates. With the advent of economic development, a society's high death rate will begin to decline, owing to such factors as the implementation of public health measures, better diet, and control of epidemics. This creates a period of rapid population growth as the continued high birth rate exceeds the lowering death rate. Gradually, the use of various contraceptive methods and the conscious decision among sectors of the population to limit the number of their offspring produce a decline in the birth rate to a level where population growth is greatly reduced.

In the United States, the decline in both death and birth rates over the last century has been pronounced (see Table 2.3). Between 1875 and 1960 the death rate dropped from 20 per 1,000 population to 10 per 1,000. Concomitantly, the average life expectancy has increased dramatically, from forty years for a woman born in 1850 to seventy-three years in 1960. Equally important in this regard is the sharp decline in infant mortality rates. At the beginning of our period, parents could expect one of every five children born to die before the first birthday. At the same time, the shift in the birth rate in the United States has also been striking, with the number of children born per 1,000 women in the population declining from a high of 52 in 1840 to 23 by 1960 (see Table 2.4).

What these demographic changes imply for women is not difficult to discern. Compared with American women of a century earlier, whose entire adult life was spent in bearing and caring for young children, women in 1960 were living significantly longer, having far fewer children, and enjoying the reasonable expectation that the children they did bear would survive to adulthood. Thus women were spending an increasingly smaller proportion of their adult lives in the bearing and care of young children. By the time she was thirty the modern American woman who had married at the age of twenty and had had her two or three children soon thereafter found herself with no young children dependent on her care for most of the day with forty years of expected life ahead of her.[18]

Education

Yet another phenomenon associated with economic development is an increase in the extent of training and education in the population. Table 2.6a indicates that school enrollment for the white population increased from approximately 50 percent in 1850 to almost 90 percent in 1960. The increase in black school enrollment has been even more pronounced. In addition, the increasing educational level of the population is attested to by an increase in the number of higher degrees conferred in the United States (see Table 2.6b). While less than 10,000 degrees were granted in 1870, by 1960 that number had grown to almost half a million. Thus the process of economic development is associated not only with the exposure of large portions of the population to at least some schooling, but also with a dramatic increase in level of educational attainment for the population as a whole.

Despite overall progress in education in the United States, it is important to note some differences by sex, particularly in the level of educational attainment.[19] While our data show roughly similar percentages of males and females enrolled in school, an examination of the distribution of degrees conferred by institutions of higher education demonstrates the relatively poor educational position of women. In 1900, for example, the first date for which we have data, women were granted less than one-fifth of all degrees and only 6 percent of the highest degrees.[20] By 1960, even though the situation had improved, women received only one-third of all higher degrees granted, and a mere 10 percent of all doctorates or equivalent degrees (see Table 2.6b). Thus, although the process of economic development was associated with an improvement in the education of large numbers of both men and women in American society during our period, women consistently lag behind men in their attained levels of education.

The implications of increasing educational attainment in a population during the process of economic development are usually discussed only in terms of presumed rises in levels of productivity. That is, it is argued that higher levels of educational attainment result from economic growth and at the same time serve as a spur to further economic development through increased skills and productivity of workers.[21] Nonetheless, the spread and increase in educational attainment has other, perhaps less easily documented, implications for a society and its people, and some of these associated changes have been especially important for women's position.

26

Educational systems can be seen as a force for social order and stability in their ability to mute or eliminate differences among groups in a society by teaching common skills and by transmitting the dominant cultural "core values."[22] By exposing various groups to similar socialization processes and by offering them similar skills, the educational system tends to integrate them by emphasizing their similarities. This process of "cultural homogenization erodes the isolation of various groups"[23] and can inculcate a sense of common purpose, similar attitudes, and social solidarity.[24] Thus one result of the inclusion of women in the expansion of the educational system during the century was a decrease in or a muting of a variety of differences in basic attitudes, abilities, and skills between them and males.[25]

In addition to its role as an integrative or stabilizing force in society, however, education is often regarded as a major source of social conflict and social change. As Burton Clark states, "Education has become a peculiarly creative force in society . . . creating the knowledge that opens new vistas, and undermines existing social and political structures." Education "can create attitudes critical of the established ways and acquaint the young with the ideals and insitutions of freedom."[26] The increasing access to higher levels of educational attainment during our period may have had such an impact on women, stimulating an increased openness to changing roles and a greater willingness to question the traditional social and economic structure and, most importantly, their own position and roles.[27] Thus, educational expansion can be viewed as contributing to the decreasing differences between men's and women's skills and attitudes through their exposure to common educational processes, and also to the increased tolerance of both sexes to processes of rapid social change and to the likelihood that traditional aspects of society would be challenged.

Still another implication of widespread education is related to its effects on the family. During the century after 1850, the relationship of the family to the process of education changed. At the beginning of the period the education of children and transmission of cultural values was traditionally performed primarily by the family unit, and it was often seen as part of the mother's role.[28] With the development of an education system as a separate institution this important and often time-consuming task was removed from the control of family and mothers. At the same time, the physical removal of children from the home, and thus from the need for parental supervision for a substantial proportion of each day, afforded women a larger amount of potential leisure time.

Finally, the expansion of education had important implications for women's entrance into the labor force in that it gave women the opportunity to acquire skills that might secure them paid jobs. Similarly, the absence of children from the home during school hours gave mothers the time and opportunity to engage in work away from their residences. More recently, as college education has become more common, a family's increased financial burden in providing it has served as a further incentive for women to go to work. In numerous ways, then, the growth and spread of education has had significant implications for women's changing position in American society.

Women's Work

It is often noted that the spread of education during the process of economic development is closely associated with changing labor needs of the society's economic institutions.[29] The need for continued technological advance, which is dependent on research activities, as well as the demand for ever higher levels of occupational and professional skill trigger educational expansion. Economic development is associated, as we have seen, with a shift toward increasing industrialization and urbanization, and also with a profound readjustment in the structure of occupations. Not only do the industries in which people are employed undergo transformation, but the jobs they do alter as well. Specifically, economic development is associated with an increase of white-collar jobs and a relative decrease of blue-collar ones. Old occupations disappear and new ones spring up, often creating unemployment among certain groups of workers, but also generating demand for new workers with different skills. Table 2.7 indicates that for the labor force as a whole, growth trends during the period 1900-1960 were clearly in favor of increases in white-collar occupations. Although fewer than one in five workers was classified as white-collar in 1900, by 1960 over 40 percent of all workers were engaged in white-collar occupations. During this same period manual workers held steady at slightly over one-third of the labor force, while the proportion of service workers increased only from 9 to 12 percent.

Although the early stages of development brought a decline in the economic role of women, dramatic changes occurred in the occupational distribution, size, and demographic composition of the female sector of the labor force between 1890 and 1960 (Tables 2.7 and 2.8). The percentage of women in the labor force rose dramatically, from 18 percent of all women in 1890 to 36 percent in 1960, and by 1960 the typical woman worker was no longer the young and single woman but was a mature and married one. In 1890 only 13 percent of women workers were married, and in 1900 the median age of women workers was twenty-six; by 1960 a full 60 percent of all working women was married, and in 1965 the median age of female workers was forty-one.[30] Thus, our period was marked not only by an increase in the proportion of American women who worked, but also by a dramatic shift in their average age and marital status.

In summarizing the changes that occurred during this period in the distribution of women workers in various occupations, Smuts states that there was "a sharp decline in the relative importance of manual work on farm, in factory, and in household service occupations; and sharp increases in the importance of clerical and sales work, teaching and nursing, and non-household service jobs."[31] The increase in the white-collar category is most striking. At the turn of the century only a small proportion of women in the labor force were classified as white-collar workers, but by 1960 55 percent of all women workers held white-collar jobs.[32] Although the specific occupations in which women are employed have changed during the process of economic development, the segregation of women workers in particular types of occupations has not changed since the turn of the century.[33] At that time, 42 percent of women workers were engaged in occupations in which more than 80 percent of their coworkers were female; in 1960 a similar percentage of women worked in female-dominated occupations.[34] Approximately one-fourth of all women employed in 1960 were secretaries, saleswomen in retail trade, private household workers, or teachers in elementary schools.[35]

With respect to wages, data supplied by Smuts indicate that men and women have been paid differently for the same work throughout this period. For example, in 1895, men's wages averaged about one-third higher than those paid to women;[36] in 1960, women engaged in occupational categories similar to those of men earned only 38 to 58 percent of what men did.[37] Thus the practice of paying women lower wages for the same work seems to be a continuing characteristic of the United States labor force.

The economic implications for women of the development process in the period 1850-1960 are evident from the data examined above.

Whether an increasing demand for women workers in occupations classified as "female" motivated their entrance into the labor force, or whether such changes as longer life spans, fewer children, widespread education, or the transfer of traditional family functions to the public sphere encouraged them to seek work outside the home, it is clear that labor force participation had become an important component of the adult lives of an ever larger proportion of American women.[38]

IDEOLOGICAL CHANGE

We have already touched on some of the numerous changes in the structure of society that are associated with economic development. While some scholars of economic development have tended to emphasize these structural transformations, others have noted that development is also associated with ideological changes in attitudes and ideas, or what sociologists often refer to as the norms and values of society.[39] The concern here is with those aspects of social change that affect the images of "proper" behavior for groups that fulfill different roles in the society, the ideals of behavior that are most valued by the society, and the expectations and obligations that are considered appropriate for different social positions.[40]

In exploring the relationship between ideology and economic development on a macro level, Weber emphasized the growing "rationalization" of society and the decline of "traditionalism," both of which are associated with the emergence of capitalism.[41] He suggests that capitalism is linked ideologically with the rise of individualism, with new importance accorded to work and monetary success as socially accepted indications of one's self-worth, and with the positive value placed on innovation and change of all kinds.[42] Thus the process of development typically involves changed social norms or redefinitions of proper behavior, new ideals and values, and the emergence of a new ideological hegemony. It should be noted that there is a longstanding controversy in the literature between those who interpret Weber's argument to mean that changed ideas and values cause or at least predate structural changes,[43] and those who interpret his work as an addendum to Marx's argument that the primary causal element is structural change.[44]

In order to understand more fully the process of social change in society and its particular implications for women, I shall examine aspects of the ideology of the period 1850-1960. In this way I hope to obtain a view of people's ideas and attitudes about themselves, about the society around them, and especially about the position of women in society. For information about this aspect of society and its importance in social change, I shall turn from statistical measures of social phenomena to historical accounts of how individuals viewed their society, their world, and particularly the changes that were occurring around them.

The Family and Children

One set of attitudes that has received attention from sociologists centers on the changing importance and nature of the family.[45] There is evidence that such attitudes are linked to the development process. William Goode's work, for example, suggests that associated with industrialization is a new "ideology of the conjugal family [which] proclaims the right of the individual to choose his or her own spouse, place to live, and even which kind of obligations to accept, as against the acceptance of others' decisions."[46] Thus, Goode argues that with economic development the ideology of the family typically asserts "the worth of the individual as against inherited elements of wealth or ethnic group," and as against the claims of parents or kin, who traditionally controlled the evaluation of an individual's worth and the decisions made for him or her. Goode sees autonomous choice of mate as a particularly important development as well as the emergence of new criteria for selection that focus on the emotional involvement of the conjugal couple. Thus, the hallmarks of the new ideology of the family include the following: an emphasis on individual rights in forming the conjugal family, with the emphasis on love between the man and woman; a belief in the right of an individual to change his or her family life if it is unpleasant; a belief that these decisions should be made in the best interests of the couple and not of their respective families; and a growing egalitarianism within the conjugal family.[47] Goode suggests that these trends have implications for the position of women and children within the family, since with a more egalitarian ideology "sex status and seniority are less relevant than the 'human' qualities of warmth, emotionality, etc., which are not based on age or sex."[48] Thus a new ideological hegemony associated with the process of economic development serves to weaken the traditional norms,—what Goode calls the "self-evident rightness of the older system"—and at the same time provides new ideas and values by which people can both guide and legitimate their behavior.

Closely connected with changing ideas regarding the family is the development of new ideologies concerning the role of children in the family and their proper care.[49] There is evidence that during our period the family was becoming more "specialized" with respect to the functions it fulfilled.[50] Parsons, for example, argues that with the process of development, the socialization of children and the psychological and emotional fulfillment of individual members becomes the major function of the family. Thus the "proper" care of children, in order to ensure their "normal" psychological and emotional development, becomes increasingly important. In this period, then, "the idea of motherhood as a fulltime occupation for all women came into fashion, reinforcing the ties of women to the home."[51] This change in attitudes toward children is reflected in the emergence of a "professional" approach to child care. Peter Filene suggests that from 1890 to 1920 a child care movement developed in the United States, which for the first time focused on the role of the mother as "a scientific vocation that required intelligence and training."[52] In sum, children, although fewer in number in the average family, were viewed as emotionally fragile creatures whose psychological development depended on constant vigilance and proper care on the part of their mothers.

Thus during our period there is evidence of a more sentimental attitude toward children and of greater maternal responsibility for their emotional well-being.[53] Children became the central focus of an ideology stressing the need for "professional" mothering.

Sex Roles

Was the process of economic development also associated with changing attitudes toward men's and women's roles? It seems clear that change did occur in this regard, and although the literature on the subject offers considerably more information on female sex-role expectations, some information is available on the changes in ideas surrounding men's roles after the mid-nineteenth century. Filene, for example, provides us with an overview of the shifting ideals of manliness and masculinity during the period. The ideal man during the Victorian period was "self-reliant, strong, resolute, courageous, honest—traits that people summed up simply as character." At home, he provided a "benevolent patriarchy" and "governed absolutely but justly."[54] By the end of the nineteenth century, the individuals who best embodied these virtues were businessmen, "the men who fight the battles of life where they must now be fought, in the markets of the world. . . ."[55] Success, and therefore manliness, was equated not only with hard work, but also with money and an abundance of material goods.

In Filene's account the changes that occurred in the ideal of masculinity were closely linked to alterations in the structure of the economy, which were produced by a rapid process of development. With the growth of bureaucracies and giant corporations, there emerged a need for a more cooperative mode of interaction with others in the economic, political, and even familial spheres.[56] The ideal of the autonomous, self-reliant male began to fade as those qualities became less functional to the task of earning a living and as new ideals of cooperation and conformity came to predominate. The new image of marriage and family life as a partnership, in which "the modern father had to earn rather than presume respect from his family,"[57] was further encouraged by the ideal of egalitarianism in family relationships noted by Goode.[58] Thus a new ideological view of manliness began to emerge during our period, although older norms and ideals persisted alongside the new.[59]

With respect to change in the ideology of women's roles and femininity between the mid-nineteenth and mid-twentieth centuries the major shift was from the exclusive identification of femininity with motherhood and domesticity to a broader definition that includes other aspects of social interaction and behavior. The Victorian ideal of femininity extolled "piety, purity, domesticity, and submissiveness as quintessentially female traits," with the assumption that men and women were indeed opposites whose lives and nature relegated them to completely separate spheres.[60] Needless to say, women's sphere was the home.

The development of new attitudes that legitimated the emergence of women from the home is the first evidence of changing definitions of femininity. Evidence of these changing attitudes is provided by the emergence of the women's "club" movement near the turn of the century, as well as women's involvement in social reform of various kinds, including abolition, the social purity movement—both the Women's Christian Temperance Union and the American Purity Alliance—and the struggle for socialism in the United States.[61] Participation in club activities and involvement in social movements are important indications of the changing position of women and the changing ideas concerning legitimate behavior consistent with femininity. Furthermore, the growth of clubs, and especially women's involvement in the abolition movement, were central for the emergence of the first American feminist movement.

A detailed discussion of early feminism is beyond the scope of this overview of the century after 1850. However, a brief exploration of the origins of that movement may be helpful. William O'Neill hypothesizes several contributing factors to the rise of feminism. First, he cites the extraordinary social ferment that characterized the United States in the two decades prior to the emergence of feminism in 1848. "Religion, politics, philanthropy, education, and, indeed, almost every part of the national life experienced great changes, or attempted changes."[62] In addition to creating an atmosphere in which the idea of change was legitimated, this reforming spirit afforded women new opportunities to become engaged in activities outside the home. Second, O'Neill points to structural changes, especially in the organization of the family, that generated strains for women. He cites as crucial the demographic changes associated with economic development, such as the decline in the birth rate and the consequent shrinking of family size, and the turning inward of family life to privacy and domesticity. The contradictions of women's role and the resulting tensions and strains were caused by "the gap between women's narrowed sphere and men's expanding one."[63] These contradictions were most strongly felt by middle-class women, whose position in society had encouraged participation in clubs and social movements and whose birth rate had declined most precipitously, leaving them with the leisure time to engage in extrafamilial activities. It was these women who created the phenomenon of early feminism and whose work laid the foundation for the later emergence of the suffrage movement.

Although the feminist movement collapsed with the gaining of suffrage—and had lost much of its feminist thrust well before that victory— it was an important force for spreading and legitimating a new image of women, of the family, and of marriage among American women and men. Often unsophisticated in their own analysis of society, the early feminists nonetheless articulated a new ideology with respect to both men's and women's roles. This ideology emphasized the increasing disaffection of middle-class women from exclusive identification with domesticity and motherhood. In addition, the emergence of a new social movement demonstrated that women could organize themselves in order to strive for what they perceived to be their own interests.[64]

Women Workers

Although there is increasing evidence of tolerant attitudes toward women's activity and involvement outside the domestic sphere in the

early twentieth century, often the justification of such activity was its
similarity to or its being merely an extension of women's home roles.
Involvement in social reform and clubs was thought to bring to the
society as a whole the "tempering influence of women's compassion,
spirituality, and moral sensitivity."[65] As Filene puts it, women were
"merely moving their pedestals to a new location" by being allowed "to
carry into the masculine realm their talents for keeping an orderly household and rearing virtuous children."[66] Married women's participation
in the labor force was, however, not as easily justified in this manner
and far less tolerated. One of the hallmarks of the "true lady" of the
Victorian period was her leisure: she should not work at all, and certainly not for wages. Only in the case of special circumstances, such as
widowhood, spinsterhood, or severe poverty, was women's work legitimate, according to the dominant ideology, and such necessity was to be
pitied.[67] In all other regards, according to Smuts, women's "work was
viewed as a threat to moral standards, to the economic foundations of
the family, and to the self-esteem of men."[68]

Nevertheless, there is some evidence of changing attitudes and an increasing acceptance of the norm of female participation in the labor
force. Smuts suggests that the period from World War I through World
War II was crucial in changing attitudes of both women and employers
in favor of female participation, since women were told that it was
"their patriotic duty to take a job."[69] The new norm of acceptance, or
at least of tolerance, of women in the labor force took hold during this
period, and work was no longer seen as completely antithetical to femininity.[70] Oppenheimer's work provides evidence of this change by com-
paring attitudes expressed in public opinion polls from the mid-1930s
with those revealed in a 1960 survey. In 1936 only 15 percent of the
persons questioned approved of married women having full-time jobs
outside the home; in 1960, 34 percent approved.[71] Thus, gradually,
and not altogether smoothly, the ideology surrounding women's place
and the definition of femininity underwent change.

During this period, the Victorian doctrine of separate spheres, of the
conception of males and females as human beings with different values,
expectations, personalities, and needs was challanged by a new ideology
of equality and similarity. The growing legitimacy of married women's
participation in the labor force and of their involvement in areas outside of the traditional Victorian sphere, a more egalitarian ideal of
marital relationships, the growth of scientific motherhood, a re-definition
of femininity that no longer emphasized exclusive preoccupation with

domesticity—all of these changes were in evidence during the one hundred years we have examined.

CONCLUSION

In this chapter I have traced the structural and ideological changes that affected the position of women in American society during the period from 1850 to 1960. As is characteristic of a period of rapid economic development such as was generated in American society in that century, many aspects of the organizational, demographic, and ideological structure of the society were altered. The changes that occurred in both institutional and ideological spheres did not happen all at once, and the process of change was not as smooth as it may seem in retrospect. Old norms and ideologies proved especially resistant to change. Filene, for example, notes that the ideal of the "new woman" of the early twentieth century was attacked as responsible for the destruction of the family, the increasing divorce rate, and immorality, and was viewed by many as "the enemy of marriage, the home and therefore civilization."[72] Conflicts were in evidence not only between the old values and the new ones emerging alongside them, but also between ideology and the actual behavior of people in society. Structural changes occurred rapidly as the birth rate declined, longevity increased, women became more educated, and economic development necessitated new occupations and workers. Conflicts arose between new behavioral patterns and old ideas about the nature and proper behavior of men, women, and children, the importance and role of the family, and the purpose and meaning of marital relationships. The early feminist movement served to challange many of those old ideas, but despite its struggles, feminism was not widely accepted as a hegemonic ideology of true equality in American society. As a result, what Ogburn has referred to as "cultural lag" was in evidence during much of this period.[73] Despite some changes in attitude, cultural norms continued to insist that women's place was in the home, and, resisting radical challanges to traditional definitions of femininity, this ideology remained hegemonic. This traditional attitude, however, stood in increasingly stark contrast to the changes in women's position that had already occurred in the economy, in the family, and in the society as whole.

The process of economic development and social change in the years between 1850 and 1960 was not only rapid but was also widespread and affected women in a multitude of ways. Although ideology and be-havior often seemed contradictory, the changes that were set in motion affected and presaged continuing alterations in women's position in American society after 1960. It is to the analysis of those changes—structural, cultural, and psychological—that I now turn.

NOTES

1. C. Wright Mills, *The Sociological Imagination* (New York: Oxford University Press, 1959).

2. Richard A. Easterlin, "Economic Growth: An Overview," in *The International Encyclopedia of the Social Sciences*, 1-17 (New York: Macmillan, 1968), 4:395-408. See also Kuznets, *Population, Capital, and Growth*.

3. Joan Huber, "Toward a Sociotechnological Theory of the Women's Movement," *Social Problems*, 23 (1976):371-88.

4. Rural is defined as places having a population of less than 2,500 individuals.

5. Among the most important sources for this view are: Ivy Pinchbeck, *Women, Workers and the Industrial Revolution, 1750-1850* (London: George Routledge and Sons, Ltd., 1930); Robert W. Smuts, *Women and Work in America* (New York: Columbia University Press, 1959); and Alice Clark, *The Working Life of Women in the Seventeenth Century* (New York: E. P. Dutton, 1919).

6. Smuts, *Women and Work*, p. 8.

7. Oakley, *Woman's Work*, pp. 14-16.

8. For a fascinating discussion of the changes in women's roles that are occurring in societies currently experiencing economic development see Esther Boserup, *Women's Role in Economic Development* (New York: St. Martin's Press, 1970).

9. Easterlin, "Economic Growth," refers to this as the "monetization of the econo-my." See also William Goode, *World Revolution and Family Patterns* (New York: Free Press, 1963), and Peter Filene, *Him/Her/Self* (New York: Harcourt Brace Jovanovich, 1975).

10. Heather Ross and Isabel Sawhill, *Time of Transition: The Growth of Families Headed by Women* (Washington D.C.: The Urban Institute, 1975).

11. John Demos, "Myths and Realities in the History of American Family-Life" in Henry Gruenbaum and Jacob Christ (eds.) *Contemporary Marriage: Structure, Dynamics and Therapy* (Boston: Little, Brown, 1975) pp. 9-31.

12. This issue has recently received attention from historians. According to Barbara Sicherman, in her summary review of the scholarship on women's history during the last dec-ade, "The single most important issue is how women's status has changed with industrializa-tion. Historians have favorably contrasted women's position in pre-industrial society . . . with the one-way relationship of economic dependence that developed when middle-class women ceased to engage in forms of labor labeled productive." Sicherman, "American History: A Re-view Essay," *Signs*, 1 (1975):463.

13. Arlene Skolnick, "The Construction of Childhood," in Skolnick, *The Intimate Environment* (Boston: Little, Brown, 1973); Edward Shorter, *The Making of the Modern Family* (New York: Basic Books, 1975); Talcott Parsons and Robert F. Bales, *Family, Socializa-tion and Interaction Process* (Glencoe: Free Press, 1955).

14. Filene, *Him/Her/Self*; Skolnick, "Construction of Childhood." In his *The Uncom-mited* (New York: Delta, 1960), Kenneth Keniston suggests that the need for the family world to be separate from the rest of society was influenced by the increasing depersonalization and alienation of work in an industrialized society; individuals needed a place to which they could escape or retreat. See also Goode, *World Revolution*, p. 14; Christopher Lasch, *Haven in a*

Heartless World: The Family Beseiged, (New York: Basic Books, 1977).

15. A. Clark, *Working Life*, p. 39.

16. But on this point see Goode, *World Revolution*.

17. Jeanne Clare Ridley, "Effects of Population Change on the Roles and Status of Women: Perspective and Speculation," in Constantina Safilios-Rothschild (ed.), *Toward a Sociology of Women* (Lexington: Xerox, 1972), pp. 372-86.

18. Paul C. Glick, *American Families* (New York: Wiley, 1957).

19. Alice Rossi and Ann Calderwood (eds.), *Academic Women on the Move* (New York: Russell Sage Foundation, 1973).

20. A doctorate or the equivalent is considered the "highest degree."

21. C. Arnold Anderson and Mary Jean Bowman (eds.), *Education and Economic Development* (Chicago: Aldine, 1965).

22. Burton R. Clark, "Sociology of Education," in Robert E. L. Faris (ed.), *Handbook of Modern Sociology* (Chicago: Rand McNally, 1964), pp. 734-69. The education of immigrants is a classic example of this process.

23. Burton R. Clark, "Education: The Study of Educational Systems," in *International Encyclopedia of the Social Sciences*, 4:514-20.

24. Samuel Bowles and Herbert Gintis, *Schooling in Capitalist America* (New York: Basic Books, 1976). This book is important for its critical view of the integrative function of schooling. The authors argue that the educational system protects the social order by socializing various social groups and classes to accept the authoritarian and unequal class structure that characterizes capitalist America both inside and outside the classroom.

25. Of course this does not contradict the argument that schools often separate and teach different skills to boys and girls (homemaking or serving in contrast to woodworking or industrial skills). See Chapter 3 below for further discussion.

26. B. R. Clark, "Educational Systems," p. 514.

27. See Chapter 7 below for a discussion of the origins of the women's liberation movement among the student population.

28. H. Schelsky, "Family and School in Modern Society," in A. H. Halsey et al. (eds.), *Education, Economy and Society: A Reader in the Sociology of Education* (New York: Free Press, 1961), pp. 414-20.

29. Easterlin, "Economic Growth"; Halsey et al., *Economy and Society*, pp. 15-54.

30. The data on median age of women workers are from Women's Bureau, *1965 Handbook on Women Workers*, Bulletin No. 290 (Washington, D.C.: U.S. Department of Labor, 1965), and Valerie Kincade Oppenheimer, *The Female Labor Force in the United States: Demographic and Economic Factors Governing its Growth and Changing Composition*, Population Monograph No. 5 (Berkeley: University of California Institute of International Studies, 1970), p. 8. The exception to this picture of married women's nonparticipation in the labor force is Negro women, approximately one-fourth of whom worked for wages in 1890. Smuts, *Women and Work*, p. 56.

31. Smuts, *Women and Work*, p. 35.

32. Edith Abbott, *Women in Industry: A Study in American History*, (New York: D. Appleton, 1924).

33. Oppenheimer, *Female Labor Force*, p. 71.

34. Oppenheimer's data show that approximately half of all women workers are employed in occupations that are classified as female dominated, that is, in which 70 percent or more of the workers are female.

35. Women's Bureau, *1965 Handbook*, p. 91.

36. Smuts, *Women and Work*, p. 91.

37. Women's Bureau, *1965 Handbook*, p. 128.

38. The causes of female labor force participation is an actively disputed issue in the social science literature. For differing viewpoints see: Smuts, *Women and Work*; Glen Cain, *Married Women in the Labor Force: An Economic Analysis* (Chicago: University of Chicago Press, 1966); James A. Sweet, *Women in the Labor Force* (New York: Seminar Press, 1973).

39. Bert F. Hoselitz, "Economic Growth: Noneconomic Aspects," in *International Encyclopedia of the Social Sciences*, 4:422-29.

40. This use of *ideology* to mean norms and values, ideas and attitudes has no negative or pejorative content. The term *hegemony* refers to the same concept. The sociological definition of a role is a position in society to which norms are attached.

41. Max Weber, *The Protestant Ethic and the Spirit of Capitalism*, ed. Talcott Parsons (New York: Charles Scribner's Sons, 1958). See also Talcott Parsons (ed.), *The Theory of Social and Economic Organization* (Glencoe: Free Press, 1957), and Parsons, *The Social System* (Glencoe: Free Press, 1951). See Chapter 1 for a discussion of Weber.

42. Weber, *Protestant Ethic*. See also Hoselitz, "Economic Growth," for further clarification of Weber's concepts.

43. Parsons, *Social System*.

44. H. Gerth and C. W. Mills, *From Max Weber: Essays in Sociology* (New York: Oxford University Press, 1958).

45. Goode, *World Revolution*.

46. *Ibid.*, pp. 1, 19. Goode defines the "conjugal family" as one that places more emphasis on the unit of couple and children, and less on kinship ties with other relatives.

47. For a recent discussion, see Edward Shorter, *Making of the Modern Family*.

48. Goode, *World Revolution*, p. 21.

49. *Ibid.*, p. 19. Goode discusses the "fit" of this ideological pattern with the new demands associated with an industrialized urbanized economic system. He notes especially the importance of a geographically mobile labor force, criteria for employment that are independent of family "connections," the characteristic social mobility (upward as well as downward)— all of which imply a severing of ties with extended kin and an emphasis on emotionality in husband-wife relationships, which helps to compensate for an increasingly bureaucratic, impersonal work world see pp. 10-18. For an excellent overview of the literature in this area, see Arlene Skolnick, "Construction of Childhood," pp. 313-54.

50. Parsons and Bales, *Family, Socialization*, pp. 3-33.

51. Oakley, *Woman's Work*, p. 56.

52. Filene, *Him/Her/Self*, pp. 45, 46; see also Ann Oakley, *The Sociology of Housework* (New York: Pantheon, 1974). The work of Philippe Aries must be mentioned for its path-breaking exploration of the social construction of childhood and the changing nature of ideas about proper behavior and care of children. Philippe Aries, *Centuries of Childhood: A Social History of Family Life* (New York: Random House, 1962).

53. Sicherman, "American History Review Essay," p. 469.

54. Filene, *Him/Her/Self*, p. 78; see also Chapter 3 ("Men and Manliness").

55. *Ibid.*, p. 80.

56. David Riesman, *The Lonely Crowd: A Study of the Changing American Character* (New Haven: Yale University Press, 1950).

57. Filene, *Him/Her/Self*, p. 163.

58. Goode, *World Revolution*.

59. Filene's work is excellent in its illustration of the erratic nature of the development of new ideologies. He ably demonstrates that new norms are threatened by and are in constant struggle against the older definitions and ideals of tradition.

60. Barbara Walter, "The Cult of True Womanhood, 1820-1860," *American Quarterly*, 18 (1966):151-74.

61. Filene, *Him/Her/Self*. See also Smuts, *Women and Work*, pp. 125-26, who argues that club activity "represents progress against the effort to confine women strictly to maternal and wifely duties."

62. William L. O'Neill, *The Woman Movement: Feminism in the United States and England* (Chicago: Quadrangle, 1969). p. 19. See also O'Neill, *Everyone Was Brave* (Chicago: Quadrangle, 1969), and Aileen S. Kraditor, *The Ideas of the Woman Suffrage Movement, 1890-1920* (New York: Columbia University Press, 1965).

63. O'Neill, *The Woman Movement*, p. 17.

64. O'Neill, *Everyone Was Brave*.

65. Smuts, *Women and Work*, p. 129.

66. Filene, *Him/Her/Self*, pp. 14, 35.

67. Oppenheimer, *Female Labor Force*, p. 42.

68. Smuts, *Women and Work*, p. 113.

69. *Ibid.*, p. 146. Also see Jean Lipman-Blumen, "Role De-Differentiation as a System Response to Crisis: Occupational and Political Roles of Women, "*Sociological Inquiry*, 43 (1973):105-29.

70. Smuts, *Women and Work*, p. 150. He notes, however, that many negative attitudes still persist.

71. Oppenheimer's data indicate that a steady proportion of respondents, approximately 45 percent, disapprove over the time period. Oppenheimer, *Female Labor Force*.

72. Filene, *Him/Her/Self*, p. 45.

73. William F. Ogburn, "Cultural Lag as Theory" in *William F. Ogburn and Social Change: Selected Essays*, ed. Otis D. Duncan (Chicago: University of Chicago Press, 1964) pp. 86-95. In *The Feminine Mystique*, Betty Friedan explores a period (the 1950s) during which changes in ideology seem to have come to an abrupt halt or even regressed to attitudes characteristic of the pre-1920 period, with emphasis on motherhood and domesticity becoming dominant.

TABLES

Table 2.1

PERCENTAGE DISTRIBUTION OF U.S. POPULATION IN
URBAN AND RURAL AREAS, 1800-1960

Year	Urban*	Rural**
1800	6.1	93.9
1850	15.3	84.7
1880	28.2	71.8
1900	39.7	60.3
1910	45.7	54.3
1920	51.2	48.8
1930	56.2	43.8
1940	56.5	43.5
1950	59.1	40.9
1960	63.0	37.0

SOURCES: *The Statistical History of the United States from Colonial Times to the Present* (Stamford: Fairfield Publishers, 1965), p. 14; *Statistical Abstract of the United States, 1962* (Washington, D.C.: Bureau of the Census, 1962), p. 21.

*Urban is defined as a place of 2,500 or more individuals.
**Rural is defined as a place of less than 2,500 individuals.

Table 2.2

PERCENTAGE DISTRIBUTION OF GAINFULLY EMPLOYED WORKERS,
BY FARM AND NONFARM OCCUPATIONS, 1820-1960

Year	Farm	Nonfarm
1820	71.8	28.2
1830	70.5	29.5
1840	68.6	31.4
1850	63.7	36.3
1870	53.0	47.0
1900	37.5	62.5
1910	31.0	69.0
1920	27.0	73.0
1930	21.4	78.6
1940	17.4	82.6
1950	11.8	88.2
1960	8.2	91.8

SOURCES: *Statistical History of the U.S.,* pp. 72, 74; *Statistical Abstract, 1962,* p. 218.

Table 2.3

MORTALITY EXPERIENCE OF THE U.S. POPULATION
BY SEX AND RACE, 1850-1960

Year	No. Deaths per 1,000 Population		No. Infant Deaths per 1,000 Live Births	Years of Life Expectancy at Birth	
	Male	*Female*		*Male*	*Female*
1850	**	**	131.1*	38.3*	40.5
1875	21.8*	20.5*	156.3*		
1900					
Whites	17.7	16.3			
Nonwhites	25.7	24.4			
Both			141.4*	46.3	48.3
1915					
Whites	13.7	12.0			
Nonwhites	20.2	20.8			
Both			99.9	52.5	56.8
1920					
Whites	13.0	12.1			
Nonwhites	17.8	17.5			
Both			85.8	53.6	54.6
1930					
Whites	11.7	9.8			
Nonwhites	17.4	15.3			
Both			64.6	58.1	61.6
1940					
Whites	11.6	9.2			
Nonwhites	15.1	12.6			
Both			47.0	60.8	65.2
1950					
Whites	10.9	8.0			
Nonwhites	12.5	9.9			
Both			29.2	65.7	71.3
1956					
Whites	10.8	7.8			
Nonwhites	11.4	8.8			
Both			26.0	66.7	73.0
1960					
Whites	10.9	8.0			
Nonwhites	11.4	8.6			
Both			25.2	66.5	73.0

SOURCES: *Statistical History of the U.S.,* pp. 25, 27; *Statistical Abstract, 1962,* pp. 61, 63.

*Data available for Massachusetts only.

**Data not available.

Table 2.4

FERTILITY EXPERIENCE OF THE U.S. POPULATION BY RACE, 1800-1960

Year	*Total Live Births per 1,000 Women Aged 15-44*	*No. Children under Age 5 per 1,000 Women Aged 20-44*
1800	**	1,342
1840	51.8	1,085
1880		
Whites		780
Nonwhites		1,090
Total	39.8	
1900		
Whites		666
Nonwhites		845
Total	32.3	
1910		
Whites		631
Nonwhites		736
Total	30.1	
1920		
Whites	26.9	604
Nonwhites	35.0	608
1930		
Whites	20.6	506
Nonwhites	27.5	554
1940		
Whites	18.6	419
Nonwhites	26.7	513
1950		
Whites	23.0	587
Nonwhites	33.3	706
1956		
Whites	24.0	**
Nonwhites	35.4	**
1960	23.7	**

SOURCES: *Statistical History of the U.S.,* pp. 23, 24; *Statistical Abstract, 1962,* p. 54.

**Data not available.

Table 2.5

MARITAL EXPERIENCE OF THE U.S. POPULATION,
BY SEX, 1890-1960

Year	Median Age at First Marriage		Divorce Rate per 1,000 Population*	% Married***		% Single***	
	Male	Female		Male	Female	Male	Female
1890	**	**	**	61.2	59.4	32.8	24.3
1900	**	**	**	59.9	58.7	33.1	25.0
1920	24.6	21.2	1.6	61.3	60.4	31.8	24.1
1930	24.3	21.3	1.6	62.1	61.2	30.9	23.7
1940	24.3	21.5	2.0	62.8	61.0	31.1	24.3
1950	22.8	20.3	2.6	68.0	66.1	26.2	19.6
1956	22.3	20.1	2.3	70.0	67.4	24.7	18.5
1960	22.8	20.3	2.2	70.0	67.8	24.8	18.4

SOURCES: *Statistical History of the U.S.*, pp. 15, 30; *Statistical Abstract, 1962*, pp. 37, 71.

*Includes reported annulments.
**Data not available.
***Omits widowed and divorced persons.

Table 2.6

A. EDUCATIONAL EXPERIENCE, BY RACE AND SEX, 1850-1960

Year	*School Enrollment Per 100 Population*	
	Male	*Female*
1850		
White	59.0	53.3
Nonwhite	2.0	1.8
1900		
White	53.4	53.9
Nonwhite	29.4	32.8
1920		
White	65.6	65.8
Nonwhite	52.5	54.5
1930		
White	71.4	70.9
Nonwhite	59.7	60.8
1940		
White	75.9	75.4
Nonwhite	67.5	69.2
1950		
White	79.7	78.9
Nonwhite	74.7	74.9
1956		
White	89.4	86.1
Nonwhite	83.6	83.5
1960		
White	90.6	87.3
Nonwhite	86.6	85.7

SOURCE: *Historical Statistics of the United States, Colonial Times to 1970 Bicentennial Edition, Part I* (Washington, D.C.: Bureau of the Census, 1975), pp. 369-70.

B. PERCENTAGE DISTRIBUTION OF HIGHER DEGREES CONFERRED, BY SEX, 1890-1960

Year	All Degrees		Bachelor's or First Professional		Master's or Second Professional		Doctorate or Equivalent	
	Male	Female	Male	Female	Male	Female	Male	Female
1890	**	**	82.7	17.3	**	**	98.7	1.3
1900	81.1	18.9	80.9	19.1	80.9	19.1	94.0	6.0
1910	77.3	22.7	77.3	22.7	73.6	26.4	90.1	9.9
1920	66.3	33.7	65.8	34.2	69.8	30.2	84.9	15.1
1930	60.5	39.5	60.1	39.9	59.6	40.4	84.6	15.4
1940	59.5	40.5	58.7	41.3	61.8	38.2	87.0	13.0
1950	75.7	24.3	76.1	23.9	70.8	29.2	90.3	9.7
1960	65.8	34.2	64.7	35.3	68.4	31.6	89.5	10.5

SOURCE: *Historical Statistics*, pp. 385-86.

**Data not available.

Table 2.7

PERCENTAGE DISTRIBUTION OF ACTIVE LABOR FORCE,
BY OCCUPATION AND SEX, 1900-1960

Occupation	1900	1910	1920	1930	1940	1950	1960
Both Sexes							
White Collar							
professional, technical, and kindred	4.3	4.7	5.4	6.8	7.5	8.6	11.4
managers	5.8	6.6	6.6	7.4	7.3	8.7	10.7
clerical	3.1	5.3	8.0	8.9	9.6	12.3	14.9
sales	4.5	4.7	4.9	6.3	6.7	7.0	6.4
total	17.6	21.4	24.9	29.4	31.1	36.6	43.4
Manual							
craftsmen	10.5	11.6	13.0	12.8	12.0	14.1	13.0
operatives	12.8	14.6	15.6	15.8	18.4	20.4	18.2
laborers	12.5	12.0	11.6	11.0	9.4	6.6	5.4
total	35.9	38.2	40.2	39.6	39.8	41.1	36.6
Service							
private household	5.4	5.0	3.3	4.1	4.7	2.6	
all other service	3.6	4.6	4.5	5.7	7.1	7.9	
total	9.0	9.6	7.8	9.8	11.7	10.5	12.2
Farm							
farmers and managers	19.8	16.5	15.3	12.4	10.4	7.4	
laborers and foremen	17.7	14.4	11.7	8.8	6.9	4.4	
total	37.5	30.8	27.1	21.2	17.4	11.8	7.8
Women							
White Collar							
professional, technical, and kindred	8.2	9.8	11.7	13.8	12.8	12.2	12.3
managers	1.4	2.0	2.3	2.7	3.3	4.3	5.0
clerical	4.0	9.2	18.7	20.9	21.5	27.4	30.3
sales	4.2	5.1	6.3	6.8	7.4	8.6	7.7
total	17.8	26.1	38.8	44.2	44.9	52.5	55.3
Manual							
craftsmen	1.4	1.4	1.2	1.0	1.1	1.5	1.0
operatives	23.8	22.9	20.2	17.4	19.5	20.0	15.2
laborers	2.6	1.4	2.4	1.5	1.1	0.9	0.4
total	27.8	25.7	23.8	19.9	21.6	22.4	16.6
Service							
private household	29.1	24.0	15.8	17.8	18.1	8.9	
all other service	6.4	8.4	8.1	9.7	11.3	12.6	
total	35.5	32.4	23.9	27.5	29.4	21.5	23.7
Farm							
farmers and managers	5.8	3.8	3.2	2.4	1.2	0.7	
laborers and foremen	13.1	12.0	10.3	6.0	2.7	2.9	
total	18.9	15.8	13.5	8.4	4.1	3.6	4.4

SOURCES: *Statistical History of the United States,* p. 74; *Statistical Abstract of the United States, 1975,* p. 359.

Table 2.8

PARTICIPATION IN THE CIVILIAN LABOR FORCE,
BY SEX AND MARITAL STATUS OF WOMEN, 1890-1960

Year	Labor Force Participation		Marital Status of Female Labor Force		
	Male (%)	Female (%)	Married (%)	Single (%)	Other* (%)
1890	84.3	18.2	13.9	68.2	17.9
1920	84.6	22.7	23.0	77.0	**
1940	79.7	25.8	35.9	49.0	15.0
1950	81.6	29.9	52.2	31.9	15.0
1960	80.4	35.7	59.9	24.0	16.1

SOURCE: *Historical Statistics,* pp. 132-33.

*Includes divorced or widowed women.
**Data not available.

Chapter 3
Women, Personality, and Socialization

My discussion of social change and its effect on women after 1960 will begin at the micro level with an exploration of the relationship between personality and social change. Many of the studies that have examined change and personality emphasize the importance of individual personalities in causing major social change. In this approach, often referred to as the "great man" theory of history, historical and social change is understood as a series of events brought about primarily by single individuals who are geniuses, political leaders, assassins, or innovators of one kind or another. The search for the causes of a particular instance of social change results in biographical accounts of these individuals, and an examination of the differences between these "heroes" and "ordinary" people who have played no major role in social changes. These differences then are posited as the major variable explaining the special role of "great men" in historical change.

My approach to personality and social change will be different, for I shall concentrate on the concept of collective or social personality rather than on that of individual personality. Freudian theory, on which much of my discussion of personality is based, never loses sight of the uniqueness of each individual, but at the same time it stresses similarities in the sources of and influences on personality development. Freud's paradigm of the importance of early childhood experiences and the existence of developmental stages, parental repression, and the unconscious is an attempt to analyze universal processes, conflicts, and needs that significantly influence the personality development of all individuals.

The concept of the collective personality seeks to emphasize the similar personality characteristics among groups of individuals living in a particular culture and social structure at a particular historical moment. My interest is in the way the collective female personality is shaped by society and affected by its changes.[1] Social personality can be viewed

49

as both cause and effect in its relation to social change. On the one hand, social and historical changes in areas such as the economy, the political system, or the structure of the family can stimulate changes in the kind of social personality prevalent in a given society. On the other hand, personality can itself be a cause of social change. This may occur, for example, in cases when pressure for changes in the society's culture or institutions is exerted by personality needs that are often unconscious and that are unfulfilled or only partially met by a particular sociocultural system. Thus the collective personality is subject to change from pressures emanating from major structural change, but changes or conflicts on the level of personality can also create tendencies toward change in society's institutions.

After a brief discussion of anthropological and historical evidence of the existence of and differences among collective personality types in different societies at different periods, I shall turn to an examination of the nature and sources of the traditional collective feminine personality. I argue that this personality, which was created by the process of socialization, was characteristic of women in American society at the beginning of the 1960s. In addition, I shall explore dysfunctions and mechanisms of change pertaining to the female personality. These gave rise to a new social personality which began to emerge in American society during the middle 1960s and 1970s.

ANTHROPOLOGY AND HISTORY

Social personality is linked to the historical period, the locale, and the culture and social system into which a human being is born. Because little of human behavior is instinctual, humans as a species have a vast repertoire of potential personality characteristics that can be developed. Humans are also unique in that to a great extent their personality characteristics and behavioral patterns are learned from social interaction with other humans, a process referred to as socialization. As Erik Erikson has stated, "Man's inborn instincts are drive fragments to be assembled, given meanings and organized during a prolonged childhood."[2] Societies and cultures differ greatly in the way they assemble those fragments. They are similar, however, in their overall goal, which is the development of social personalities that exhibit desired regularities and that equip individuals to survive in the society into which they are born.

Anthropologists and social historians have provided us with a rich literature documenting the diverse ways in which human groups at different times and in different cultures fulfill this common goal. Human gestures and even biological changes vary or are given wholly different meanings among sundry societies. Anthropologist Weston LaBarre shows, for example, that gestures that may seem to be instinctual are in fact developed and used differently in various cultures. Shaking the head up and down and smiling signifies the affirmative in our culture, while among the Abyssinians the same response is communicated by throwing the head back and raising the eyebrows; similarly, among some African tribes smiling is more likely to express embarrassment or discomfiture than positive feelings.[3] Certain universal biological processes are also given diverse meanings in different societies. Margaret Mead's classic study of adolescence demonstrates the wide discrepancies in the treatment of the onset of female puberty and menses.[4] She reports, for example, that northern California Indian tribal societies fear such changes in young women, "stressing particularly the danger which the girl could do the community at this time." In contrast, among the Yuki Indians, puberty is greeted with high hopes for the great potential power of the pubescent female to enhance the community's life by magically increasing the harvest. In contrast to the behavior among the Samoans, where, Mead states, there are no changes in a girl's status or relationships attendant upon puberty, adults in the Gilbert Islands of the western Pacific confine their daughters for up to eighteen months in the gloomy inner cubicle of a special house called a *ko.*

Anthropological research has also illuminated striking differences among cultures in their ideas and norms about what constitutes the acceptable, proper, and "natural" role behavior of women and men. Again Mead's research is of particular importance. In *Sex and Temperament in Three Primitive Societies,* she reports that among two of the three New Guinean tribes she studied there was no expectation that men and women would exhibit different personalities, temperaments, or abilities. However, these two tribes differed in the nature of the social personality characteristic of their members. Among the Mundugamor, competitive, violent, aggressively sexed, and nonnurturant behavior was found among both men and women. Sexually undifferentiated social personalities were also apparent in the second tribe, the Arapesh, among whom the personality characteristics valued, expected, and developed in all adults were those of cooperation, nurturance, and gentleness. Finally, among the third tribe, the Tchambuli, Mead found that men and women were thought to have "naturally" different social personalities. Mead describes Tchambuli women as self-assertive, vigorously efficient, and unadorned. In contrast, men depend on women for support, food, and affection. Among the Tchambuli, men are personally sensitive, wary of one another—even catty—and spend most of their time discussing and taking part in various artistic activities, such as carving, painting, and dancing. Thus cultures can differ in the social personalities they create and encourage in their people, and also in their expectations of similar or dissimilar social personalities for men and women.[5]

In a more recent and strikingly provocative study, *Men and Women*, anthropologist Ernestine Friedl brings together diverse field evidence of the nature of sex roles and personality characteristics in various societies. Friedl contends that male and female differences in power, privilege, and self-esteem differ across societies, and that these differences are tied to the society's material structure and the level of technology upon which it depends for subsistence. She concludes that "the position of men and women in the social structure among foragers and horticulturalists has consequences for the quality of the relationships between the sexes, and for cultural beliefs about maleness and femaleness and sexuality."[6]

Historians have also examined data that demonstrate cultural differences, but their emphasis is more often on changes within the same society over time. Particularly relevant to our study is the work of social historians who have explored change in the cultural expectations attached to sex roles. Observation of one society at different points in time may yield evidence of changes in cultural ideas (norms) of what constitutes "proper and acceptable" behavior for men and women. This sort of research reveals that dramatic changes have occurred over time in the United States with respect to sex roles. In the era prior to 1919, as we have seen, cultural norms encouraged women to be fragile, incompetent, and sexual, while the proper personality for men was characterized by self-reliance, strength, courage, and dominance in the home. In the period since the 1920s the same society has evidenced very different expectations, with men expected to be significantly less aggressive and ambitious than in the past, and encouraged to develop some nurturant traits as part of their social personalities. At the same time, the social personality encouraged in women began to emphasize more autonomous and assertive characteristics than had been true prior to 1920.[7]

In another example, Edward Shorter provides a picture of the changes in the social personality of mothers between the fifteenth and seventeenth centuries in France. At the beginning of the period, mothers were regularly indifferent to their children and even harsh in their care of infants. Shorter reports that "wakeful children were commonly knocked into the sleep of insensibility" and that there existed "a well-nigh universal practice of leaving it [the infant] alone for long stretches of time," during which the child was permitted "to stew in its own excrement for hours on end, tightly wound in swaddling clothes." By the end of seventeenth century, this behavior pattern began to change, and there emerged the expectation for a new type of maternal personality, which expressed love for infants and children and placed the happiness and welfare of offspring above all other considerations.[8]

Thus the sociocultural characteristics of a society are crucially important in determining which of a wide range of personality characteristics will tend to characterize the social personalities of its people. Not only is a society capable of encouraging certain selected characteristics and of discouraging others, thus producing a high degree of regularity in the social personalities developed in that context, but cultures also differ among themselves in their choices of desirable traits. Furthermore, evidence suggests that in many cultures the nature of these characteristics varies over time, with different historical periods distinguished by a unique configuration of traits characteristic of its social personalities.

PARENTS AND SOCIALIZATION

In exploring the relationship between personality and social change in the case of American women during the period after 1960, I shall begin by analyzing the development of the female social personality at the beginning of this period. As noted in the theoretical discussion of Freudian theory in Chapter 1, the model that I use in this endeavor is one that hypothesizes that society will attempt to repress those characteristics viewed as deviating from or threatening some aspect of the society or the individual's expected future role in that society. For Freud, the repression of characteristics and drives is of particular importance in understanding the development of human personality, and he claims that the most powerful repression occurs during childhood at the hands of the child's parents (or primary adult caretakers). It is of course true that the social personality is also shaped by those traits or behavioral characteristics that are not repressed.

Childhood socialization, then, is to a large extent future oriented. Its goal generally is to prepare children for life as adults in the society by teaching codes of behavior and by controlling deviant tendencies. Socialization is not, however, necessarily uniform for all children in a culture. In our society different traits are encouraged and repressed among specific groups of children, and sex is an important criterion for distinguishing such traits. Parents, as primary early caretakers, respond to these circumstances by treating their children differently according to sex from earliest infancy.[9] As Eleanor Maccoby and Carol Jacklin point out, American parents generally have fairly clear, although not always well-articulated, ideas of what characteristics should be repressed and/or encouraged in their children:

> A scene from the early musical "Carousel" epitomizes (in somewhat caricatured form) some of the feelings that parents have about bringing up sons as opposed to daughters. A young man discovers he is to be a father. He rhapsodizes about what kind of son he expects to have. The boy will be tall and tough as a tree, and no one will dare to boss him around; it will be all right for his mother to teach him manners but she mustn't make a sissy out of him. He'll be good at wrestling and will be able to herd cattle, run a riverboat, drive spikes, etc. Then the prospective father realizes, with a start, that the child may be a girl. The music changes to a gentle theme. She will have ribbons in her hair, she will be sweet and petite (just like her mother), and suitors will flock around her. There's a slightly discordant note, introduced for comic relief from sentimentality, when the expectant father brags that she'll be half again as bright as girls are meant to be; but then he returns to the main theme: she must be protected, and he must find enough money to raise her in a setting where she will meet the right kind of man to marry.[10]

Parents respond to the culture's ideas of expected sex role differences through actual behavior as well as fantasy. Much care, for example, is taken to distinguish boy babies from girl babies by appropriate colors in clothing and blankets, room decorations, and playthings. If the parents should fail to provide such signals as to the child's sex, it is likely that friends or relatives will ask for verbal identification before interaction with the infant occurs. Michael Lewis notes that the sex of a child is so important culturally that expectant parents spend a great deal of effort in attempting to predict the sex of their future offspring.[11]

Although the research is not definitive, there have been some consistent findings reported with respect to parental treatment of infants by sex. For example, studies have reported that parents talk to girl infants more than to boys and handle them more often. Also, parents seem to try to elicit "gross motor behavior" more often from their infant sons than from their daughters, handling their sons roughly and pulling their arms and legs vigorously. Maccoby and Jacklin assert that "the continuing theme appears to be that girls are treated as though they were more fragile than boys."[12] This attitude is reflected in the evidence that fathers are more apprehensive about the physical well-being of infant daughters than of sons, while mothers in another study expressed more worry about physical danger to infant daughters than to sons.

As children grow older the differences in parental treatment by sex continue, although the forms change. Walter Mischel suggests that the most consistent and general distinctions between the sexes in personality development are in the area of aggression, with girls encouraged to exhibit nonaggressive, dependent personality characteristics and boys taught to repress dependency and show aggressive behavior.[13] Research by David Aberle and Kaspar Naegele found, for example, that middle-class fathers are satisfied by different characteristics in their male and female children, even at fairly young ages. Satisfactions with respect to girls center on their being "pretty, nice, affectionate, and well-liked," while the same fathers are best satisfied when their sons show ability "to be responsible, to show initiative and to stand up for themselves."[14] Miriam Johnson's and Elizabeth Goodenough's findings are similar, demonstrating that fathers generally encourage adaptive, dependent, and passive traits in their daughters, with the goal that the girls should be "pleasing to others," and even sexually attrative within the limits of what is appropriate for a child. These same fathers carry out instrumental or goal-oriented behavior vis-à-vis their sons, encouraging excellence in performance and competence, particularly in nonfamilial settings, and guiding their sons away from "sissy" or feminine behavior.[15] Mothers also expect different behavior in their boy and girl children. C.Y. Nakamura and M.M. Roger found that mothers of boys had higher expectations of practical autonomy in their children than did mothers of girls.[16] Thus it seems that parents have different expectations of and exhibit varied behavior with respect to their male and female children, repressing and encouraging different personality traits in them.

Freudian Theory and the Parents' Role

From the above it is evident that at the beginning of our period, parents in American society expected the future roles of their sons and daughters to differ significantly and therefore treated their children differently. In stressing the importance of the parents in the early childhood socialization process, Freudian theory suggests that such differential parental treatment will result in personality differences between boys and girls. Since the parents constitute the primary object in a young child's emotional life, their expectations and desires are rendered extremely influential in shaping behavior. Thus it is not only the parents' physical power over children, which itself is not unimportant, but also their ability to manipulate implicitly or explicitly the emotional ties and dependence of their children on their love and care that accounts for their special influence.

According to Freudian theory, thoughts and wishes of which we are not aware have consequences for our personalities just as much as do the conscious acts of individuals toward us. The unconscious, for Freud, is a realm that is particularly important for understanding parent-child interaction and the consequences for the child's personality development. To reiterate Freud's idea, instinctual, largely unconscious drives and desires, the id, are repressed and/or channeled to socially approved ends during the process of socialization. The crucial factor in the success of this endeavor is fear on the part of the child of its parents' wrath. Freud suggested that this fear is triggered by the child's growing recognition that many of his/her desires and drives are viewed as "bad" by the adults on whom he/she is dependent.

The most important fear in small boys, according to Freud, is that their sexual desire for their mothers will be answered with violence, specifically castration. The competition with the father figure for the mother's love generates such fear on the part of the boy that he responds by identifying with the male adult in order to avoid punishment. Instead of attempting to replace the father, the boy shifts his goal to the socially approved end of being "just like Dad." There is in the male child, says Freud, an unconscious recognition that by controlling his id, repressing his desires for sexual relations with his mother, he will at once avoid castration and eventually, upon maturity, be allowed to fulfill his desires with a woman, as has his father.

This model of the successful resolution of the Oedipus crisis is the major example of the way in which fear of parental punishment generates a repressive or punishing mechanism (the superego) within the individual personality, modeled after the parents' own ideas of proper behavior. Moreover, this superego is the embodiment of the culture's norms regarding a wide range of attitudes and behaviors. Even at the stage where the developed superego enables the child to repress his id, he is of course still responsive to external prohibition by parents or other authority figures, but such control is largely internalized as part of the individual's own personality by the age of seven or eight. The mechanism of such a significant change in the locus of emotional and behavioral control is the child's identification with the parents' norms and values, triggered by an often unconscious sexual "showdown" between the boy and his father over that most socially unacceptable of all desires, maternal incest. Thus not only parents' actions, but also their interaction with their child's unconscious desires and wishes have implications that significantly influence the development of personality.

Female Personality Development

As we saw earlier, Freud argued that the development of the female's personality is significantly different from that of the male's in that the young girl experiences nothing comparable to the boy's fear of castration. As a result, her motivation to identify with parental norms, to develop a strongly repressive superego, and to channel or sublimate id energy to socially acceptable goals is less well developed than that of her brother. Freud suggests that this basic difference between males and females, centered on anatomy, is responsible for women's less important contributions to art, literature, and civilization throughout history (poor sublimation), their tendency toward feelings of inferiority (lack of a penis), and their passive, masochistic, and narcissistic personality modes (weak superego).[17]

Recent revisions of Freudian theory, particularly as it pertains to female personality development, have argued that while Freud's descriptive account of the female personality was largely accurate, he overestimated the importance of biology in the development of femininity.[18] If we assume that the most important mechanism Freud identified was the influence of parents on their children, we shift the focus of investigation from anatomy to an analysis of identification with and repression by parental proscriptions, norms, and expectations. Thus parental influence becomes a primary mechanism of personality development for female children, much as in Freud's own model for

male children. In other words, I am reasserting the importance of
Freud's insight that the crucial element in personality development is
children's identification with their parents and their parents' expectations and prohibitions. As the same time, however, I am suggesting a
revision of Freud's work by asserting that this model be employed in
analyzing and understanding the development of not only male but
also female personality, as well as the differences between them.

I suggest that the fear of parental rejection and of parents' power to
punish socially undesirable id drives is a reality for all children, whether
that fear takes a specific "castration" form or not. Such fears produce
a psychic and emotional process by which children, against their own
wishes and desires, are forced to repress or rechannel (sublimate) their
desires for gratification of libido and, through a process of identification,
to take on their parents' conceptions of socially acceptable ideas and
behavior. The development of the superego is the second stage in the
process by which society enforces its conceptions of right and wrong,
proper and improper behavior on its members. First, parents as primary
caretakers control their children directly, and second, after much psychic
pain, fear, and struggle, the children themselves develop the capacity to
intrapsychically repress those behaviors and ideas which are unacceptable
in their society. Thus the culture's expectations and proscriptions,
through the mechanism of parental love and identification, ultimately
become inculcated into and part of its children's personalities.

How then can the differences in personality between males and females be understood? I have posited similar psychological and social
processes of identification, repression, and conformity for all children,
and yet argue that male and female personalities differ. The answer
lies in the disparate cultural conceptions of what forms of behavior are
socially acceptable for females as compared with those for males. Even
the small amount of research summarized in this chapter reveals that
significant differences exist in both the expectations upon which parents
act and also in their actual treatment of their children. The adult roles
that the culture expects females to fulfill, which center on nurturance,
homemaking, and child care differ greatly from the protective, achievement, and extrafamilial roles that men are expected to fulfill. The
socialization process is oriented toward equipping children to successfully fulfill anticipated roles, and differential socialization by sex reflects that future orientation. When boys identify with parents and
develop superegos that repress aspects of themselves, part of what is

repressed is those characteristics that the society deems appropriate to femininity. Similarly, through their exposure to the cultural definition of femininity, girls learn to repress by mechanisms finally established in their own personalities those ideas, modes of behavior, and desires that the culture has labeled masculine.

It should be noted that the process by which the personalities of children develop the capacity to control and repress what the culture deems inappropriate does not imply that those original id desires are totally destroyed. A unique contribution of Freudian theory is to suggest that the process of repression and sublimation—the conflict between the id and the superego, the individual and his/her culture—is a constant struggle that lasts throughout the individual's life. Here the importance of the unconscious is crucial, for socially unacceptable drives and tendencies remain part of the psychic structure and personality of all individuals, no matter how well "socialized." Thus in Freud's view individuals are not passive recipients of their society's prescriptions, and the price of conformity to the culture and of control of the id is a high one. The struggle between id and superego produces or at least contributes to guilt, anxiety, and sometimes neuroses and even more severe forms of mental illness. With respect to sex role socialization, this implies that original tendencies in all members of society, which Freud suggests include aspects of *both* culturally defined masculinity and femininity, remain in a struggle with a culture that through the superego punishes any straying from "appropriate" forms of masculinity or femininity. I shall return to this conflict built into the personality in my discussion of personality change later in this chapter.

In sum, I have pointed to the enormous importance of parents as mediators between the id-dominated pre-Oedipal child and the culture's insistence that its members conform to a common set of norms and values. Particularly important for our study is the expectation inherent in these norms that boys and girls, destined for different adult roles, should exhibit different behavior modes, attitudes, and personality traits. According to the Freudian model, by the time of the resolution of the Oedipal stage—about age seven or eight—the boy child has developed a superego that generally ensures his conformity to culturally defined masculinity and his repression of so-called feminine characteristics. I have suggested that by this stage the girl child has similarly developed a superego that punishes deviation from culturally prescribed femininity. Parents' own socialization experiences, which have influenced their ideas of the proper behavior for boys and girls, are thus transferred to the next generation, enhancing order and stability in society and regularity in the social personality of its male and female members.

OTHER AGENCIES OF SOCIALIZATION

Of course parental upbringing is not the only agency of socialization that influences the development of personality in a society as complex as ours. Many of the traditional functions performed by parents with respect to their children have been transferred to institutions that specialize, for example, in educational or religious training, recreation or social activities. Contacts with other children become increasingly important as children and then teenagers learn more about and interact with the world outside their own families. According to Freudian theory, however, the primary emotional and psychic importance of parents in the child's life is not displaced by any one of these nonfamilial socializers. The early years of socialization lay a foundation of sex role expectations that is not easily challenged or profoundly shaken until adulthood, if then. Sexual identity and ideas of sex differences are already well developed by the time children begin to be seriously influenced by forces other than their own parents and family.[19]

Nevertheless, as other agencies do play a role in the socialization process, I shall undertake a brief examination of the influence of the most important ones. This discussion will also be useful in highlighting the wider culture's conceptions of "proper" masculinity and femininity. These norms, of course, at once reflect, reinforce, and contribute to parents' ideas of acceptable sex role behavior. The belief that there is a dominant set of fairly homogeneous norms and values in a society is not a new one. Such a hegemonic ideology provides consistency and reinforcement of the expectations of parents, teachers, and peer groups in enforcing conformity to sex role expectations.

Language

The importance of language as a mechanism of socialization has received considerable attention in the literature.[20] Through its ability to create special needs and ways of thinking and feeling specific to a particular culture, language communicates a culture-bound view of reality, and, with respect to individual development, helps to create attitudes and feelings toward others and oneself. As Gordon Allport points out, some words and concepts are exceedingly powerful in generating emotions in both the speaker and listener. He offers the following example:

> Ask yourself how you feel and what thoughts you have when you read the words "school teacher" and then "school marm." Certainly the second phrase calls up something more strict, more ridiculous, more disagreeable than the former. Here are four innocent letters: M-A-R-M. But they make us shudder a bit, laugh a bit, and scorn a bit. They call up an image of a spare, humorless, irritable old maid. They do not tell us she is an individual human being with sorrows and troubles of her own. They force her instantly into a rejective category.[21]

Thus language has the ability to communicate a culture's view of specific groups and to affect the attitudes of outsiders as well as the self-image and personality development of members of the group itself. The personality development of boys and girls is deeply influenced by the language they learn.

What then is the image of women communicated to children by the English language? Barrie Thorne and Nancy Henley argue that

> language helps enact and transmit every type of inequality, including that between the sexes; . . . in the culture of English speakers, men are more highly regarded than women. The male is associated with the universal, the general, the subsuming; the female is more often excluded or is the special case. Words associated with males more often have positive connotations; they convey notions of power, prestige, and leadership. In contrast, female words are more often negative, conveying weakness, inferiority, immaturity, a sense of the trivial. Terms applied to women are narrower in reference, and they are more likely to assume derogatory sexual connotations which overshadow their meanings.[22]

An interesting experiment conducted by Inge Broverman and her colleagues shows the evaluation implicit in many sex-linked adjectives in the English language.[23] Respondents in this now famous study were asked to list characteristics that they believed to be linked to sex, that is, different between men and women. Each of these characteristics (listed in Table 3.1) was then separately judged by a different group of respondents in terms of its "social desirability." Respondents were asked, "How desirable is this characteristic for an adult in our society?" Adjectives associated with masculinity, such as independent, aggressive, rational, virile, or brave, consistently received significantly higher desirability scores than did those associated with femininity, such as submissive, illogical, helpless, passive, or subjective. Thus the English language tends to include words and concepts that place boys and girls, and men and women into separate categories—thus emphasizing differences—and that implicitly (and sometimes explicitly) grant females secondary status. The results of this male bias in the language can be expected to be felt in the process of socialization and in the development of self-image and identity for both boys and girls in American society. The universality and hegemony of language create categories that seem natural and that predispose members of the culture of which it is part to think of men and women as different and unequal, dominant or inferior, desirable or undesirable.

Children's Literature

As an embodiment of a culture, written language is a particularly important agency of socialization. Both inside and outside of educational institutions, books are recognized as important influences on children's conceptions of the nature of society, what it expects of them, and how they may be sanctioned for deviance. In examining the images of men and women and boys and girls reflected in books from which children learn, Lenore Weitzman found, for example, that in prize-winning preschool picture books published between 1967 and 1972, women are greatly underrepresented in the titles, central roles, and illustrations.[24] Where women do appear,

> Their characterization reinforced traditional sex-role stereotypes: boys are active while girls are passive; boys lead and rescue others while girls follow and serve others . . . men engage in a wide variety of occupations while women are presented only as wives and mothers . . . little girls receive attention and praise for their attractiveness while boys are admired for their achievements and cleverness.[25]

Textbooks used in grades one through twelve reveal similar findings. In reading and spelling, mathematics, science, and social studies books, Weitzman argues, the image of women is a limited one. Either women are almost totally absent—only 6 percent of pictures in science texts include adult women—or the roles in which women are depicted are largely limited to home and mother roles.

Media

Children in a technologically advanced society such as ours learn from an array of media sources in addition to books. Television in particular is increasingly important in transmitting cultural norms, values, and prescriptions to children who spend a great deal of time in front of their home sets. Different roles of men and women, and differential behavior and abilities of boys and girls, are communicated by television. For example, in one popular traditional cartoon show, Popeye, the male hero, eats spinach and is transformed into the savior and protector of a weak and helpless woman, Olive Oyl. Even the more recent television shows for children have been criticized for their reinforcement of the image of men and boys as achievers, adventurers, and heros and their depiction of women as helpless, passive, or engaged in roles limited to those of wives and mothers.[26]

Analyses of other cultural agencies of socialization reach similar conclusions. For example, examination of the images of women in popular American song lyrics in the last two decades, in advertisements, and even in dominant aspects of Western art and literature suggests that these forms of cultural expression and communication reflect and further create sex-typed norms and expectations by depicting women, if at all, exclusively as homemakers, mothers and/or sex objects.[27] Thus the most popular and predominant cultural agencies, whether geared to children or to adults, emphasize the differences between men and women and the limited nature of women's role options.

Peer Groups

The influence of peer groups is another important determinant of the behavior, goals, and personality development of young people, especially as adolescence approaches. The strength of the peer group in enforcing and reinforcing norms is discussed at length in James Coleman's classic study of adolescence in America, where he asserts that in the high school subculture, desirable traits are highly sex-typed.[28] For boys, athletic interest and ability and academic success are the avenues to prestige, while for girls, popularity, and especially popularity with boys, is the dominant method for achieving social prestige. Such prestige and recognition among peers are especially important during adolescence, as youngsters begin to search for sources of self-esteem and identity outside their own families. As do other agencies of socialization, the peer group works to enforce its norms upon its members and, especially at puberty, seeks to encourage the abandonment of characteristics deemed inappropriate for the proper adult sex role. Girls specifically are encouraged to give up "tomboy" behavior, which may have been tolerated prior to adolescence, and to get on with the business of learning to be feminine.

Coleman suggests that for female adolescents, physical attractiveness, "beauty," is the key to the popularity to which they aspire. The importance of beauty as a means to attain popularity is especially crucial during the sophomore and junior years in high school, according to Coleman, when dating begins in a serious fashion. The peer group sets, and seeks to enforce, a set of norms—a successful dating personality— which for girls focuses on the most external and superficial aspects of the self. In order to gain prestige among peers, adolescent females are pressed to emphasize physical attractiveness and appearance and to deemphasize or repress such attributes as intelligence or competence. Good looks are thus a prerequisite for girls' attaining popularity, and only by adhering to these norms will they avoid the negative sanctions available to their peers in the form of rejection, exclusion, and mockery.

At adolescence, then, the peer group emerges as a particularly important agency of socialization, with sanctioning power to reinforce behavior, aspirations, and attitudes. Here again the rigid sex typing of males and females is encouraged in preparation for adult roles. For girls, peer group pressure during this time tends to communicate that female identity and individual self-esteem are primarily dependent on superficial physical characteristics and on popularity with boys. Only then will girls be considered "feminine" and "successful" according to cultural standards.

School

Although schools are not the only social institutions responsible for the development of intellectual functioning, they clearly play an important role in that regard. Although most boys and girls in the United States attend the same schools, there has traditionally been a considerable degree of segregation by sex within each school. Boys and girls are told to line up separately, often are seated separately in classrooms, and even at young ages are exposed to sharply different physical education programs. By junior high school there has been routine separation for certain subjects—boys take shop or woodwork, while girls are given courses in home economics, sewing, or cooking—and during high school there is increasing specialization by sex in the area of electives and vocational training.[29] Nancy Frazier and Myra Sadlek found that career guidance, which is usually performed by school counselors, encourages traditional sex-typed aspirations.[30] Girls are channeled into courses that will presumably prepare them for homemaking roles or sex-typed jobs, while boys are guided toward training for "masculine" occupations. The staffing of elementary and secondary schools in American society itself reinforces the conception that the sexes should prepare for and will achieve different educational goals. Even as recently as 1965, for example, 85 percent of elementary school teachers were female, while 79 percent of elementary school principles were male.[31] In other words, authority figures were male, and women fulfilled the more nurturant roles in the primary school setting.

For those women who aspire to and enroll in institutions of higher education, a variety of institutionalized obstacles to equality between the sexes and to high achievement for women are evident. Pamela Roby's research documents structural barriers that "hinder or halt female students in their efforts to obtain college or university educations."[32] Practices that amount to outright discrimination against women in student admissions and financial aid, counseling that stresses women's traditional roles, degree requirements that demand full-time study or campus residence, and the lack of faculty women to serve as role models all contribute, in Roby's view, to the special burdens placed on women in institutions of higher education. Table 2.6 indicates that the proportion of women students compared with men declines at each increasing level of educational attainment. The evidence that educational institutions differentiate students by sex, treat them differently, and, perhaps most important, assume that training and educational achievement is more important for boys (men) than for girls (women) indicates that sexual inequality is experienced and taught in schools.

IMPLICATIONS FOR PERSONALITY

What sort of female personality emerges from the interaction of these agencies of socialization, which both assume and create differences between boys and girls? I have suggested that those characteristics listed in Table 3.1 that are stereotyped as uniquely female can be understood as the result of the differential socialization experiences of male and female children. The culture, society, institutions, and agencies of socialization expect females to exhibit "feminine" personality characteristics, and they frequently create a series of situations and pressures by which these expectations ultimately become reality. In other words, a self-fulfilling prophesy is generated. Some of these sex-linked personality characteristics, however, have been judged as harmful, either to the individuals involved or to the society as a whole.[33] In this section I shall concentrate on three developmental aspects of the female personality that are believed to embody such negative consequences: the process of identity formation, the emergence of self-esteem, and the development of achievement motivation.

Most psychologists agree that the process of individual identity formation is a crucial part of the maturation process and of the development of a healthy adult personality. A healthy adult personality may be defined in many different ways, of course, but the definition used here is the widely accepted formulation of Abraham Maslow.[34] Maslow's work suggests that adult psychic health can be defined as a drive for self-actualization, for mastery of the environment, and for fulfillment of one's potential as a human being. The development of such a self-actualizing adult personality is closely linked to the earlier process of building a strong and independent identity. Much of our understanding of this developmental process rests on the research of neo-Freudian psychologist Erik Erikson.[35] Like Freud, Erikson argues that personality development involves a series of conflicts or crises. One of the most important, and the crisis characteristic of adolescence, is the identity crisis. Its successful resolution, according to Erikson, is necessary for the development of a healthy adult personality. The adolescent must wrestle with the questions, "Who am I?" and "How do I appear to others?" To resolve this set of conflicts, the young person must choose a set of goals, specifically an adult role—"occupation" or "career," in Erikson's terms— that will give security, meaning, and fulfillment through life.

When we examine Erikson's model of identity development as it applies to adolescent girls, there is some evidence of problems. Because the adult role of women, as culturally prescribed, is a fixed one of wife and mother, which does not involve the weighing and sorting out of alternatives, girls may develop less clear or weaker identities than might be true for boys. The process of testing out a range of potential identities or "careers" is an important male developmental experience during adolescence that is culturally denied or at least undeveloped for females. Thus we find evidence in the psychological literature of special problems among female adolescents, related to the aborted development of a strong individual identity.

Adolescent psychologists Elizabeth Douvan and Carol Kay have detailed the nature of identity problems that emerge from the fixed nature of the female adult sex role of wife and mother.[36] On the one hand, they suggest that the identity developed in response to such expectations depends relatively little on the individual involved. Rather than being self-generated—a response to the question "Who am I?"—adult female identity depends largely on the characteristics of the man and children to whom the female is attached. Her identity is as someone's wife and someone's mother, not as a separate individual. On the other hand, the method by which that identity is attained precludes active planning, preparation, or initiation. In our culture, the role of the female is passive, since norms dictate that the man should choose the woman he marries, and the process of attaining the adult female status of wife is infused with spontaneity and romance rather than planning and preparation. As Douvan and Kay succinctly state:

> The sexual identity, so critical for feminine development, permits no orderly or conscious effort. It is a mysterious and romantic issue freighted with fiction, mystique and illusion. The real core of feminine settlement [identity]—living in intimacy with a beloved man—is a future prospect for which there is no rehearsal. Girls in contrast [to boys] are absorbed much more in fantasy, particularly fantasy about boys and popularity, marriage and love.[37]

Thus the assignment of a single acceptable adult role to women may discourage or even prevent the adolescent girl from engaging in the inner search necessary for the development of a strong, independent sense of identity. This assertion is supported by Douvan's and Kay's evidence that females at adolescence are more dependent on their peers for their own sense of self and self-esteem, and that they remain more sensitive than males to others' opinions of them. As one researcher states, "society teaches girls to stake *themselves* on making an agreeable impression on others . . . ."[38] The fixed goal of wife and mother at once predisposes girls to focus on the most external attributes of the self, particularly physical appearance, and to expect to receive their inner identity from another, depending on him to decide who and what she is. The socialization of girls in preparation for their culturally prescribed adult role thus seems to be an important factor in their greater dependency and weaker inner sense of self and strength in comparison with males. If Erikson, Maslow, and others are correct in their assertions that a strong sense of self-identity is developed from an inner struggle during adolescence to choose a "self" and is also crucial for the development of a healthy, self-actualized adult personality, women seem to be at a distinct disadvantage in this regard, since their sex role discourages or even prevents this development.

A second personality characteristic that has been examined extensively in the light of sex differences is that of self-esteem, the individual's view of how much he or she is worth or valued as an individual. People who have low self-esteem often evidence psychological feelings of inadequacy, inferiority, and even self-hatred. That girls evidence overall lower self-esteem than do boys is suggested by a number of studies, which often assert that this lower self-esteem is linked to sex role differentiation in society. In a recent summary of the psychological literature, Reesa Vaughter concludes that consistent findings show that "successful socialization into the feminine role is accompanied by low levels of self-regard."[39] Studies have indicated, for example, that significantly greater numbers of girls than boys report that they would prefer to be a member of the "opposite" sex.[40] Among the explanations offered by girls for such a choice are the assertions that "male" activities, such as sports, are more fun, that males have characteristics that are valuable and/or valued, such as bravery, independence, and strength, and that the male role has more power or privileges (or both) associated with it than does the female role. And as we have already seen in Table 3.1, adults also consistently rate more of those qualities associated with the "ideal male" as more valuable than the qualities associated with the "ideal female."[41] According to Vaughter, "The theme that the masculinity of men is more highly valued than the femininity of women is one of the most consistent themes to be found in the research data."[42] What is so striking here is that not only men but also, and even especially, women consistently devalue the attributes of members of the female sex.

If women's abilities and qualities are not valued highly, if girls think it better to be boys because they have "all the fun," if women are prejudiced negatively against other women, thinking them incompetent, petty, passive, or uninteresting, especially as compared with men, it would not be surprising to suggest that they tend to hold these feelings about themselves as well. In addition the adult role prescribed for women of wife, mother, and housewife is itself clearly accorded little prestige or power in society.[43] Women who fill these roles seem to be especially susceptible to feelings of little worth, as indicated by the classic response to questioners, "I'm *only* a housewife." Thus low self-esteem among females, which interferes with self-actualization and may contribute to such feelings as self-hatred and inferiority, is linked to the process of sex role socialization, the division of men and women into prescribed and mutually exclusive adult sex roles, the social pressures on both sexes to remain within the society's definition of those roles, and the social devaluation of the female role.

Finally, a third personality characteristic hypothesized as overrepresented in the female population is low achievement motivation. Matina Horner's famous study of college students posited that women's lower motivation to achieve, as compared with men's, was a response to a situation in which "competition, independence, competence, intellectual achievement, and leadership reflect positively on mental health but are basically inconsistent or in conflict with femininity."[44] Girls are taught during their socialization experiences that femininity, and therefore their success and identity as females, is threatened or may be destroyed by achievement. Although a subsequent study failed to find evidence of Horner's "fear of success" as a personality characteristic of females, the researchers suggest that this hypothesized characteristic "may certainly exist," but that Horner's research methods may have been flawed.[45] Despite questions about the validity of Horner's specific study, such disproportionately female behavior as "playing dumb" or reducing occupational and intellectual aspirations implies a conflict between traditional concepts of femininity and achievement, particularly in areas defined socially as "male."[46] For women who remain "ambitious" and who do achieve in these areas, the existence of conflict both with existing norms and with aspects of their own socialization experiences may produce rejection or ridicule from members of society and/or personal anxiety about their own femininity.

The constrictions surrounding female personality development have especially important implications for women's educational attainment and intellectual development. Consistent findings link girls' less developed intellectual abilities and lower levels of educational achievement, as compared with boys', to the process of differential sex role socialization.[47] In a review of this literature, Eleanor Maccoby concludes that such personality traits as conformity, dependence, and passivity interfere with important aspects of intellectual functioning. In particular, intellectual creativity and originality are viewed as inconsistent with and are rarely developed by dependent and/or conformist personalities. Since these latter personality traits are thought to be more appropriate for girls than for boys, and thus encouraged as part of the development of femininity, Maccoby suggests that sex role socialization may interfere with and inhibit girls' intellectual development and functioning.

To these inhibiting socialization practices we must also add the pressures against intellectual development exerted by other agencies of socialization. As mentioned earlier, strong peer group pressure emphasizes popularity as a girl's most important goal and views intellectual ability and academic achievement as contradictory to this goal. The schools themselves reinforce differences by sex in academic aspirations, specific areas of academic specialization, and career planning. Female achievement is questioned on a general level, but achievement in fields that are culturally defined as "male" is viewed with particular horror.

The specific period in life at which female underachievement becomes evident provides data consistent with this argument, for it is at puberty— the period at which agencies of socialization begin to exert serious pressure on girls to adhere to their "proper" sex role in behavior and aspirations—that we see the sharpest rise in underachievement among girls.[48] By the time girls reach college age, barriers to academic success may have been internalized. The fear that achievement is in conflict with socially prescribed femininity may become a part of a woman's own personality and inhibit intellectual development and achievement. This situation is aptly described by an M.I.T. student quoted by sociologist Alice Rossi:

> For years I have had to fight to retain my interest in aeronautics. My high school teacher said I was crazy to even think of going into aeronautical engineering. My mother said I'd never find a man willing to marry a woman who likes to "tinker with motors," as she put it. My professors say I won't get a job in industry and should switch to another engineering speciality.[49]

The socialization process discussed above distinguishes between the sexes, tends to create in women those personality characteristics least conducive to intellectual development, and creates barriers to women's academic achievement and success by defining such success as contradictory and threatening to socially defined femininity.

In sum, the traditional definition of femininity, and a socialization process that involves different expectations for the sexes in behavior, attitudes, and personality characteristics produce an adult female social personality that, in comparison with that of males, tends to be at once more dependent, more passive and less achievement oriented, and also tends to lack self-esteem, a strong inner identity, and the ability to fulfill intellectual potential. I do not mean to overstate the case in this regard. Not all women have such characteristics, just as all men do not possess equally high self-esteem or achievement motivation. The concept of a collective personality, however, as noted earlier, attempts to explain the personality characteristics that the institutional structure, socialization practices, and cultural expectations encourage among individuals in a given society at a given time. The claim here is that the socialization process and structure of our society tend to encourage the production of specific male and female personality types, and that differences between them are in the directions indicated in the preceding section.

In addition to elucidating the social personality traditionally encouraged in American women I have argued that some of those characteristics are demonstrably harmful to women themselves, and to the people with whom they interact. The tendency to develop personalities characterized by low self-esteem, poor inner identity, or low aspirations—the "normal" outcome of adjustment to femininity—puts harmful limits on the attainment of a mature, healthy individual adult personality. But the loss to society through such a socialization process should also be noted. A society that promotes such personalities in women, not only prevents them from developing their full potential as human beings and from feeling that they are worthwhile and valuable people, but it also limits the contribution they might make to the wider society. The importance of parents in this differential socialization has been emphasized in the preceding discussion. Ultimately, however, the assumptions and expectations shared by all agencies of socialization, as embodied in the ideology and institutions of the society, are the sources of such repression.

CHANGE IN SOCIAL PERSONALITY

The previous discussion of social personality makes use of a model that emphasizes socialization as a process essentially conservative in nature. From this perspective, socialization is viewed as a mechanism that transmits and enforces the dominant sociocultural norms and social structure by teaching or constraining (or both) individuals to fulfill what the society sees as their proper and/or necessary adult roles. In a society in which male and female adult roles are significantly different, sex-typed socialization ensures the repression in each sex of those attributes and characteristics deemed inappropriate. Girls learn to repress and thus do not develop those traits, interests, and abilities that are deemed the prerogative of males and that are identified as masculine; similarly, males avoid or hide any glimmering of culturally defined femininity in their own personalities. In a given society this type of socialization creates inferiority or blocks the development of mature, healthy personalities in one sex, such "personal" problems are viewed as less important than the overall stable functioning of the stratified and sex-differentiated system of adult roles.

It is obvious that from this perspective individuals are locked into whatever personalities the culture and its institutions deem proper. As we have seen, Freudian theory suggests that this process is extremely successful in achieving its goal because primary socialization is instituted so early in life, and because its chief agencies are the at once beloved and all powerful individuals in the life of the child, namely, its parents. Since the parents themselves are products and part of the wider culture, those characteristics encouraged as well as repressed by parents in their children are likely to produce social personalities that conform to the culture's perceived needs and expectations. Deviance from this collective personality type brings negative sanctions ranging from gossip and guilt to actual ostracism from the society. In this way, socialization limits, or even prevents, the development of tendencies toward social change, and effectively preserves the social personality, norms, and institutions of the society.

Many critics have charged that this model depicts what Dennis Wrong has called an "oversocialized conception of man."[50] Wrong argues that such a model incorrectly assumes that human beings are infinitely malleable, remain passive in the face of sociocultural demands, and never act successfully to change their societies' norms or institutions. Yet change in society does occur, and ultimately, it is individuals who create such change. Freudian theory offers an explanation of this contradictory situation in which society's attempt to conserve its normative and institutional structure by socializing individuals into conformity is nonetheless sometimes challenged by groups of individuals pressing for change. For Freud, the personality is not only the embodiment of social and cultural repression, but also the locus of possible change. The unconscious retains the memory of socially unacceptable desires that were repressed during the process of socialization, and these desires remain in conflict with the socialized and conformist ego and superego. According to Freud, the memory of and potential for socially unacceptable ideas, behaviors, and aspirations is therefore always present in the human psyche.

Although Freud himself was not primarily concerned with the process of change, and thus left largely unanswered the question of how this potential for change can and does become actualized in certain groups, in certain societies, and in certain periods of history, several scholars working in the Freudian tradition have examined these issues more closely. Erik Erikson, for example, suggests that in times of major sociocultural change, the traditional social personality is no longer able to fulfill new institutional or cultural demands adequately. A conflict is thus generated, which may initiate a collective search for personality characteristics or, in Erikson's terms, a new social identity that is more compatible with the changed structural circumstances. Certain individuals or groups of individuals may be likely to experience more intensely the strains between the new structure and the traditional personality. It is those individuals and groups who can be expected, under certain conditions, to initiate and/or endorse the development of a new social personality which may include previously repressed characteristics.[51]

Erikson's own work in psychohistory tends to focus on single individuals, such as Martin Luther and Ghandi, who in his view individually triggered searches for a new social identity in response to changed structural circumstances in their societies. But in my view, Erikson's model of specially sensitized individuals whose search for identity culminates in widespread social personality and cultural change may also be applied to larger groups of individuals, no one of whom may be singled out as a charismatic leader. If certain individuals are positioned in society to feel more acutely than others the contradictions of and need for new personal qualities, it is possible that they might come together to press for change. No one of them could be viewed as the initiator, but the convergence of such people and their ability to communicate and act with one another might produce a movement that could, among other things, press for acceptance of new personality characteristics and the abandonment of the traditional social personality.

A second and complementary application of Freudian insights suggests that social personality may change even without the major structural upheavals hypothesized by Erikson. In this model, the inner conflict created by repression serves to produce an explosive reaction on the part of some individuals, culminating in changes in social personality. In his classic formulation, Freud suggests that such unresolved inner conflict most often shows itself as mental illness—both psychoses and neuroses— when social repression becomes unbearable. However, Herbert Marcuse, a neo-Freudian, suggests that sometimes such "surplus repression" may trigger movements for social change and even revolution, rather than individual illness. This might occur when enough individuals, finding the socialization process oppressive, affirm and incorporate into their personalities "unacceptable" characteristics.[52] Repression itself, then, has at least the potential of generating a number of nonconformist individuals, who, through a social movement, may demand changes in the structure, institutions, and culture of the society in order to accommodate the new social personality they embody.

In sum, personality can be viewed as a mechanism for social change. Since the process of socialization and repression is not entirely successful, there is at least the possibility that in response to major structural changes, as Erikson argues, or in reaction to unbearably large amounts of repression, as Marcuse suggests, at least some members of society may search for personality characteristics different from those inculcated by the society. If this happens, and if these individuals form a large enough group and/or are strategically placed in the society, a social movement may be generated that presses for the legitimacy of a new social personality. Thus, although the socialization is a conservative force, producing a social personality that will conform to and preserve traditional norms and institutions, there lies within the process of personality development the seeds of conflict, resistance, and revolt, which at certain times may initiate or at least reinforce changes within the very society that gave substance to that personality. In Chapters 6 and 7 we shall explore the implications of this model and test its applicability to the emergence of the women's liberation movement in the early 1960s.

CONCLUSION

The importance of society in developing a particular social personality and the ways in which the components of personality change over time have been explored in this chapter. Using Freudian theory as the model of personality development, I have examined the conservative nature of socialization processes, which through parents, schools, peer groups, and media transmit the dominant culture's norms and values by teaching individuals to fulfill what society views as their "proper" roles. For both women and men this has meant the repression of characteristics associated with traditional stereotypes of the "opposite" sex. The success of socialization as a mechanism that maintains the hegemonic collective personality is attested to by the infrequency with which major new social personalities are developed in societies and by the strength and frequency of the resistance of individuals whose identities and self-conceptions are threatened by such attempts at change.

At certain points in history, however, dramatic changes do occur in the nature of the accepted social personality. Such change is always potentially possible, according to Freud, because the repression of undesirable characteristics is never entirely complete or successful. The memory of those repressed needs and desires remains alive in the unconscious and is a force both for anxiety and for conflict with the agencies of repression.

NOTES

1. Alex Inkeles, Eugenia Hanfmann, and Helen Beier, "Model Personality and Adjustment to the Soviet Social-Political System," in Robert Endelman (ed.), *Personality and Social Life* (New York: Random House, 1967), pp. 210-32.

2. Erik Erikson, *Childhood and Society*, 2d ed. (New York: W. W. Norton, 1963), p. 95.

3. Weston LaBarre, "The Cultural Basis of Emotions and Gestures," in Gerald Starr (ed.), *Social Structure and Personality* (Boston: Little, Brown, 1974), pp. 74-80.

4. Margaret Mead, "Adolescence in Primitive and Modern Society," in V. F. Calverton and S. D. Schmalhausen (eds.), *The New Generation* (New York: Macauley, 1930), pp. 169-88.

5. Margaret Mead, *Sex and Temperament in Three Primitive Cultures* (New York: Morrow, 1963).

6. Ernestine Friedl, *Women and Men: An Anthropologist's View* (New York: Holt, Rinehart and Winston, 1975) p. 138.

7. Filene, *Him/Her/Self*, pp. 7-10, 78.

8. Shorter, *Making of the Modern Family*, pp. 168-204 (Chapter 5, "Mothers and Infants"). See also Aries, *Centuries of Childhood*.

9. Although much of it has become available only in the last decade, at present there is an abundance of largely psychological literature reporting on personality differences between male and female children and discussing differential personality development and socialization by sex. See especially Eleanor E. Maccoby (ed.), *The Development of Sex Differences* (Stanford: Stanford University Press, 1966), and Eleanor E. Maccoby and Carol N. Jacklin (eds.), *The Psychology of Sex Differences* (Stanford: Stanford University Press, 1974).

10. Maccoby and Jacklin (eds.), *Psychology of Sex Differences*, p. 303. The musical *Carousel* was first produced in 1945.

11. Michael Lewis, "Parents and Children: Sex Role Development," *School Review*, 80 (1972):228-40. Lewis notes the "folk" methods of determining the fetus's sex, such as its activity level or its position in the womb.

12. Maccoby and Jacklin (eds.), *Psychology of Sex Differences*, pp. 309, 311.

13. Walter Mischel, "A Social Learning View of Sex Differences in Behavior," in Maccoby (ed.), *Development of Sex Differences*, pp. 56-81. Of course, only a certain amount of aggression in children is tolerated in our culture. The emphasis here is on the relative emphasis on agression in boys compared to girls.

14. David F. Aberle and Kaspar D. Naegele, "Middle Class Fathers' Occupational Role and Attitudes towards Children," *American Journal of Orthopsychiatry*, 22 (1952):366-78.

15. Miriam M. Johnson, "Sex Role Learning in the Nuclear Family," *Child Development*, 34 (1963):319-33; Elizabeth Goodenough, "Interest in Persons as an Aspect of Sex Differences in the Early Years," *Genetic Psychology Monographs*, 55 (1957):287-323.

16. C. Y. Nakamura and M. M. Rogers, "Parents' Expectations of Autonomous Behavior and Children's Autonomy," *Developmental Psychology*, 1 (1969):613-17.

17. Freud, *Civilization and its Discontents*; see also Freud, *New Introductory Lectures*.

18. Mitchell, *Psychoanalysis and Feminism*.

19. Lawrence Kohlberg, "A Cognitive-Developmental Analysis of Children's Sex Role Concepts and Attitudes," in Maccoby (ed.), *Development of Sex Differences*, p. 87. Kohlberg suggests that sex identity may be established as early as age three and that it is difficult to change thereafter.

20. See, for example, Barrie Thorne and Nancy Henley (eds.), *Language and Sex: Difference and Dominance* (Rowley: Newbury House, 1975), and Robin Lakoff, *Language and Woman's Place* (New York: Harper & Row, 1975).

21. Gordon W. Allport, *The Nature of Prejudice* (New York: Doubleday, 1954), p. 177.

22. Thorne and Henley (eds.), *Language and Sex*, p. 15.

23. Inge Broverman, Susan Vogel, Donald Broverman, Frank Clarkson, and Paul Rosencrantz, "Sex Role Stereotypes: A Current Appraisal," *Journal of Social Issues*, 28 (1972): 59-78.

24. Lenore Weitzman, "Sex Role Socialization," in Jo Freeman (ed.), *Women: A Feminist Perspective* (Palo Alto: Mayfield Publishers, 1975), pp. 105-44.

25. Weitzman et al., "Sex Role Socialization in Picture Books for Pre-School Children," *American Journal of Sociology*, 77, no. 6 (1972):125-50.

26. Richard Levinson, "From Olive Oyl to Sweet Polly Purebred: Sex Role Stereotypes and Televised Cartoons," *Journal of Popular Culture*, 9 (1975):561-72; Jo Ann Gardner, "Sesame Street and Sex Role Stereotypes," *Women*, 1 (1970):10-14.

27. Kay Reinartz, "The Paper Doll: Images of American Women in Popular Songs," in Freeman (ed.), *Women*, pp. 293-308; Alice E. Courtney and Thomas W. Whipple, "Women in T.V. Commercials," *Journal of Communication*, 24, no. 2 (1974):110-18; Lyvia M. Brown, "Sexism in Western Art," in Freeman (ed.), *Women*, pp. 309-22.

28. James Coleman, *The Adolescent Society* (New York: Free Press, 1961), esp. pp. 143-72.

29. Nancy Frazier and Myra Sadlek, *Sexism in School and Society*, (New York: Harper & Row, 1973), p. 132.

30. *Ibid.*, p. 138.

31. Pauline Gough, *Sexism: New Issue in Education* (Bloomington: Phi Delta Kappa Educational Foundation, 1976), p. 23.

32. Pamela Roby, "Structural and Internalized Barriers to Women in Higher Education," in Safilios-Rothschild (ed.), *Toward a Sociology of Women*, p. 122.

33. Inge Broverman et al., "Sex Role Stereotypes and Clinical Judgments of Mental Health," *Journal of Consulting and Clinical Psychology*, 34 (1970):1-7.

34. Abraham Maslow, *Motivation and Personality* (New York: Harper & Row, 1954). See especially Chapter 2, "Self-Actualizing People: A Study of Psychological Health."

35. Erikson, *Childhood and Society*, esp. Chapter 7 ("Eight Ages of Man"). See also Erik H. Erikson, *Identity, Youth and Crisis* (New York: W. W. Norton, 1968), pp. 128-33.

36. Elizabeth Douvan and Carol Kay, "Motivational Factors in College Entrance," in Nevitt Sanford (ed.), *The American College* (New York: Wiley, 1962), pp. 199-224.

37. *Ibid.*, p. 202.

38. Florence Rosenberg and Roberta Simmons, "Sex Differences in Self-Concept at Adolescence," *Sex Roles*, 1 (1975):147-59.

39. Reesa M. Vaughter, "Psychology: Review Essay," *Signs*, 2 (1976):127.

40. Sharon C. Nash, "The Relationship among Sex-Role Stereotyping, Sex Role Preference, and Sex Differences in Spatial Visualization," *Sex Roles*, 1 (1975):15-32 (1975).

41. Broverman et al., "Clinical Judgments of Mental Health."

42. Vaughter, "Review Essay," p. 128.

43. Oakley, *Woman's Work*.

44. Matina Horner, "Toward an Understanding of Achievement Related Conflicts in Women," in M.T.S. Mednick, S. S. Tangri, L. W. Hoffman (eds.), *Women and Achievement* (New York: Wiley, 1975), pp. 206-20. For a discussion of Horner's original experiment, see Lois W. Hoffman, "Fear of Success in Males and Females: 1965 and 1971," in *ibid.*, pp. 221-22.

45. Adeline Levine and Janice Crumine, "Women and the Fear of Success: A Problem in Replication," *American Journal of Sociology* 80 (1975):964-74.

46. Sharon Sutherland, "The Unambitious Female: Women's Low Professional Aspirations," *Signs*, 3 (1978):774-94.

47. Eleanor E. Maccoby, "Sex Differences in Intellectual Functioning," in Maccoby (ed.), *Development of Sex Differences*. pp. 25-55.

48. M. C. Shaw and J. T. McCuen, "The Onset of Academic Underachievement in Bright Children," *Journal of Educational Psychology*, 51 (1960):103-8.

49. Alice Rossi, "Job Discrimination and What Women Can Do About It," *Atlantic* 225 (March 1970):99.

50. Dennis Wrong, "The Oversocialized Conception of Man in Modern Sociology," *American Sociological Review*, 26 (1961):183-93.

51. Erik Erikson, *Young Man Luther: A Study in Psychoanalysis and History* (New York: W. W. Norton, 1972). For an interesting discussion of the issues of personality and social change, see Alex Inkeles, "Continuity and Change in the Interaction of Personal and Socio-Cultural Systems," in Bernard Barber and Alex Inkeles, *Stability and Social Change* (Boston: Little, Brown, 1971), pp. 265-81.

52. Herbert Marcuse, *Eros and Civilization: A Philosophic Inquiry into Freud* (Boston: Beacon, 1955). See also Marcuse, *An Essay on Liberation* (Boston: Beacon, 1969).

TABLES

Table 3.1

STEREOTYPIC SEX ROLE ITEMS

Feminine	Masculine
Competency Cluster: Masculine Pole Is More Desirable	
Not at all aggressive	Very aggressive
Not at all independent	Very independent
Very emotional	Not at all emotional
Does not hide emotions at all	Almost always hides emotions
Very subjective	Very objective
Very easily influenced	Not at all easily influenced
Very submissive	Very dominant
Dislikes math and science very much	Likes math and science very much
Very excitable in a minor crisis	Not at all excitable in a minor crisis
Very passive	Very active
Not at all competitive	Very competitive
Very illogical	Very logical
Very home oriented	Very worldly
Not at all skilled in business	Very skilled in business
Very sneaky	Very direct
Does not know the way of the world	Knows the way of the world
Feelings easily hurt	Feelings not easily hurt
Not at all adventurous	Very adventurous
Has difficulty making decisions	Can make decisions easily
Cries very easily	Never cries
Almost never acts as a leader	Almost always acts as a leader
Not at all self-confident	Very self-confident
Very uncomfortable about being aggressive	Not at all uncomfortable about being aggressive
Not at all ambitious	Very ambitious
Unable to separate feelings from ideas	Easily able to separate feelings from ideas
Very dependent	Not at all dependent
Very conceited about appearance	Never conceited about appearance
*Thinks women are always superior to men	*Thinks men are always superior to women
*Does not talk freely about sex with men	*Talks freely about sex with men
*Doesn't use harsh language at all	*Uses very harsh language
Very talkative	Not at all talkative
Very tactful	Very blunt
Very gentle	Very rough
Very aware of feelings of others	Not at all aware of feelings of others
Very religious	Not at all religious
Very interested in own appearance	Not at all interested in own appearance
Very neat in habits	Very sloppy in habits
Very quiet	Very loud
Very strong need for security	Very little need for security
Enjoys art and literature	Does not enjoy art and literature at all
Easily expresses tender feelings	Does not express tender feelings at all easily

SOURCE: Broverman et al., "Sex Role Stereotypes: A Current Appraisal," *Journal of Social Issues,* 28(1972): 63.

*These items are omitted in table contained in Broverman et al., "Sex Role Stereotypes and Clinical Judgements of Mental Health," *Journal of Consulting Psychology,* 34(1970): 3.

Chapter 4
Women
and the Economy

THE ECONOMIC POSITION OF WOMEN

The importance of economic change is widely acknowledged by social scientists as central to changes in other institutions and to changes in cultural aspects of society as well. To be sure, economic institutions, which emerge in society in order to organize the production and distribution of goods and services, are not alone responsible for change in other aspects of the overall social structure or culture. Nevertheless, the importance of the economic system and the social relations it molds are felt in institutions as diverse as the family, the educational system, and the political system. In discussing the impact of the economy and its changes on women, I shall emphasize a macro analysis of society. Furthermore, in light of the rapidity of technological change and the continuous development experienced in the economy, the focus of the discussion will be on change rather than on stability. There are, however, some aspects of the economy in general, and of women's position in the economy specifically, that have been resistant to change, and I shall be concerned to explore these as well. First, I shall examine the impact of the economy on and its interaction with the process of socialization and personality formation among women, and second, the implications for the American labor movement of women's economic position.

Theoretical Framework

The theoretical work of Karl Marx provides a framework for an analysis of the impact of economic institutions on wider social change. Marx was not an economic determinist, that is, he did not suggest that the organization of production is the single source of social change.[1] He did, however, believe that the influence of economic institutions is central to an understanding of a group's status in society and of the broader process of social change. The nature of a group's relation to the process of production, according to Marx, is a central determinant of its position, power, and status in society. Applying this framework, Marxists have suggested that the isolation of women in home and family roles and their exclusion from direct participation in the economic system in return for wages are the central sources of women's secondary status in all other aspects of social life. As early as 1884 in *The Origin of the Family, Private Property and the State,* Engels, stated:

> To emancipate woman and make her the equal of man is and remains an impossibility so long as the woman is shut out from social productive labor and restricted to private domestic labor. The emancipation of women will only be possible when woman can take part in production on a large social scale, and domestic work no longer claims anything but an insignificant amount of her time. And only now has that become possible through modern large-scale industry, which does not merely permit of the employment of female labor over a wide range, but positively demands it, while it also tends towards ending private domestic labor by changing it more and more into a public industry.[2]

More recently, those neo-Marxists who have focused exclusively on the sources of women's inferior status in modern capitalist society have made much the same argument. Margaret Benston, for example, noting the importance in modern capitalist society of direct access to income as a crucial criterion of individual worth, personal and political power, and social prestige, suggests that women as a group are "denied an active place in the market and thus have little control over the conditions that govern their lives."[3] Thus Marxist theory suggests that an analysis of the economic institutions of capitalist society provides insights toward an understanding of women's overall secondary status.

Marxism provides a theory of social movements as well as an understanding of the relative status and power of social groups. Marx argued that with capitalist development, the growth of a working-class or proletariat movement provides the impetus for revolutionary social change.[4] He also proposed that the rise of industrial production, made possible by technological innovation, brought with it an end to the isolation of farmers and peasants from one another. Moreover, urbanization and the concentration of workers in factories under similar conditions would generate strong feelings of solidarity among them. Marx believed that such a set of circumstances, built into the economic development of capitalism, would create strong pressure for revolutionary social change as the workers become increasingly conscious of their shared economic exploitation. In Marxist theory, the development of a working class, living and working in close relationship with one another under exploitative economic conditions, was the necessary prelude to the development of a political movement capable of drastically changing society for the better. Economic change—in this case, the development of a proletariat under capitalism—paves the way for wider change through the mediation of a political movement.

It is this model that Engels and Benston had in mind when they asserted the importance of economic change in general, and the increase of a female labor force activity in particular, as central to broader change in women's social position. According to the model, if technological and economic change produces a decrease in women's isolation in home and family roles and also an increase in their participation as workers, such changes would be expected to generate pressure for social change in other aspects of women's lives. Following Marx, we might expect that the development of a social movement of women workers would be the specific mechanism of wider social change in women's status. Such a sociopolitical movement might of course take a variety of forms. It might focus on the issue of women as workers as only one aspect of a broader concern with a variety of women's concerns in society. Alternatively, growing numbers of women workers might produce or contribute to a social movement focused on general work-related issues common to all workers, with the special concerns of women emerging as one of several focuses of the larger working-class movement. Whatever the nature of the specific social movement, the model hypothesizes that the development of political consciousness and activity among women is dependent upon prior economic changes. The development of such a movement, according to Marxist theory, is deeply influenced by or even contingent upon women's involvement in the economic institutions of the society through their participation in the labor force.

Women and Work, 1960-1976

The history of female labor force activity in the United States has been a dynamic one, especially in the decades following World War II.[5] Not only were the absolute numbers of women workers steadily growing before 1960, but the typical woman worker by that year was not a single, young, and poorly educated woman, as was true in the 1920s, for example, but rather an older, married woman whose children were generally grown.

In the period from 1960 to 1976, growth in the female labor force continued, bringing ever increasing numbers of women into a direct relation with the labor market (Tables 4.1-4.7). Higher proportions of women worked full time and year round than ever before. The most recent data indicate that by 1976, close to one-half of all American women of working age were in the labor force, and 57 percent had actually worked or looked for work during the year.[6] The characteristics of employed women also continued to change. The greatest increases in labor force activity in this period were registered by younger, well-educated, married women with young children, whose husbands were also working and earning relatively high incomes. Overall trends, however, indicate that during our period women's relative income position deteriorated, with the gap between male and female median incomes and unemployment rates widening. In addition, concentration of women in female-dominated occupations and continuing underrepresentation and/or exclusion of women from many "male" occupations has continued.

Table 4.2 indicates that the most dynamic and rapidly growing portion of the female labor force is comprised of young married mothers. It is important to recognize that older married women, who were the more typical women workers at the beginning of our period, have not been displaced by these additions. As Table 4.2 shows, the rates of labor force participation have actually risen between 1960 and 1976 among older married women as well as among single and divorced women. Yet in spite of this general increase, the median age of women workers declined from forty-one years in 1960 to thirty-six years in 1974, reflecting the disproportionate increase of younger working women. Consequently, the number of families with two or more persons in the labor force has increased dramatically. While in 1960 only 38 percent of all families included two workers, by 1975 this proportion was almost 50 percent, and women who worked full time, year round were contributing approximately two-fifths of total family income.[7]

Although the overall proportion of employed married women was growing, it was those women whose husbands earned relatively high incomes who entered the labor force in greatest numbers between 1960 and 1975 (Table 4.2). Indeed, women whose husbands' incomes were in the lowest categories were slightly less likely to be employed in 1975 than in 1960. In addition, overall high rates of labor force participation during our period were especially characteristic of women who were heads of families (54 percent in 1974).[8]

After 1960, the female labor force also changed significantly in racial composition and level of educational attainment. The labor force participation rate of white women has risen dramatically in our period, while that of nonwhite women has remained fairly stable. As a result, the large gap that separated the participation rates of white and nonwhite women in 1960 had closed significantly by 1976 (Table 4.2). Finally, the level of educational attainment of women in the labor force has steadily risen between 1960 and 1976. At the beginning of the period, only a small majority of working women had been educated beyond the third year of high school (Table 4.3). By 1976, however, 90 percent of working women had at least graduated from high school, and one out of four had received some college training.

Thus the demographic composition of the female labor force altered between 1960 and 1976, owing to the addition to the ranks of working women of younger, married, white mothers with relatively high levels of education, whose husbands earned high salaries. Were there also important patterns of change during this period in the specific types of jobs in which these newcomers and those women with longer work histories were employed? To answer this question we must examine the occupational structure of the female labor force. As revealed in Table 4.4, there has been a long-term tendency for the labor force in the United States to be occupationally segregated by sex. This pattern was present at the beginning of the 1960s and has remained a characteristic of the labor market. The pattern of female employment in 1976 indicated that women were concentrated largely in white-collar work, with the largest single proportion (more than 30 percent) in the single category of clerical workers. The extent of segregation of women workers into "female" jobs is suggested by Table 4.5, which lists occupational classifications in which women constituted more than 90 percent of the workers in 1973.

Some changes that occurred in the occupational distribution of the female labor force in the post 1960 period deserve mention. On the one hand, there were tendencies toward increasing the concentration of women in certain occupations, the most striking example being the 5 percent growth in the proportion of women classified as clerical workers. On the other hand, the same period indicated a small but significant influx of women workers into predominantly "male" occupations, and of male workers into female-dominated categories. For example, a number of women entered the skilled trades as carpenters, auto mechanics, and machinists, with the increase amounting to 80 percent in the decade 1960-1970—twice the rate of increase of women in all other occupations and eight times the rate of increase for men in skilled trades.[9] During the same period, men were making inroads into predominantly female occupations. The growth rate of male librarians, for example, was double that of women, while the employment of male telephone operators grew at a rate four times that of women.[10] These changes have not as yet significantly affected the sex-segregated occupational structure characterizing the United States labor force, but they may be viewed as small trends in the direction of a less rigid structure.

One of the most dramatic recent changes in the occupational distribution of female workers has been the shift in the occupations of employed black women. While over one-third of all employed black women worked in private households in 1960, by 1976 only 9 percent of black working women were classified in this category. The data in Table 4.4 indicate a significant increase during the same period in the proportion of black women employed in clerical jobs (from 9 percent to 26 percent). Thus, changes of enormous significance were occurring during our period in the occupational distribution of black employed women. The net result was an ever-increasing similarity in the occupational distribution of black and white women in the labor force.

In describing the female labor force, we must explore not only its own internal changes, but also its position and dynamics in relation to the male sector of the labor force. Table 4.6 shows the wide discrepancy between the median income of male as compared with that of female workers—a gap that has persisted and even increased between the early 1960s and the mid-1970s (Fig 4.1). This wage and salary differential exists, regardless of educational level, for all major occupational categories, and by 1974 the size of the gap amounted to a difference of $5,000 in favor of men. In terms of median wages, minority women are the worst off. Although the median income of minority men was significantly lower than that of white men, it was nevertheless higher than that of either white or minority women during the entire period from 1960 to 1974.

Not only do women workers, taken as a group, have a substantially lower median income than employed men, but the female labor force also contains a higher percentage of unemployed workers (Table 4.7). Between 1960 and 1976 the gap between male and female unemployment rates has increased, and as Figure 4.2 indicates, women account for an increasing proportion of all unemployed persons. Black workers' rates of unemployment are considerably higher than those of white workers, with black women having the highest overall rates since 1965 (Table 4.7).[11] Moreover, men and women also differ substantially in the reported reasons for their unemployment. Table 4.7 shows that in 1974 the proportions of women and men who were unemployed because they left their last job differed only slightly. On the other hand, the proportion of women unemployed because they were reentering or just entering the labor market was twice that of men, while the proportion of men unemployed because they lost their last job was half again that of women.

The female labor force has undergone changes in size, demographic composition, and occupational distribution since 1960. Yet certain characterisitcs of that labor force, such as concentration in female-dominated occupations, have persisted, as has women's disadvantaged position when compared with the male labor force on such variables as unemployment rates, median income, and participation in prestigious and highly rewarded occupational categories.

Analysis of Trends

I now turn from a description of labor force trends in the period from 1960 to the present to an analysis of the determinants of those trends. In this section I shall explore the motivating factors that influence women to join the labor force, the reasons women work in particular occupations once the decision to work has been made, and the factors that explain the inferior wage position of working women.

Attempts to explain the rapid expansion of the female labor force in the United States after 1960 have come largely from economists, whose explanations emphasize the importance of theories of supply and demand. According to such theories, change in female participation rates could hypothetically result from women's increased willingness to seek employment in the labor market (supply factors); alternatively, such change might be stimulated by the need of employers to hire increasing numbers of workers (demand factors). In fact, according to Hilda Kahne and Andrew Kohen, empirical work has generally supported both demand and supply factors as contributing to the increase in female participation rates.[12]

On the supply side, several different factors can be identified as creating an expansion of the female labor force. One explanation suggests that an increase in wages will produce a response involving increased female labor force participation. Economists would describe this as a movement along the female labor force supply function. The earning capacity of women is thus hypothesized as a factor that is directly related to labor force participation: the more a woman can earn, the more likely she is to seek employment. A second argument from the supply side stresses the importance of education as a variable that affects labor supply. At a given wage level, the higher the educational attainment of women, the greater the likelihood that they will seek work. Thus in a period of increasing female educational attainment, it is hypothesized, a growing proportion of females will offer themselves in the labor market.

A final supply factor that has been found to affect the decisions of women to work is the number and ages of their children.[13] Children, especially young children, have been found to have a negative influence on the employment of their mothers. Women with fewer and/or older children are more likely to be willing or able to search for employment. Thus in a period of declining fertility, labor force participation among women would be expected to increase.

According to Kahne and Kohen, the period 1960-1975 shows evidence of change in all three of these supply factors: the wages paid to women rose, women's overall level of educational attainment increased, and the birth rate declined precipitously. These factors interwined in their effects on the supply of women in the labor market. Since each supply factor alone would tend to influence women to seek employment, it is reasonable to assume that after 1960 these changes combined to produce a steady and rapid expansion in the supply of female workers.

To understand changing labor force participation, demand factors should also be examined. An increased demand for workers may reflect basic industrial and occupational growth that produces new jobs and/or industries. Along with an overall expansion of the labor force, economic growth sometimes produces a demand for workers with specific attributes and/or skills. The rapid post World War II economic growth was concentrated in clerical, service, and white-collar occupations, and the demand for new workers in these occupations was met largely by workers new to the labor force rather than from within the existing labor pool.[14] The period after 1960 witnessed continuing growth in the size of the labor force, largely in these same occupational categories. To what extent the demand was specifically for female workers, or whether women simply supplied themselves disproportionately at this point remains unclear. However, demand factors—the need for more workers for new occupations—was surely an important factor in influencing increased numbers of women to become members of the labor force.

Between 1960 and the present, then, women were increasingly needed as workers as the result of steady industrial and occupational growth, and at the same time a variety of supply factors converged—higher educational attainment, higher wages, and fewer children—so that women as a group were increasingly willing to join the labor force. When women entered the labor force during this period, however, they found themselves in a disadvantageous position relative to men, and largely concentrated in sex-segregated occupations. It is to an explanation of these characteristics of female labor force participation that we now turn.

The subject of segregated occupational structures has received considerable attention from economists.[15] Although scholars agree that there is segregation in the labor force, there are differences among the explanations of its sources. Again, the differing theories can be divided into those that emphasize demand factors and those that focus on the importance of the segregated supply of workers.[16] Demand arguments state that men discriminate against women as a group by their ability to exclude women from some jobs and to give them access to others. Such discrimination can take many different forms, but the result is that women as a group are excluded from certain "male" jobs and occupations or from the training necessary for those jobs, and are demanded as workers for other categories of jobs and/or given training to equip them only for those "female" occupations. Just who are the men responsible for such discrimination and what are their motivations? Theories vary, but some of the suggested reasons for discrimination include: male employers believe that women are inferior workers, that women have "natural" abilities in certain areas, or that women cannot handle the responsibility of demanding occupations or jobs, and they therefore exclude women from some jobs and demand them for others; capitalist employers want to promote and intensify divisions in the working class, in this case by dividing men from women, in order to prevent the development of a unified class of workers; capitalist employers want to minimize wages, and by segregating males and females into different occupations they are able to pay women lower wages than would otherwise be feasible; male workers want to retain the best (highest paying, most prestigious) jobs for themselves or members of their own sex and therefore pressure employers through union practices and other mechanisms to exclude women from certain jobs. Regardless of these variations, all explanations from the demand side place the blame for the sex segregation of the labor force on men whose policies as employers or workers succeed in producing a dual labor market in which women are trained and demanded only for "female" occupations.

A second group of theories emphasizes supply factors as critical in explaining the sex segregation of the labor force, suggesting that women themselves choose to train for and apply to only certain jobs and that they avoid other kinds of occupations. If women make themselves available for a specific group of "female" jobs and avoid "male" occupations, sex segregation of the labor force is not surprising. As was true for demand theory, there are differing explanations as to why women behave in this manner, but the most powerful of these emphasizes sex-role differentiation in the process of socialization. According to this argument, the traditional process of socialization encourages women to lower their aspirations for careers, to avoid situations in which they compete with men, and to view work as a secondary focus of their identities and adult lives. In a society in which definitions of femininity focus on domestic and wife-mother roles, girls are taught to seek fulfillment in this sphere or to aspire only to roles that are consistent with that definition of femininity. In addition, training for women is only encouraged or even available for occupational roles that those agencies of socialization, primarily schools, believe to be consistent with the domestic focus of women's adult lives. According to supply theories, the disproportionate willingness of women to apply for such occupations as secretary, nurse, or elementary school teacher is linked to the service orientation, and therefore "feminine" definition by society, of those particular occupations.

It is neither necessary nor possible to choose among these explanations of occupational segregation by sex. However, following Kahne and Kohen, if we view these explanations not as mutually exclusive but rather as mutually reinforcing, we can conclude that male and employer discrimination in demand and female socialization that leads women to supply themselves only for the same segregated jobs for which they are demanded together produce the occupational segregation by sex that has persisted over time as a defining characteristic of the American labor force.

Research concerning the sources of occupational segregation by sex has been accompanied by exploration of the implications of such segregation. Such separation of occupations by sex not only restricts the choice of both men and women to those jobs that are considered appropriate to their sex. In addition such occupational segregation has a more profoundly negative impact on women in that it confines them to occupations that are more likely to be lower paid and less prestigious than those reserved for men. Since women are prepared or prepare only for a relatively small number of occupations, there tends to be severe overcrowding in those fields, which depresses wages and contributes to the relatively high female unemployment rates shown in Table 4.7. Economist Victor Fuchs has concluded that occupational segregation by sex is the principal manifest form of discrimination against women and the "principal explanation for the lower wages of females" as a group.[17] Thus occupational segregation has a profoundly negative impact on the position of the female labor force when compared with that of male workers in terms of lower wages, higher unemployment rates, and concentration in low prestige positions.

Although the segregation of occupations is the most important contributor to women's disadvantaged economic position as compared with men, it is not the only factor of importance. Economists have often noted the negative impact of the cyclical nature of the work histories typical of women workers.[18] Figure 4.3 clearly shows that, compared with employed men, whose work histories indicate steady labor force participation after about age 30 until retirement, women's employment experience is quite different. The female labor force shows two peaks of participation by age, the first between the ages of about 17 and 19, and the second considerably later, between the ages of 40 and 55. Traditionally, it seems that women have entered the labor force in large numbers at relatively young ages, left in large numbers between the ages of 20 and 40, and then reenteered until retirement.

The obvious source of such a pattern of intermittent labor force activity is women's special responsibility for domestic duties, which are not counted as labor force activity because they are not reimbursed by wages. Women's adult role, as defined in our culture, includes not only bearing but also rearing offspring, and this task has produced conflict with and withdrawal from labor force participation. I shall discuss the precise nature of home-work conflicts in the next chapter in my examination of working mothers, but it is clear that the demands of each role often make it extremely difficult or even impossible for women to fulfill the demands of the other adequately.

There are clear economic disadvantages for individuals whose work histories indicate movement in and out of the labor force, regardless of the reasons for such movement. In the first place, individuals with intermittent work histories lose possibilities for promotions, fringe benefits, pensions, and seniority. Moreover, the level of unemployment among such individuals is invariably high, for as Table 4.7 indicates, an important source of unemployment is the attempt to reenter the labor force. Individuals with intermittent histories may be considered "inferior" workers, and the demand for such workers, particularly in highly paid or prestigious occupations, may be low or nonexistent. Finally, the same family-related factors that account for women's interrupted work histories are also largely responsible for their overrepresentation in part-time employment, which pays notoriously poor wages and provides few if any benefits and little job security (Fig. 4.1).

In a society in which women are expected to rear their own children and where alternative child-rearing methods are scarce and/or perceived as inadequate, women have a built-in disadvantage in the labor market as compared with men, who usually have no such special domestic responsibilities. Although the pattern of cyclical work histories for women seems less predominant in the most recent period since women increasingly work even when their children are young (Table 4.2), it is nonetheless true that the dominant sex role expectations for adult women are in direct conflict with the prerequisites for "success" in the labor market.

WOMEN'S WORK AND SOCIAL CHANGE

In my discussion of female labor force expansion, I have stressed the continuity of women's disadvantaged position in the labor force as compared with that of men. The view that women's position in the economy has not improved even in the recent decade and a half is supported by data that indicate consistently high unemployment rates for women, the persistence of occupational segregation by sex, and an increase in the wage gap between men and women who are full-time, year-round workers. Indeed, Kahne and Kohen conclude that at the beginning of 1976, "Despite all the rhetoric, women's position has not changed much [relative to men]."[19]

From another point of view, however, women's involvement and position in the American economy has changed dramatically in the period between 1960 and 1976. Furthermore, this change in the economic sphere can be viewed not only as an indicator but also as a source of the more complex social change that has been occurring in the position of American women. In this view, women's entrance into the labor force in large numbers creates the possibility of the emergence of new tensions and pressures for wider social change.

Pressures for social change generated by alterations in women's position in the economy may be felt in either material or ideological (normative) aspects of society, or in both. For example, change in women's economic role may stimulate a rise or a drop in the level of birth rates, or may exert pressure on the norms relating to and the practices associated with socialization and personality development. Alterations in the economic status of women may also be hypothesized as important factors in the creation of or changes in a social movement or movements. In the remainder of this chapter I shall trace the effects of alterations in women's position in the economy on socialization practices and norms and on the composition and impact of the American labor movement. Possible effects of such economic changes on the family will be explored in Chapter 5, and their influence with respect to the emergence and nature of the women's liberation movement will be examined in Chapters 6 and 7.

Effects on Socialization

Significant changes in patterns of female employment are likely to be felt in the sphere of socialization practices. The process of socialization is future oriented to a considerable degree; that is, society attempts to inculcate those social and personal characteristics that are deemed necessary for the future role that a given individual is likely to play. Growth in female employment—part of broader change in women's economic position—changes the future role expectations of women in that it becomes increasingly likely that women's adult roles will include participation in the labor force. Thus the socialization process, which had not previously equipped this sector of the population for such work roles, is under some pressure to provide for this new circumstance in addition to the more traditional preparation for domestic roles.

As noted above, the period from 1960 to the present has been characterized by continuing expansion of the female labor force and of the number of women who engage in uninterrupted employment throughout their adult lives. We would expect that various agencies of socialization were under increasing pressure during this period to provide women as well as men with those characteristics necessary to an adult role of which work was an important component. To this end, we might hypothesize that agencies of socialization would deemphasize the sex role differences that had traditionally been a hallmark of the socialization process. Presumably schools, media, literature, and family life all might be affected by this new structural change in women's adult role expectations. If agencies of socialization responded to these demands to emphasize and teach similarities rather than differences between the sexes, females as well as males would be able to function adequately as adult members of the labor force.

One clear way of determining the existence and extent of such changes in socialization is to look at data from the institution of socialization that is most responsible for equipping young people for work roles. When we examine data such as that in Table 4.8 on the proportions of women finishing high school, attending college, and receiving degrees of higher education between 1960 and 1975, we see significant changes. Especially above the level of three years of high school, women's educational attainment has risen dramatically. Particularly striking is the growth during this period in the number of women receiving prestigious professional degrees.

Although change is evident in women's educational attainment, so too is the fact that women, even as recently as 1976, received only a small proportion of higher degrees granted. One explanation for such a situation may be that change does not occur overnight and that a period of fifteen years is not long enough to reveal the full range of equalizing tendencies set in motion by women's increased labor force participation. Another explanation, however, takes into account the importance of specific characteristics of female employment. Although employment creates pressures for equivalent sex role socialization for men and women, the segregated nature of the occupational structure of the American labor force may significantly reduce this equalizing tendency. If women and men are always segregated in occupations that demand significantly different skills, personal attributes, and commitment, for example, we might expect that the socialization process would continue to create and reinforce differences between men and women, since such differences might be viewed as consistent with the needs of their work roles. Some scholars have argued that women's work roles in the occupationally segregated labor force are merely extensions of their traditional "feminine" or domestic roles in the home.[20] The jobs in which women are concentrated reflect traditional feminine roles of help, service, and child care. If nursing, teaching, and clerical work are viewed in this manner, it is at least possible that traditional female personality characteristics may be thought to be requirements for these work roles, much as they were considered necessary to the demands of traditional female adult roles. Viewed in this way, employment of women in "women's" jobs may create little or no pressure for equalization of the differential socialization processes to which boys and girls are exposed.

In sum, the growth of female employment exerts direct pressure on the socialization process to adjust itself to new adult role requirements of women by moving away from distinct socialization patterns for boys and girls, since both must be equipped by society to fulfill work roles as adults. Such pressure for change, however, is not unambiguous, because the specific nature of a sex-segregated labor force may reduce or even cancel it altogether. In this view, all children must be equipped for work roles, but when the specific nature of those roles is differentiated by sex, different skills and social and personality characteristics may be judged necessary for men and women workers.

Women and the Labor Movement

Increases in female labor force participation and change in women's economic role may influence social change through their implications for the strengthening or weakening of the labor movement in American society. In this section I shall consider the relationship between women and the American labor movement from 1960 to the present time, and the likelihood that the effects of women's changing economic position on broader social change will be mediated through the growth of a sexually integrated labor movement.

American working women have a long history of membership in trade unions, and they have often played important and even heroic roles in labor struggles in the past.[21] Yet alongside the record of active female participation in union organizing and activity, there is also a history of discrimination on the part of unions against women as well as against other minority and immigrant groups.[22] The expansion of the female labor force after 1960 brought with it a growth in female union membership and also a rise in the proportion of female union members. While in 1960 approximately 18 percent of all union members were women, by 1972, 22 percent of the total membership was female. Although the growth of female union membership has continued, it is significantly lower than the proportion of women in the labor force as a whole. Women were and are presently underrepresented in the ranks of organized labor in the United States.

In addition, the pattern of female membership in unions parallels the segregated distribution of women by occupation. As recently as 1975, three-quarters of all women union members belonged to only twenty-one unions. Finally, even in those unions where women comprise a significant proportion of the membership, women are underrepresented in leadership positions. Heidi Wertheimer reports that only 5 percent of all governing positions of any kind in American unions are held by women. The sources of such underrepresentation are not clear. Whether women's relatively low participation as both members and leaders of trade unions is the result of discrimination against women on the part of male-dominated unions, of patterns of union organizing that make organization of segregated female occupations more difficult, or of characteristics of working women that make them less willing than their male counterparts to join or participate actively in unions cannot be judged at this point.

Despite women's underrepresentation, it is at least plausible to argue that the labor movement might nonetheless provide a social organization or movement through which the changes in the position of women in the American economy might be translated into broader social change. In the context of rising female employment, the existence of a viable and well-established labor movement might be viewed by women workers as an adequate mechanism for ameliorating exploitative working conditions. According to this hypothetical model, female and male workers, increasingly finding themselves in similar conditions at work, might develop communication, awareness, and solidarity across sex lines. The union movement would be the mechanism for uniting them and directing their common struggle against the capitalist class. Indeed, this is precisely the model that Marx himself and later Marxists projected. As each new group became part of the proletariat, class consciousness and worker solidarity generated by common conditions and close communication would be strong enough to overcome all other divisions, whether racial, geographical, or sexual. Such a labor movement, according to Marx's model, would not only press for changes in working conditions, pay, and job security, but would also constitute a political movement that eventually would revolutionize society by replacing capitalism with socialism. Although such a revolutionary outcome is not necessarily implied here, a labor movement that united the sexes would increase the bargaining power of all workers vis-à-vis capital and have profound implications for the rapidity and nature of social change in the society. Thus the change in women's economic position has the potential for strengthening and expanding the labor movement, and thus indirectly affecting the structure of institutions and culture in American society.

However, this theoretical model is rendered less plausible when two circumstances are considered. First, the American labor movement has not recently proved itself able to increase significantly the proportion of union members, male or female, in the labor force. The proportion of the total labor force in the United States that is unionized has actually declined from a high of 34.7 percent in 1954 to 31.4 percent in 1960, and to only 26.7 percent in 1972.[23] Whether this poor record is caused by the increasing bureaucratization of a union hierarchy that has made its peace with capital, or by the difficulty of organizing any but the largest manufacturing firms (most of which were unionized well before the present period) is not clear. However, this weakness makes it likely that the majority of employed women will not be organized by the existing union structure in the near future.

A second factor that raises serious questions about the role of a sex unified labor force as the major source of social change in the position of women centers on women's evaluation of the labor movement as a vehicle for expressing their newly emerging consciousness and solidarity as women. The union's existence clearly legitimates and provides a model for womens' development of an awareness of and a way to protest against unsatisfactory working conditions. However it may be perceived as an inadequate mechanism for expressing work-related dissatisfactions specific to women workers, or for building a social movement that speaks to other concerns, only indirectly related to work, of which women have developed awareness. Thus women may fear that their oppression as women with respect to such traditional issues as wages, promotions, and hiring may be neglected by a male-dominated union structure. Furthermore, such a labor movement may not recognize the importance of such nontraditional needs as day care, parenting leaves, flexible work schedules, and other indirectly work-related concerns about which women are likely to be more aware than men. Finally, women workers may fear that they will be treated as "second-class" citizens within such a movement, or that their participation in an already established and male-dominated labor union movement will lessen the feelings of support and solidarity that they have established with one another.

Thus both the weakness of the union movement in the United States and women's potential dissatisfaction with it as a vehicle for achieving changes they desire as women as well as workers, are obstacles to the labor movement's role in affecting broader social changes in women's position.

CONCLUSION

In this chapter I have explored the changes that have occurred in the economic position of women in the United States from 1960 to the present. The expansion of the female labor force has been a steady trend during the period, and employment has increasingly become an integral part of the adult lives of women. Such change in economic institutions, I have argued, can create tensions in the society and generate pressures for change in socialization practices, as well as in the economy itself. Tensions emerging from the changing economic position of women also have the potential for creating other changes in the wider society. Such pressures may be mediated through a social movement, which would serve to translate the effects of economic changes into the consciousness of groups of people who then organize themselves to pursue the goal of altering society in specific ways. In Chapter 7 I shall further explore these questions of the emergence and nature of social movements when I discuss the effects of women's changing economic position on the rise of the women's liberation movement. What is clear from this discussion, however, is that the rapid and continued expansion of the female labor force, which is a form of significant economic change, helped to generate pressures for further social change in the position of women in American society.

NOTES

1. See "Frederich Engels' Letter to Joseph Bloch," in Tucker (ed.), *Marx-Engels Reader*, pp. 640-42.
2. Engels, *Origin of the Family*, p. 148.
3. Benston, "Political Economy of Women's Liberation,"
4. Karl Marx, "Address of the Central Committee to the Communist League," in Tucker (ed.), *Marx-Engels Reader*, pp. 366-73.
5. The most complete source of data for this investigation, and the source relied upon unless otherwise noted, is: Women's Bureau, *1975 Handbook on Women Workers*, Bulletin 297 (Washington, D.C.: U.S. Department of Labor, 1975).
6. U.S. Department of Labor, "News," June 9, 1977, p. 3.
7. For information on two-earner families see Howard Hayghe, *Families and the Rise of Working Wives*, U.S. Department of Labor, Special Force Report No. 189 (Washington, D.C., 1976), pp. 12-14. *The New York Times* of March 8, 1977, reported that in 47 percent of American families in 1975 husbands and wives both worked.
8. U.S. Department of Labor, *Women Workers Today* (Washington, D.C.: Women's Bureau, 1976), p. 10.
9. *1975 Handbook on Women Workers*, pp. 92-94.
10. *Ibid.*, p. 94.
11. A detailed examination of the data indicates that unemployment rates for black females were also higher than those for black males in 1963 and 1964. *Handbook for Labor Statistics, 1975 Reference Edition, Bulletin 1865* (Washington, D.C.: U.S. Government Printing Office, 1975) p. 146.
12. Hilda Kahne and Andrew I. Kohen, "Review Essay: Economic Perspectives on the Roles of Women in the American Economy," *Journal of Economic Literature*, 13 (1975): 1249-92.
13. Sweet, *Women in the Labor Force*.
14. Kahne and Kohen, "Economic Perspectives," p. 1225.
15. David M. Gordon, *Theories of Poverty and Underemployment* (Lexington: D. C.

Heath, 1972), Chapter 4 ("Dual Labor Market Theory"). Much of the work on segregated labor markets has focused on black-white differences.

16. Kahne and Kohen, "Economic Perspectives." Much of this discussion is based on their excellent summary of the literature.

17. Victor Fuchs, "Differences in Hourly Earnings between Men and Women," *Monthly Labor Review*, 94, no. 5 (1971):9-15. Also see Larry E. Suter and Herman P. Miller, "Income Differences between Men and Career Women," *American Journal of Sociology*, 78 (1973): 962-74.

18. Juanita Kreps, *Sex in the Marketplace* (Baltimore: Johns Hopkins University Press, 1971), pp. 28-33.

19. Kahne and Kohen, "Economic Perspectives," p. 1274.

20. Ann Oakley, *Woman's Work*, pp. 72-75.

21. Barbara M. Wertheimer, "Search for a Partnership Role: Women in Labor Unions Today," in Jane Roberts Chapman (ed.), *Economic Independence for Women: The Foundation for Equal Rights* (Beverly Hills: Sage, 1976), pp. 183-209. All data cited in this section, unless otherwise noted, are from Wertheimer.

22. Heidi Hartmann, "Capitalism, Patriarchy, and Job Segregation by Sex," in Martha Blaxall and Barbara Reagan (eds.), *Women and the Workplace: The Implications of Occupational Segregation* (Chicago: University of Chicago Press, 1976), pp. 137-70.

23. *Handbook of Labor Statistics, 1975*, p. 389.

TABLES

Table 4.1

A. CIVILIAN LABOR FORCE PARTICIPATION RATES FOR FEMALES AGED 16 AND OVER, 1947-1976

Year	Whites	Negro and Other Races	Total
1947	28.7	41.0	31.8
1948	30.3	39.9	32.7
1949	29.9	40.1	33.2
1950	31.1	42.1	33.9
1951	31.8	41.5	34.7
1952	31.9	39.7	34.8
1953	32.3	39.6	34.5
1954	32.4	42.5	34.6
1955	32.9	41.2	35.7
1956	34.2	42.7	36.9
1957	34.1	43.7	36.9
1958	**	**	37.1
1959	**	**	37.2
1960	36.5	48.2	37.8
1961	36.9	48.3	38.1
1962	36.7	48.0	38.0
1963	37.2	48.1	38.3
1964	37.5	48.5	38.7
1965	38.1	48.6	39.3
1966	39.2	49.3	40.3
1967	40.1	49.5	41.1
1968	40.7	49.3	41.6
1969	41.8	49.8	42.7
1970	42.6	49.5	43.4
1971	42.6	49.2	43.4
1972	43.2	48.7	43.9
1973	44.1	49.1	44.7
1974	45.2	49.1	45.7
1975	44.6	48.6	45.1
1976	46.9	50.2	47.4

SOURCES: *Handbook of Labor Statistics, 1975 — Reference Edition, Bulletin 1865* (Washington, D.C.: U.S. Government Printing Office, 1975), pp. 35-38; *Statistical History of the U.S.,* p. 72; *Handbook of Labor Statistics, 1977, Bulletin 1966 Labor Statistics,* (Washington, D.C.: Government Printing Office, 1977), pp. 29-32.

**Data not available.

B. WOMEN AS A PERCENTAGE OF THE TOTAL CIVILIAN LABOR FORCE

Year	(%)
1950	29.0
1965	33.4
1970	38.1
1974	39.4
1975	39.9
1976	40.5

SOURCES: *Statistical Abstract of the United States, 1976* (Washington, D.C.: Bureau of the Census, 1976), p. 335; *Statistical Abstract of the United States, 1977* (Washington, D.C.: Bureau of the Census, 1977), pp. 387, 393.

C. STATUS OF THE FEMALE LABOR FORCE, 1967 AND 1976

Work Experience	1967	1976
Full time (%)	81.0	78.7
Part time (%)	19.0	21.3

SOURCE: *Handbook of Labor Statistics, 1977*, p. 64.

Table 4.2

LABOR FORCE PARTICIPATION RATES
BY SELECTED DEMOGRAPHIC CHARACTERISTICS:
FEMALE LABOR FORCE SELECTED YEARS, 1960-1976

Characteristic	Labor Force Participation Rate				
	1960	1963	1974	1975	1976[1]
Marital Status[a]					
single	44.1		57.2		61.0
married (husband present)	30.5		43.0		45.3
married (husband absent)	51.8		55.2		
widowed	29.8		24.8		40.5[2]
divorced	71.6		72.9		
total	34.8		45.2		47.4
Age[b]					
16-17	23.7		34.0		40.7
18-19	48.0		54.1		59.2
20-24	45.4		61.4		65.2
25-34	35.9		51.8		57.2
35-44	44.3		54.6		57.8
45-54	49.5		54.9		55.0
55-64	37.4		41.0		41.1
65+	10.8		8.3		8.2
Age of Children[c 3]					
no children under age 18	34.7		43.0		43.8
children aged 6-17 only	39.0		51.2		53.7
children under age 6	18.6		34.4		37.4
Race[d]					
white	36.5		45.2		46.9
Negro and other	48.2		49.1		50.2
Husband's Income[e]					
under $3,000		33.4		35.5	
3,000-4,999		39.1		35.8	
5,000-6,999		38.2		43.3	
7,000-9,999		31.2		49.3	
10,000 and over		24.8		43.4	

SOURCES: a. *1975 Handbook on Women Workers,* p. 18; b. *ibid.,* p. 12; c. *Handbook of Labor Statistics, 1975,* p. 57; d. *ibid.,* Table 41; e. *1965 Handbook on Women Workers,* p. 29, and *1975 Handbook on Women Workers,* p. 23.

[1] Data for 1976 from *Handbook of Labor Statistics, 1977,* pp. 24, 30, 31, 33, 52.

[2] Combined rate for married (husband absent), widowed, and divorced.

[3] For married women with husbands present.

Table 4.3

A. EDUCATIONAL ATTAINMENT OF WOMEN IN THE CIVILIAN LABOR FORCE, 1959-1976

| Year | Elementary | | High School | | College | | Average Years of Education |
	Less than 5 yrs. (%)	5-8 yrs. (%)	1-3 yrs. (%)	4 yrs. (%)	1-3 yrs. (%)	4 yrs. (%)	
1959	3.5	21.1	18.8	37.6	9.6	7.9	12.2
1962	3.0	18.8	18.8	38.7	11.2	9.5	12.2
1965	2.4	16.6	18.7	41.9	10.4	10.0	12.3
1970	1.5	12.2	16.9	45.5	13.2	10.7	12.4
1974	1.2	8.6	18.1	44.2	15.2	12.8	12.5
1976	1.0	7.4	17.1	44.6	15.9	14.0	12.6

SOURCES: *Handbook of Labor Statistics, 1975*, p. 55; *Handbook of Labor Statistics, 1977*, p. 51.

B. LABOR FORCE PARTICIPATION RATES OF WOMEN, BY EDUCATIONAL LEVEL, 1962 AND 1974

Year	Elementary 8 years	High School 1-3 yrs.	High School Graduate	College Graduate	Graduate Study (at least 1 yr. beyond college)
1962	30.1	37.8	43.2	57.3*	
1974	25.0	40.0	50.0	61.0	70.0

SOURCES: for 1962, Janice Fanning Madden, *The Economics of Sex Discrimination* (Lexington: D.C. Heath, 1973); for 1974, *1975 Handbook of Women Workers*, pp. 187-88.

*Includes both college graduate and graduate study.

Table 4.4

OCCUPATIONAL DISTRIBUTION, BY SEX AND RACE, 1960 AND 1976

	1960		1976	
	Whites	Negro and Other Races	Whites	Negro and Other Races
Occupation	(%)	(%)	(%)	(%)
	Males		*Males*	
Professional, technical, and kindred	11.6	3.9	15.3	9.6
Managers, administrators	**	**	15.0	5.8
Sales	6.2	1.4	6.4	2.4
Clerical	7.3	5.9	6.2	7.6
Craft and kindred	19.9	9.7	21.1	15.3
Operatives	19.1	24.5	16.8	24.7
Nonfarm laborers	6.4	22.5	6.8	14.3
Service workers (except private households)	5.5	14.8	7.9	16.6
Private household workers	*	0.3	*	0.2
Farm workers and farmers	**	**	4.6	3.6
	Females		*Females*	
Professional, technical, and kindred	13.3	6.2	16.2	14.2
Managers, administrators	**	**	5.9	2.8
Sales	8.6	1.5	7.3	2.5
Clerical	33.3	9.3	36.2	26.0
Craft and kindred	1.1	0.5	1.6	1.1
Operatives	15.4	14.3	11.3	15.7
Nonfarm laborers	0.3	0.6	1.1	1.4
Service workers (except private households)	13.8	21.6	16.8	26.0
Private household workers	5.1	34.8	2.2	9.4
Farm workers and farmers	**	**	1.4	0.8

SOURCES: for 1960, *Handbook of Labor Statistics, 1975,* pp. 41, 68, 72; for 1976, *Handbook of Labor Statistics, 1977,* p. 61.

*Less than 0.05%.

**Data not available.

Table 4.5

OCCUPATIONS IN WHICH WOMEN WERE MORE THAN 90 PERCENT
OF EMPLOYEES IN 1973

Occupation	*Female Percentage of Total Employment*
Professionals	
registered nurses	97.8
kindergarten and	
pre-kindergarten teachers	97.9
Clerical	
keypunch operators	90.9
receptionists	96.9
secretaries	99.1
teachers' aides	90.4
telephone operators	95.9
typists	96.6
Operatives	
dressmakers and seamstresses	
(except factory)	96.3
sewers and stitchers	95.5
Service	
child care workers	
(private household workers)	98.3
private household cleaners	
and servants	98.3
lodging quarters cleaners	96.6
dental assistants	98.2
practical nurses	96.4
child care workers	
(not private household)	95.5
hairdressers and cosmotologists	91.8

SOURCE: *1975 Handbook on Women Workers,* p. 89.

Note: In 1973, "more than 2/5 of all women workers were employed in
10 occupations—secretary, retail sales worker, bookkeeper, private
household worker, elementary school teacher, waitress, typist,
cashier, sewer and stitcher, and registered nurse. Each of these
occupations employed more than 800,000 women." *1975 Handbook on Women Workers,* p. 91.

Table 4.6

A. MEDIAN INCOME BY SEX AND RACE
(YEAR-ROUND, FULL-TIME WORKERS)

	Women		Men	
Year	*Whites*	*Minority Races*	*Whites*	*Minority Races*
1960	$3,410	$2,372	$5,662	$3,789
1965	3,991	2,816	6,704	4,277
1970	5,490	4,674	9,373	6,598
1973	6,544	5,772	11,633	8,363
1974	6,772*		11,835**	

SOURCE: *1975 Handbook on Women Workers,* p. 136

*All women.
**All men.

B. WOMEN'S MEDIAN SALARY AS A PERCENTAGE OF MEN'S,
BY SELECTED OCCUPATIONAL GROUPS, 1962 AND 1973

Year	*Professional*	*Managerial*	*Clerical*	*Sales*	*Operatives*	*Service**
1962	66.1	57.8	68.6	43.6	59.4	51.8
1973	63.6	52.8	60.9	37.8	56.4	57.8

SOURCE: *1975 Handbook on Women Workers,* p. 130.

*Except private household.

C. MEDIAN INCOME IN 1973, BY EDUCATIONAL ATTAINMENT AND SEX
(YEAR-ROUND, FULL-TIME WORKERS AGED 25
AND OVER AS OF MARCH 1974)

Educational Attainment	*Median Income*		*Women's Median Income as a % of Men's*
	Women	*Men*	
Elementary School			
less than 6 years	$4,369	$7,521	58.1
8 years	5,135	9,406	54.6
High School			
1-3 years	5,513	10,401	53.0
4 years	6,623	12,017	55.1
College			
1-3 years	7,593	13,090	58.0
4 years or more	9,771	16,576	58.9
Total	6,791	12,088	56.2

SOURCE: *1975 Handbook on Women Workers,* p. 134.

Table 4.7

A. ANNUAL AVERAGE UNEMPLOYMENT RATES,
BY SEX AND RACE, 1960-1976
(PERSONS AGED 16 AND OVER)

Year	Women			Men		
	Whites	*Negro and Other Races*	*Total*	*Whites*	*Negro and Other Races*	*Total*
1960	5.3	9.4	5.9	4.8	10.7	5.4
1965	5.0	9.2	5.5	3.6	7.4	4.0
1970	5.4	9.3	5.9	4.0	7.3	4.4
1973	5.3	10.5	4.1	3.7	7.6	6.0
1974	6.1	10.7	6.7	4.3	9.1	4.8
1975	8.6	14.0	9.3	7.2	13.7	7.9
1976	7.9	13.6	8.6	6.4	12.7	7.0

SOURCES: *Handbook of Labor Statistics, 1975,* pp. 153-155; *Handbook of Labor Statistics, 1977,* p. 108.

B. REASONS FOR UNEMPLOYMENT, APRIL 1974
(PERSONS AGED 20 AND OVER)

Reason Given	Unemployed Women (%)	Unemployed Men (%)
Lost last job	43.1	66.9
Left last job	18.9	14.3
Reentered labor force	33.7	16.7
Never worked before	4.3	2.1

SOURCE: *1975 Handbook on Women Workers,* p. 67.

Table 4.8

A. YEARS OF SCHOOL COMPLETED, BY RACE AND SEX, 1960 AND 1975

Race	Total No. of Persons Aged 25 and Over (In Thousands)	% of Population Completing							Median School Years Completed
		Elementary			High School		College		
		0-4 yrs.	5-7 yrs.	8 yrs.	1-3 yrs.	4 yrs.	1-3 yrs.	4 yrs. or more	
				1960					
White									
males	43,259	7.4	13.7	18.7	18.9	22.2	9.1	10.3	10.7
females	46,322	6.0	11.9	17.8	19.6	29.2	9.5	6.0	11.2
total	89,581	6.7	12.8	18.1	19.3	25.8	9.3	8.1	10.9
Negro									
males	4,240	28.3	23.9	12.3	17.3	11.3	4.1	2.8	7.7
females	4,814	19.8	24.5	13.4	20.5	14.3	4.1	3.3	8.6
total	9,054	23.8	24.2	12.0	19.0	12.9	4.1	3.1	8.0
All races	99,438	8.3	13.8	17.5	19.2	24.6	8.8	7.7	10.6
				1975					
White									
males	49,259	3.6	6.8	10.5	14.0	33.1	13.6	18.4	12.5
females	54,806	3.0	6.4	10.6	15.9	41.1	12.1	11.0	12.3
total	104,065	3.3	6.6	10.6	15.0	37.3	12.8	14.5	12.4
Negro									
males	4,925	15.3	14.7	8.1	20.2	25.2	9.7	6.7	10.7
females	6,171	9.8	14.0	8.9	24.0	28.6	8.5	6.2	11.1
Total	11,096	12.3	14.3	8.5	22.3	27.1	9.0	6.4	10.9
All races	116,897	4.2	7.4	10.3	15.6	36.2	12.4	13.9	12.3

SOURCE: *Statistical Abstract of the U.S., 1976*, p. 123.

Table 4.8

B. FIRST PROFESSIONAL DEGREES CONFERRED, BY SEX, 1960 AND 1976

Year	Dentistry (D.D.S. or D.M.D.)		Medical (M.D.)		Law (L.L.B. or J.D.)	
	No.	(%)	No.	(%)	No.	(%)
1959-1960						
Males	3,221	99.2	6,645	94.5	9,010	97.5
Females	26	0.8	387	5.5	230	2.5
Total	3,247	100.0	7,032	100.0	9,240	100.0
1975-1976						
Males	5,187	95.6	11,252	83.9	26,085	80.8
Females	238	4.4	2,174	16.1	6,208	19.2
Total	5,425	100.0	13,426	100.0	32,293	100.0

SOURCES: *Digest of Education Statistics* (Washington, D.C.: Department of Health, Education, and Welfare, 1976), p. 123. *Digest of Education Statistics*, (Washington, D.C.: Department of Health, Education, and Welfare, 1978), p. 115.

FIGURES

Figure 4.1

MEN'S AND WOMEN'S INCOMES, 1957-1973

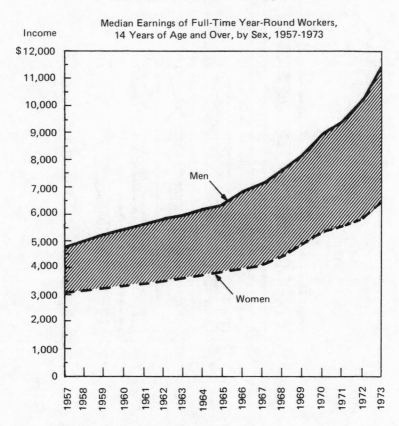

Income

Median Earnings of Full-Time Year-Round Workers,
14 Years of Age and Over, by Sex, 1957-1973

SOURCE: *1975 Handbook on Women Workers,* p. 129.

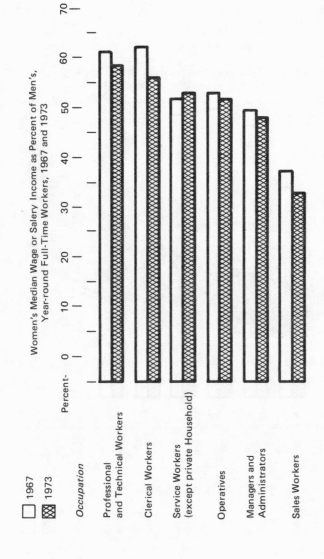

Figure 4.1 (Continued)

Women's Median Wage or Salery Income as Percent of Men's, Year-round Full-Time Workers, 1967 and 1973

1967
1973

Occupation

Professional and Technical Workers

Clerical Workers

Service Workers (except private Household)

Operatives

Managers and Administrators

Sales Workers

SOURCE: *1975 Handbook on Women Workers*, p. 131.

Figure 4.2

FEMALE UNEMPLOYMENT, 1950-1973

The Number of Unemployed Women
Has Increased Greatly, and Women Account for
an Increasing Proportion of All Unemployed Persons

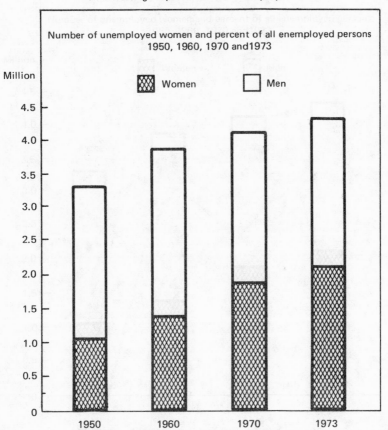

SOURCE: *1975 Handbook on Women Workers,* p.66.

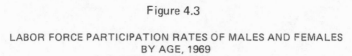

Figure 4.3

LABOR FORCE PARTICIPATION RATES OF MALES AND FEMALES
BY AGE, 1969

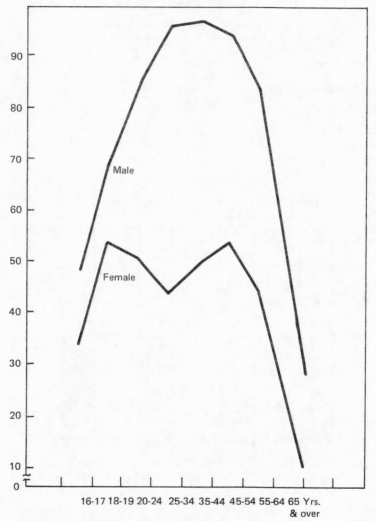

SOURCE: Juanita Kreps, *Sex in the Marketplace* (Baltimore: Johns Hopkins
University, 1971).

Chapter 5
Women
and the Family

The structure and ideology of the family are central to the position of women in American society. After all, women have been largely defined in the culture of American society as wives and mothers, and much of their lives has been structured around the bearing and care of children and the serving of husbands. However, although the family is often viewed as an unchanging institution, and although women's roles may seem stable, the family roles of Americans have in fact undergone pervasive changes between 1960 and the present.

My approach to the family's importance for women and to the implications of recent changes is not confined to either the macro or the micro level of analysis, for the family is at once intimate—involving the most personal interactions between and among individuals on the micro level—and is also an important part of the wider social structure as a whole—a major institution that must be analyzed on a macro level. Thus this chapter focuses on macro analyses of fertility changes and divorce rates, and also explores the micro area of personal relationships. The material sources of American family structure and of their changes will be examined, but consideration is also given to the importance of the ideology of the family in explaining change and resistance to change. Finally, although the American family has been characterized recently by diverse strains that are a result of the long-term process of economic development and at the same time a source of further social change, the family as an institution contains elements that resist change, which I shall also explore.

Until recently, the study of the family almost exclusively stressed that institution's unchanging nature. Especially important has been the view that the stability of the family, through a fixed set of roles determined by sex, is important for maintaining the equilibrium of the wider society. These family roles with their attendant rights and obligations,

113

traditionally have been viewed as necessary to the stability of the family unit, with the husband fulfilling the "instrumental" role of breadwinner, protector, and provider, and the wife fulfilling the "expressive" role of stabilizing internal familial relationships, focusing her full attention on the housekeeper-wife-mother functions within the family.[1]

This theory of the family, with its emphasis on the need to limit women to homemaker-mother roles for the good of the family and the society, has been roundly attacked since the early 1970s by scholars both within and outside of the field of sociology. As sociologists Arlene Skolnick and Jerome Skolnick have commented, this view of the "normal" family—a husband and wife living with their children in a separate residence away from relatives or friends—meant that "unusual family structures such as mother and children, or the experimental communes are regarded as deviant by participants as well as by the rest of the society, and are regarded as unstable and unworkable."[2] According to the Skolnicks, the implication of this traditional view is that the family would not and could not change, and that women could best contribute to their society by fulfilling "expressive" roles and thus ensuring the stability of the nuclear family.

The sources of the critique of this more traditional sociology of the family are not hard to find. In the early 1960s strains in family life and roles, and change in women's family functions in particular, became widespread in the society. Academicians who recognized and sometimes experienced firsthand these changes and strains were motivated to search for an alternative theory of the family that could explain these phenomena. What was required was an explanatory model that could include conflict and change, as well as retain aspects of the concern with stability characteristic of earlier approaches to the subject.

One means of constructing a perspective on change in the family and on women's position therein is to relate it to the process of economic development. In so doing, it is possible to focus on the long-term changes in the structure, functions, and even the ideology of the family that are associated with technological change and economic development. In this chapter I explore such major changes as the continued decline in the birth rate, changes in marital relationships, the rise in the divorce rate, the increasing incidence of alternative (nontraditional nuclear) family forms, and the decline in the number of full-time housewives in American society since 1960. In particular, I shall make use of the recent and growing literature contributed by those modern scholars working in the Marxist tradition who have addressed themselves to the sources and meaning of change in the family and whose perspective is informed by the importance of technological and economic change.[3] Following the initial discussion of changes in the family, I shall turn to an examination of the impact of these changes on women's position in the economy and on norms and practices associated with the process of socialization.

FERTILITY CHANGE

Women's traditional ascription to homemaker-mother roles means that any change in the fertility rate has important implications for a variety of aspects of women's lives. Because the period under consideration was in fact characterized by a marked decline in the birth rate, an explanation of the sources of that decline and of its implications for women's familial roles is necessary in order to understand the overall change in women's position that occurred after 1960.

Table 5.1 shows the rapid decline in the birth rate between 1960 and 1975; by 1975 the birth rate was the lowest ever recorded in the United States. This decrease is of course part of the long-term drop in birth rates that has been found to be universally characteristic of countries undergoing economic development. However, the pronounced rate of decline after 1960 appears even more dramatic when compared with the fertility rates for 1945-1957, the period of the so-called baby boom, when birth rates increased.

Economist Richard Easterlin has proposed a framework that can be used to account for the contrasting experiences of these two periods and for the decline in the birth rate in the later period.[4] As do other economists, Easterlin applies the theory of consumer choice to the issue of parents' decisions to bear children.[5] This theory suggests that the decision to bear children (assuming the knowledge and availability of contraceptive control) reflects the couple's desire for children as balanced against their income and their desires for alternative goods. Such a set of implicit calculations then leads to given levels of fertility in the society, and also to differences among income groups and among groups with varying access to alternative goods.

When this model is applied to a discussion of birth rates after 1960, one might predict rising birth rates, since income was growing rapidly during this period and more children could thus be "afforded." Easterlin argues, however, that a couple's decision rests not only on their own level of income but more importantly on what he calls their "relative economic status," which he defines as the standard of living to which a couple aspires. These aspirations are largely developed in childhood and depend primarily on the standard of living in the family in which a child was reared (family of origin). According to this model, children reared in times of prosperity in relatively affluent homes will expect a higher standard of living when they reach adulthood than will children raised in times or conditions of economic deprivation. Couples in the former group will tend therefore to have smaller families, even with rising income levels, because they feel that they cannot attain or maintain their desired standard of living and also support a large number of children. In contrast, the couples who were reared in and whose aspirations were shaped by conditions of economic hardship will feel that they can afford a relatively larger number of children on the same income as the other group because their desires for alternative goods are relatively modest.

Although Easterlin's theory is not universally accepted, one kind of evidence that tends to support his model is that the children reared during the Great Depression of the 1930s became the parents who produced the sharp rise in birth rates immediately after World War II. This generation may have had only limited expectations with respect to the standard of living they would enjoy as adults, and as a result, according to the theory, felt that they could afford a relatively large number of children. In the late 1950s and early 1960s the parenting generation bore fewer children than the previous generation because, according to Easterlin, they were reared in the relatively affluent postwar period and were motivated to curb their fertility levels in order to attain their desires for a relatively high standard of living. Thus it is not the absolute level of a couple's income that is crucial in predicting their fertility rate, but rather, their income relative to the set of aspirations developed two decades earlier in their families of origin.

In the previous chapter we discussed supply influences on the increase in female labor force participation rates after 1960. Some scholars have argued that the decline in fertility during the same period was a crucial factor in this increase. This argument maintains that a drop in the birth rate is a cause of rising labor force activity because it enables women to enter employment.[6] But it is equally plausible to hypothesize the reverse: that the decline in fertility in the 1960s is best explained as the result of increased female labor force participation.[7] The simultaneous appearance of both trends seems to indicate their interaction, but no convincing evidence has appeared to enable us to choose which of the two variables, fertility or employment, was the primary stimulus.

Easterlin's theory of relative economic status, however, may provide a solution to this dilemma. Relative economic status may not only affect fertility rates, but may also exert a causal influence on female labor force participation rates. The same mechanism that results in a curbing of fertility rates in order to attain a desired standard of living may also motivate some women to move into the labor force in order to help their families to achieve that standard. If women of childbearing age in the early 1960s had high aspirations with respect to their standard of living, it is likely that some of them would enter the labor force and also minimize their fertility in order to help their husbands to achieve such a standard.

The Easterlin hypothesis can be used to explain both rising labor force participation rates and declining fertility, thus avoiding the necessity of choosing between decreased fertility and increased labor force participation as the causal variable. On the one hand, relative economic status bears directly on the recent decline in fertility by its effect in raising parental desires for and expectations of consumer items relative to children. On the other hand, the Easterlin hypothesis also explains the increase in female labor force participation rates, since high aspirations for material goods motivate women to become employed in order to achieve the higher standard of living available to two-income families. In addition, of course, the two variables are mutually reinforcing. Each, however, can be viewed as determined by the economic aspirations of couples, which were shaped by childhood socialization experiences.

THE HOUSEWIFE-MOTHER ROLE

The sharp drop in the birth rate in the recent period may be hypothesized as creating strains in the housewife-mother role to which women were ascribed in American society. If, as we have argued, an important focus of the adult female role was mothering, a decrease in that role—implied by the decline in fertility—might be expected to create pressure for a redefinition or reassessment of that aspect of the cultural definition of women.

In fact, the decline in the mothering role implied by fewer offspring is only part of a long-term reduction in the functions fulfilled by the family.[8]   The process of economic development is associated with a shift away from the family as the locus of economic production and a decline in the responsibility of the family for formal education, religious observance, social activity, and exclusive socialization of children beyond infancy or early childhood. When I discuss the loss of functions in the "family," of course, I am primarily dealing with the roles of adult women, to whom "family" focus and functions were ascribed. With the decline in these functions, women's adult roles over time became increasingly centered on caring for the emotional well-being of their husbands and children. At the same time, and also as a result of economic development, the longevity of women (as well as men) significantly increased. In combination with the decline in fertility this meant that the period of childbearing involved a considerably smaller portion of a woman's adult lifespan. As a result of these changes—the bearing of fewer children, increased longevity, and the declining functions of the family—women's role in the family was experiencing a profound diminution. At the same time, strain was generated because the normative cultural ascription of women to full-time housewife roles remained constant, and cultural norms continued to define femininity exclusively as domesticity and motherhood.

Another major contradiction associated with housewife roles is suggested by Margaret Benston, a modern Marxist. Although the work entailed by such roles is both arduous and economically valuable, that labor goes largely unrecognized and receives no monetary recompense.[9] In the context of a society in which individual worth tends to be evaluated on the basis of occupation and income, women's home roles are of extremely low status. Nevertheless, the work performed by women in the home is necessary to the society. Through housewife roles the function of socializing young children is accomplished, and other members of the family are able to concentrate on their economic roles (husband) or on education that is geared toward preparing them for economic roles (children). The contradiction, according to Benston, lies in the contrast between the valuable and necessary work that women do and the lack of status and/or income associated with that work. To the extent that women are aware of these contradictions, she argues, they will be dissatisfied, much as are other workers who feel exploited in their labor.

Although Benston offers a theoretical model of the housewife role which highlights contradictions that could plausibly lead to dissatisfaction, she unfortunately does not suggest how or why these contradictions might increase or decrease over time or result in differential behavior. When applied to the period after 1960, however, Benston's model can help to clarify the increased strain that we have posited as associated with the housewife role. The contrast between low status and unpaid housewife roles on the one hand, and the status and income available to women in the labor force on the other hand, must have become increasingly acute as ever larger numbers of women became employed. Also, as women as a group became more highly educated, this academic achievement could potentially be translated into higher status and more interesting, higher-paying occupations.[10]   Especially for women with college degrees, higher education may have inculcated personal expectations about their ability both to achieve self-respect and to contribute to society through the use of their educations. Such expectations, when frustrated by involvement in low status and socially unrecognized housewife roles, would surely suggest increasing dissatisfaction with exclusive housewifery. Thus although Benston suggests that it was capitalism that made evident a sharp contradiction between housewife roles that conferred little status and no income, and "work" roles that offered at least a modicum of status and income for women, I would argue that these contradictions most likely became more acute and more perceived in the early 1960s because of the new opportunities for women in education and in the labor market.

In sum, there appear to have been two major structural sources of increasing dissatisfaction with exclusive housewife roles on the part of at least some American women. First, decreased family functions, increased longevity, and a sharp drop in the birth rate left women with only a small portion of the "housewife role" as traditionally defined, which filled a relatively small proportion of their adult lives. The emptiness of the housewife role and the dissatisfaction it aroused thus created a "push" factor. Second, changes in educational attainment and labor force participation rates of women created a "pull" factor in the form of alternative roles that exerted a strong appeal in contrast with low status and monetarily unrewarded housewife roles.

Finally, contradictions generated within the hegemonic ideology surrounding family life may also have contributed to increasing tensions centered on women's exclusive housewife roles. One important part of family ideology, according to Eli Zaretsky,[11] was the belief that the family and home must be completely separate from other institutions of society. In particular the family-society split—this division between "our personal lives and intimate personal experiences on the one hand, and our place in the social division of labor and our participation in impersonal and anonymous social relations"—made the home appear to be a refuge and an escape from the world. It also made the family, in Zaretsky's words, "the major institution in society given over to the personal needs of its members where . . . the individual was central and a sometimes desperate search for warmth, intimacy and mutual support prevailed."[12] This ideological belief in the family as the last refuge of individuality and emotional sustenance served to strengthen the rejection of any change in women's role in the family. If women, who were designated by the culture as the caretakers of the family's emotional health, were to vacate that role, it was believed that the family would crumble, and with it the individual's only source of emotional stability and personal fulfillment. It is in light of this ideological hegemony pertaining to the family that beliefs about the housewife role must be understood. The assumption that women were "naturally" fulfilled by their roles as wives, mothers, and housekeepers was augmented by the belief that the work women did in the home could not produce dissatisfaction, as did work in the "real" world, because women were motivated not by desire for income or status, but by love for the members of their family. Thus the ideology surrounding the family and women's role as the foundation of family life inhibited women's recognition and articulation of dissatisfaction with either family life or their prescribed roles.

As Zaretsky cleverly points out, however, the strains generated by this set of beliefs eventually helped to bring about the very changes that the ideology resisted. On the one hand, the demands placed on the family, and on women in particular as primary caretakers of the emotional life of its members, produced increased difficulties in personal relations within the family unit. No single institution could possibly fulfill all its members' emotional needs, and thus this ideological hegemony meant that many real personal needs went unfulfilled. In addition, it is a myth that the family is indeed separate and completely different from other institutions in society. The workings of economic institutions, for example, have long been recognized as having a strong effect on the quality of family life, which, for example, undergoes increased strain and disorganization during periods of high unemployment.[13] To deny these links between the family and other institutions was to reject the actual experience of people and thus discredit and weaken the ideology. Finally, although as Zaretsky points out, much of the search for personal meaning and fulfillment within the family "has been at the expense of women," the hegemonic ideology does insist that all individuals, including women, have the right to meaning and fulfullment in their lives.[14] Such meaning, according to the ideology, is available only within the family sphere, but for some women the desire for fulfillment and meaning directly contradicted the constraints imposed on them by the housewife-mother role. The ideology of personal fulfillment thus increasingly generated great tension when confronted with the traditional ascription of women to solely housewife and mother roles.

In sum, women's increasing dissatisfaction with their traditional, exclusive roles of wife, housewife, and mother had its sources in objective changes in the society and also in the contradictions and strains generated by the hegemonic ideology surrounding the family. The changes associated with economic development—the decline in fertility, increased longevity, changes in the functions of the family, and such technological innovations as washing machines, refrigerators, prepared foods, and dishwashers that lightened household chores—all served to remove much of the content of women's traditional roles in the family. At the same time, new possibilities for employment, personal development, and education for women outside of the family sphere became increasingly available. Strains surrounding the exclusive ascription of women to housewife roles were further aggravated by the ideology of the time, with its emphasis on personal fulfillment and its assumption that the family should be the exclusive provider of such fulfillment. For some women at least, it seems likely that housewife roles and family relationships were increasingly less fulfilling at precisely the time that the predominant ideology asserted the right of all individuals to personal development.

Although we do not have direct evidence of increasing dissatisfaction after 1960, a plausible case for it can be made from three different kinds of evidence. First is the theoretical argument constructed above, which suggests that structural and ideological changes within and outside of the family may have produced increasing dissatisfaction at that time. Second, the emergence of the women's liberation movement during this period provides indirect evidence of such dissatisfaction in its critique of the housewife role as women's prescribed and exclusive role and its assertion that such roles should radically change. Finally, we have a remarkable piece of literary evidence in the form of Betty Friedan's famous *Feminine Mystique*, published in 1963.

Although Friedan's work did not make use of a sophisticated method and is written in journalistic style, the book and its remarkably wide impact represent evidence of the increased dissatisfaction of at least some groups of women with their ascription to exclusively housewife-mother roles. Friedan asserts that her research, based on interviews with eighty American women in the late fifties and on her own experience, is evidence that the women's traditional roles had produced a generation of unhappy, frustrated, incomplete, and dissatisfied American women. These women, she argues, suffered from the "problem that has no name," that is, the assumption in American society that women should fulfill exclusively housewife-mother roles and that those roles alone were sufficient for the development of feminine identity and fulfillment. The lack of a name stemmed from the fear that women had of expressing their frustration and dissatisfaction with these roles. Thus Friedan argues that the true source of the strain went unarticulated, and perhaps even unrecognized, by women who lived in silent frustration and unfulfillment lest they be labeled "unfeminine." In sum, Friedan's polemical and often moving book is an indictment of traditional, exclusive housewife-mother roles and stands as indirect evidence of the reality of some women's frustration within those roles.

MARITAL RELATIONSHIPS

The period after 1960 was characterized not only by change in the size of the family unit and in the nature of the housewife role, but also by change in marital relationships. In the following sections I shall explore this phenomenon in its various forms: the increased rate of divorce, the increased incidence of unmarried adults in the society, the rising number of single-person households, and the significant changes in the quality of marital relationships.

Divorce

Table 5.3 indicates numerous changes that have occurred in the marital behavior of large numbers of American men and women since

1960. Of these demographic changes, one of the most dramatic is the more than twofold increase in the divorce rate between 1960 and 1975. Although the rate of divorce had been increasing prior to 1960, its acceleration in this period is described by Paul Glick and Arthur Norton of the Census Bureau as "a phenomenal upsurge."[15] Moreover, this trend is not specific to any one sector of the population, but holds for both white and nonwhite marriages and is no longer closely associated with such traditionally differentiating factors as level of education, income, or occupational prestige. As Norton and Glick argue, the correlation between high divorce rates and low education, low income, and low occupational prestige has dropped during this period, as relatively high rates of divorce have spread to higher socioeconomic groups.

It is considerably easier to sketch out the changes in American divorce rates than it is to explain them. As Heather Sawhill and Isabel Ross state in their 1975 survey of the literature on marital instability, "we are dealing with an area where the facts are still very much in search of a theory, and where a given set of facts may be equally consistent with several hypotheses."[16]

Some hypotheses focus on the effects of structural changes in society. A decrease in the fertility rate, for example, may be expected to result in higher divorce rates. Declining birth rates would reduce several obstacles to divorce, including the concern of many people that divorce creates special and damaging psychological and emotional traumas for young children, and the special economic burden placed on parents who divorce when their children are young and dependent. In a society with low fertility rates, more couples are likely to be childless, and small family size means that the family includes young children for a relatively small proportion of the total marital life. High fertility rates in a society where the nuclear family is alone responsible for its offspring thus imply widespread constraints on the divorce rate, while low fertility rates suggest a direct weakening of obstacles to divorce.

In addition to the effect of declining fertility on the divorce rate, another structural pressure in the direction of rising divorce rates makes itself felt through the mechanism of increased female labor force participation. It is widely acknowledged that the probability of divorce increases with increased possibilities for women to be economically self-sufficient.[17] Women's ability to earn a separate income eliminates their economic dependence on men and therefore lessens the economic constraints on men and, significantly, on women who desire a divorce.

In sum, both men and women may be more willing and/or able to dissolve an undesirable marriage if the woman is or can be employed. Both women's rising educational attainment, and the lowering of the fertility rate, of course contribute to the increased potential for divorce in this regard. The former does so by increasing the probability that women will be employed and receive adequate financial reward, and the latter does so by decreasing the burdens of childrearing, which represent an obstacle to women's participation in the labor force.

Although the structural changes discussed above exerted strong upward pressure on the divorce rate during our period, it is probable that attitudinal and normative changes also inclined it in the same direction. Norton and Glick state that "the upsurge in divorce during the last ten years has been stimulated by a growing acceptance of the principle that divorce is a reasonable and at times desirable alternative to an unhappy marriage."[18] Even in the early 1960s the stigma once attached by American culture to divorce was fading and the constraints of the dominant antidivorce ideology were probably felt with less intensity than in the past. At the same time, the ideological belief in individual development and fulfillment may have influenced the divorce rate. Not only might women look outside their familial roles for opportunities to develop their identity and their potential, but some could also plausibly view their marriages as obstacles to such development. It seems likely that the belief that individuals have a right to develop their potential and the belief that divorce is an acceptable if not desirable mechanism for achieving individual happiness or fulfillment began to converge in the early 1960s, exerting an upward pressure on the divorce rate.[19] Thus changes in ideology, as well as structural changes, contributed to the increasing divorce rate in American society during our period.

The rate of remarriage of course is closely tied to trends in the divorce rate. As more couples are divorced, more individuals become part of a pool of people for whom remarriage is at least a possibility. Thus the potential for a high rate of remarriage follows from the existence of a high divorce rate in a given society. The factors affecting whether members of that pool of divorced persons actually become involved in second (or third, fourth, etc.) marriages, however, are not clear, as this subject has so far generated relatively little research. It is plausible to suggest however that the rate of remarriage is influenced by the society's beliefs about divorce and remarriage. In a society where the stigma attached to divorce begins to fade and where people choose divorce as a means of achieving greater fulfillment or happiness in their lives, it seems likely that remarriage would be increasingly tolerated and practiced as a legitimate attempt to achieve happiness within the institution of marriage. The increase in the rate of remarriage in American society after 1960 may indicate just such a set of beliefs. In any event, the high remarriage rate certainly implies that divorce represents the rejection of a particular spouse rather than the rejection of the institution of marriage.

Singles

Data reflecting the median age of marriage, the proportion of single people in the population, and the living arrangements of singles also seem to indicate significant changes in American patterns of marriage and family building during the 1960s and early 1970s. Table 5.3 shows that the median age of marriage, a figure that generally remains stable over time, rose steadily during this period, as did the proportion of people under thirty-five years of age who were single (had never been married). Marriage itself seems to have become less of a prerequisite for young people establishing their own households, as sharply increasing numbers of never-married young people move into separate residences, often with unrelated individuals.

Again, an explanation of these changes in marital status and household formation must focus initially on the hypothesized influence of structural changes in American society. For example, the rising levels of educational attainment for both American women and men, especially with respect to university and professional training, would imply an increase in the age at first marriage, since marriages are postponed or not considered until education is completed. This would be particularly true if both partners in a couple had high educational aspirations. Similarly, the tendency for singles to establish separate households may be a factor in postponing the age of marriage. With the establishment of a separate residence, individuals have claim to the adult status and independence which previously could be attained only with marriage. Finally, the involvement of women in the labor force and their ability to support themselves financially of course implies less need to turn to marriage as a source of financial support.

Along with these structural changes, social norms over the period have altered in the direction of greater tolerance for single status,

especially for women. Peter Stein suggests "there is clearly more support now than there was a generation ago for those who continue to
defer marriage."[20] His research indicates that many singles view their
status as facilitating self-development, change, freedom of choice and
more varied opportunities than are available to married persons. Thus
while marriage remains the eventual goal of most people, structural and
ideological changes have rendered the single status increasingly legitimate and likely.

Quality of Marriage

Because we have objective statistical measures of divorce, remarriage,
and living arrangements, we can assert with confidence that widespread
changes occurred in the marital behavior of large numbers of Americans
after 1960. However, it is difficult to infer the specific nature and extent of the changes in the quality of marital relationships implied by
these measures. Although we know that there were more divorces during our period than previously, we cannot assume that this figure represents a greater number of unhappy marriages or a decline in the quality
of married life. Indeed, a large amount of evidence indicates that stable
marriages are not necessarily happy ones, since stability may derive
from economic, social, or personal reasons unrelated to the question of
happiness.[21] Thus, it may be argued that an increase in the divorce rate
indicates that marriages are less happy than in the past and that they
are subjected to increasing strains. However, it is equally plausible to
suggest that the quality of relationships remains comparatively stable
over time but that the ability to dissolve unsatisfactory unions has
increased. There is no satisfactory evidence to justify a choice between
these hypotheses, as both circumstances may in fact be contributing to
the precipitous rise in divorce rates.

Despite this lack of a definitive answer to the question of change in
the overall quality of relationships within marriage, much research has
focused on the effects on marriage of female labor force participation,
which underwent considerable change during our period. The findings
are summarized in two important collections by Lois Hoffman and Ivan
Nye, which appeared in 1963 and 1974.[22] In a theoretical article in
the early collection, Hoffman explores the changes in marital relationships that emerge with wives' employment by discussing the effects of
employment on power relationships within marriage.[23] In general it is

argued that men and women have unequal power in the marital relationship, with men retaining greater control. However, to the extent
that marital power, as is often argued, rests on differential access to
external resources, primarily in the form of income and prestige, wives'
employment could increase their power and thus change the balance of
power in marital relationships. According to Hoffman, the sources of
such an increase include the greater prestige attached to the role of
wage earner than to that of housewife, and the external monetary resources to which women are entitled through their labor. A wife's independent income would also increase her power by lessening her economic dependence on her spouse, since she could support herself in the
event of a divorce. Finally, Hoffman suggests that working outside the
home allows women social interaction and skill development that are
unobtainable in the role of housewife. These could increase the relative power of women in marriages by increasing wives' self-confidence,
their feelings of achievement and contribution, their knowledge of alternative situations in other families, and even their development of
social skills that may be useful in influencing their husbands.

Whereas Hoffman's initial discussion of this issue was largely theoretical, ten years later Stephen Bahr summarized the empirical research
carried out in the interim by stating that "in general, employed wives
tend to have greater power than non-employed wives."[24] Specifically,
it appears that the growth in wives' power is especially apparent with
respect to decisions concerning finances and the bearing and rearing of
children. According to Bahr, however, these effects are stronger for
working-class than for middle-class couples. While the empirical research over a decade tends to confirm that employment increases wom-
en's relative power in marital relationships, equality between couples
has not been attained and evidence of male dominance persists.

Although, as Hoffman points out, power relationships in marriage
may be altered as a result of female employment, this phenomenon
raises a second issue with respect to the quality of marital relationships:
What is the effect of a relative increase in female power on the overall
happiness of the marriage? Nye suggests that a shift in power relationships and in role definitions such as that caused by female labor force
participation could be expected to create tensions within the relationship, since "sociologists generally expect any role redefinitions or
power alterations to be accompanied by increased conflict because of
confusion, lack of predictability of behavior, and differing perceptions

of social norms."[25] In testing his hypothesis, however, Nye found that empirical data gathered during the decade indicate only a few negative effects at the beginning of the 1960s, mainly among working-class couples. He argues that by the early 1970s the negative effects of wives' employment on marital happiness had disappeared entirely among middle-class families and were only mildly significant among working-class families. Thus although the shifts in marital power and the redefinition of roles associated with female labor force partici-pation were expected to decrease marital happiness and increase mari-tal strain, there is little empirical evidence for such an hypothesis, with the exception of the few negative effects found in the case of working-class couples.

Available studies seem to indicate that the structural change repre-sented by increased labor force participation of married women has had only a minor effect on the quality of marital relationships after 1960. I would suggest that the lack of significant change may be owing in large part to middle-class husbands' continued access to greater financial resources than are available to their working wives, and their ability thereby to maintain a relative position of power within the marriage. Among working-class couples, female labor force participation has had some effect on both marital power relationships and marital happiness, perhaps because the difference between the husbands' and wives' rela-tive contributions to family finances are slight. But even among those working-class families, it appears that wives' employment has few ef-fects on the quality of marriage. Thus, wives' labor force activity alone does not seem to be a sufficient condition for significant alteration of the quality of marital relationships, whether with respect to power or to happiness. Rather, what Hoffman calls the "male dominance ide-ology," particularly when buttressed by a large differential in the in-comes between husband and wife, seems to reduce or even, according to Hoffman, reverse the overall impact of wives' employment in equal-izing power and, consequently, has little impact on the quality of the marriage. Although the research done on the quality of marital rela-tionships after 1960 is inadequate as a basis for any definite general conclusions, the evidence on the effect of increased wives' employment indicates that it is only a potential generator of redefinitions of roles, power, and relationships. Without other changes, for example, in ide-ology and women's earning power, increased female employment seems unlikely to affect radically the quality of intact marriages.

ALTERNATIVE FORMS OF FAMILY STRUCTURE

As I noted at the beginning of this chapter, the emphasis in the social science literature on the nuclear family as the ideal family type has contributed to the view that any other family structure is problem-ridden, inherently unstable, and less desirable. In other words, moral judgments were inextricably intertwined with analytic examinations of the family. Deviant family structures were not only "bad" in themselves, but also threatened to weaken or upset the nuclear family form. Despite the fears of many social scientists and their warnings about the dire consequences of the growth of alternative family forms, the period from 1960 to the present saw the unprecedented growth of such alternative structures.[26] I shall explore the literature concerned with the sources and implications of two of these forms: the female-headed, single-parent family, and the dual-career family.

Female-Headed Families

A female-headed family is defined by the U.S. Census Bureau as "a group of two or more persons related by blood, marriage or adoption and residing together," whose designated "head" is female. Prior to changes made for the 1980 census, the Census Bureau defined a family head as the person who is "regarded as such by the members of the group, *except that married women are not classified as heads if their husbands are living with them*" (my emphasis).[27] Thus the only way a married woman could be classified as a "head" is by having related individuals, not including her husband, living with her. Using this definition, we can see that female-headed families in the United States have been increasing rapidly since 1960, both in absolute numbers and as a proportion of all family types (Table 5.4). Heather Ross and Isabel Sawhill of the Urban Institute have brought together much of the available information on female-headed families in their book, *Time Of Transition*, and they note specific demographic trends among these families in the last decade and a half: the greatest increase in female heads of families has occurred among young women, and the reason for their status as "heads" is overwhelmingly divorce or separation rather than widowhood; there has been marked growth in the number of female-headed families with children under the age of eighteen (9 percent in 1960, 15 percent in 1974); since 1960, the number of nonwhite female-headed families with children has increased twice as fast as that of white female-headed families with children; the trend toward increasing numbers of female-headed families is characteristic at all income levels; because of the decline since 1960 in the number of male-headed families that are classified as below poverty level, the poverty population increasingly has come to consist of female-headed families; in 1974, the majority of those families with children under the age of eighteen that were classified as poor were headed by females.[28]

Ross and Sawhill view female-headed families as a transitional phenomenon, "interim entities of relatively short duration between one traditional family structure—usually a husband-wife family—and another."[29] According to their estimates, this impermanent family structure lasts for an average of about five to six years, which of course means that the data concerning such families at any given point in time are deceiving. In effect, the number of individuals who have experienced living in female-headed households is far larger than is indicated in the statistics at one point in time. Marital disruption is the primary reason for female-headed families, according to Ross and Sawhill, while remarriage usually accounts for the return to the traditional male-headed structure. In addition to divorce, other, albeit less important, contributing factors to the large number of female-headed families after 1960 are the high rate of illegitimacy and the changes in living arrangements of never-married or formerly married mothers, who in recent years have appeared more likely to set up their own households rather than to live with an already established family (such as that of a parent or sibling). Taking into account the fertility, education, and employment factors that, we have already seen, greatly contribute to higher rates of marital disruption, it is reasonable for Ross and Sawhill to state that their "central hypothesis is that the changing economic and social status of women is a major source of the behavioral evolution leading to female-headed families."[30] In a society in which the bond between mothers and children is culturally presumed to be stronger and more important than that between fathers and their offspring, increases in marital disruption result in large numbers of women and children living without men.

Female-headed families have generally been viewed as inferior to or less adequate than the traditional nuclear family unit. One criticism is prompted by the fact that, regardless of prior economic status, many female-headed families find themselves below the poverty level.[31] But is this tendency toward poverty a reflection of inadequacies inherent in the female-headed structure itself? On the one hand, the poverty of female-headed family units is a consequence of the inferior position of women in the labor force as compared with that of men. On the other hand, economic problems associated with female-headed families can be linked to extra expenditures for child care and various domestic services, which are typically carried out "free of cost" by the women in two-parent families, but which must be paid for by employed female heads. Finally, the poor performance of fathers in supporting their children after divorce or separation is also a contributing factor, since it is often the single mothers who must bear the entire cost of rearing their offspring.[32] None of these economic problems is inherent in the structure of the female-headed family unit; rather, they are the result of such factors as the weak position of women in the economy, the lack of publicly financed child care and domestic services outside the family unit, and the erratic enforcement of child support payments by the court system. Most female-headed families, regardless of prior socioeconomic status, must struggle under imposed economic disadvantages.

The other major criticism leveled at the female-headed family unit focuses on its alleged incapacity to provide adequate child rearing. Here the concern is for the possible negative effects on children of being reared in a fatherless home. Perhaps the best-known indictment of this type of family is Daniel P. Moynihan's denunciation of the black female-headed family, which centers on the assertion that "At the heart of the deterioration of the fabric of Negro society is the deterioration of the Negro family."[33] According to Moynihan, family deterioration was the result primarily of the so-called matriarchal structure of the black family, as embodied in the relatively high proportion of female-headed families among black Americans. Specifically, he argued that the female-headed family structure is associated with high levels of juvenile delinquency, poor academic and occupational achievement, and lowered aspirations, particularly among male children. These problems, according to Moynihan, are largely owing to father absence.

Critiques of the Moynihan thesis were both angry and numerous, with two major points consistently reiterated.[34] First, critics noted that Moynihan's focus on the female-headed structure as the source of pathology deemphasized the importance of poverty as a primary factor. They cited evidence indicating that for both black and nonblack families, regardless of who is at the head, poverty is strongly associated with negative social behavior on the part of children, including poor achievement, low aspirations, and criminal activity. As Ross and Sawhill have pointed out recently, close analysis of data on this question cannot distinguish the effects of poverty from the effects of father absence, and thus it is premature, if not incorrect, to suggest that father absence causes the development of social and behavioral problems among offspring in female-headed families. These same authors note their view that social and economic deprivation is the most likely source of marital instability, of father absence, and also of severe behavioral problems among children in the black ghetto community. Thus Moynihan's attack prompted his critics to question the purported pathology-generating characteristics inherent in the female-headed family. Many social scientists have come to view the poverty with which female-headed status is so often associated as a more likely causal agent of problems than father absence.

The second major rebuttal to the Moynihan thesis argues that the female-headed family structure can be interpreted as having strengths rather than weaknesses. Scholars such as Robert Staples, Andrew Billingsly, and more recently, Carol Stack have pointed to ways in which this structure has had positive effects in the black community.[35] Staples argues that the female-headed structure is "a sign of the strength and resiliency of the Black family" in the face of discrimination, poverty, and oppression, since black women have proved themselves capable of taking on new roles and functions in spite of the dominant restrictive cultural definitions of femininity. Stack points to the strong bonds of reciprocity and mutual assistance among women without husbands; they develop wider kin networks, which provide monetary and emotional support for themselves and their children. In the context of high levels of marital instability, according to Stack, such women-centered networks may provide at least as stable and adequate a family structure within which to rear children as the more acceptable nuclear family form. In addition, she objects to the assumption that children in female-headed families suffer from father absence, since in many of the families she studied, male kin—uncles and grandfathers—serve as adequate substitute fathers and role models for children.

More recent research seems to substantiate much of the anti-Moynihan critique with respect to the effects on children of living in a female-headed family. In their review of the literature, Ross and Sawhill point out that children may be better off living with their mothers alone after divorce or separation than in an intact nuclear family that is wracked by conflict, hatred, or irreconcilable differences.[36] They also note that the degree of father-absence created by a divorce varies from couple to couple. In a culture that deemphasizes paternal involvement with off-spring, divorce may not appreciably decrease the amount of time that many fathers would otherwise spend with their children. The emotional stability and behavior of children is not necessarily affected adversely either by divorce or by living in a female-headed family. In sum, there has been increasing recognition that the female-headed family is not an inherently inferior form of family structure.

Nevertheless, the problems associated with families headed by wom-en are indeed numerous and it is to be expected that such problems, regardless of their source, would generate strains for the women in-volved. The most severe and widely experienced strains are likely to be those associated with the provision of an adequate livelihood for the mother and her offspring and with the economic and social problems of surviving in conditions of poverty. A second source of strain emanates from the negative normative labeling to which women without hus-bands are exposed. Women who were socialized to believe that mar-riage was their primary goal and that the success of the marriage was their primary responsibility are likely to feel some guilt and anxiety in their husbandless state. Their children too may suffer from the view that they are different or incomplete as compared with children of intact families. Finally, the negative stereotyping of women without husbands as inadequate mothers, and as sexually deviant and/or un-stable individuals is likely to affect adversely their social contacts with others, even when they themselves have escaped the guilt engendered by their own socialization experiences. The lack of social supports— both emotional and monetary—create strains for many women who head families, with the multiple burdens of child care, income earning, and social interaction falling on their shoulders alone.

Dual-Career Families

During the 1960s and early 1970s a second alternative pattern of familial relationships was emerging and receiving attention from schol-ars. Unlike the female-headed family unit, the dual-career family pat-tern is similar in form to a nuclear family structure—husband, wife, and children residing by themselves—but is different from the traditional pattern in its internal role definitions.[37] In contrast to the culturally ascribed feminine family role of exclusive domesticity, women in dual-career families are active in full-time and demanding careers. A career can be distinguished from other types of employment by the greater time and commitment it demands and by the assumption that it has priority over many other aspects of the individual's life. Thus, it was expected that women's involvement in careers would entail more extreme departures from traditional cultural norms pertaining to family life than would be true for wives and mothers engaged in less demanding jobs.

The findings for dual-career couples, however, parallel the pattern for middle-class families that is reflected in the literature on working wives, that is, relatively minor changes in traditional male-female role definitions are occasioned by the development of the dual-career pattern. For example, Margaret Paloma and T. Neal Garland reject the "myth of the egalitarian family" in their discussion of the dual-career model. Their empirical research indicated that despite the wife's career, the primary burdens of child care and household maintenance continue to fall on her, that the husband's career needs clearly take precedence over those of his wife, and that the majority of couples interviewed reported that the man clearly is "head of the household."[38] Wives who took up a career had not only the approval but often the encouragement of their husbands; indeed, such approval seemed to be a prerequisite for the emergence of a dual-career pattern. Thus the early development of a dual-career family pattern stimulated only minor changes in the role structure of dominance and responsibility typical of marital relationships in the more traditional nuclear family, despite wives' deviance from the traditional feminine role of exclusive domesticity.

At the same time, however, research on dual-career families has shown that different strains characterize this family pattern compared to the traditional one, as the emergence of new patterns of career involvement for married women come into conflict with both ideological and structural features of traditional American families. Rhona Rapoport and Robert Rapoport label the special strains of dual-career family life as "dilemmas" and note five such conflicts of particular significance for the career wife.[39] "Role-cycling dilemmas" in dual-career families can be generated in two ways. First, role-cycling strains are produced by conflicts between the demands of the husbands' and wives' careers, and are especially severe when the wife's career threatens to interfere with the husband's needs. Tensions are also heightened in those cases where the wife's income or occupational prestige tend to supersede those of her husband. Role cycling is a special problem for the wife, who faces the constant struggle of establishing priorities among the competing claims of family and occupational responsibilities. In addition, the issues of when to have children and how many children to have may cause further anxieties for the woman in connection with the development of her career. How much career achievement should, can, or must be sacrificed for how much family involvement or responsibility sometimes also affects the husband in dual-career families, but it is largely the wife's problem, given the cultural maxim that the family is primarily her responsibility.

A second type of strain consistently reported in dual-career families is described by the Rapoports as "role overload." This dilemma is generated by the sheer amount of responsibility and work required of women who have careers and also maintain families; indeed, families and professional occupations have been called "greedy institutions" by sociologist Louis Coser.[40] Their heavy demands on time, energy, and emotions take a toll on the individual who attempts to fulfill both roles at once. Many researchers report that adequate provision for child rearing is a particularly difficult problem, since nonfamilial agencies are rarely available to assist with this task. And almost all dual-career wives report that they have little or no time to relax or enjoy leisure activities. One of Lynda Holmstrom's respondents described the typical symptoms of role overload:

> I sometimes am very tired. I work harder at being with the children and making use of my time with them, and planning it and the same with the groceries you know . . . . I'm a lot more pushed to keep onto some kind of schedule. I sometimes find that I'd just like to relax and forget the whole business (Laughter).[41]

Lack of leisure time is also associated with a fourth set of strains, "social network dilemmas." Often, dual-career couples do not have the time or energy to sustain the kinds of relationships and engage in the numerous social interactions that friends and close relatives may expect. Demands for sociability and obligations to relatives often fall most heavily on the wife, since women are culturally expected to organize social life and familial commitments. The dilemma and strain result from the difficulty the wife experiences in fulfilling this set of role obligations in addition to her career responsibilities.

Finally many women who participate in a dual-career family pattern experience "identity dilemmas" and "normative dilemmas." Virtually all researchers note the anxiety and guilt expressed by such wives with respect to their status as mothers and as females. This guilt is partly generated by their own recognition that they are deviating from the cultural norms governing motherhood and family care that they were taught as children. In addition, the society's skepticism about their family pattern and their ability to parent adequately and/or to fulfill work responsibilities satisfactorily is also a source of self-doubt and anxiety. To the extent that femininity in American culture is defined by exclusive domesticity and motherhood, self-definition is a problem for women in dual-career families who are sensitive to their own and others' tendency to view them as unfeminine and nonmaternal because of their involvement in demanding professional careers.

In spite of such strains the number of dual-career families increased substantially after 1960 as more and more women engaged in professional occupations and as more and more mothers with young children entered or reentered the labor force (Table 4.2). The Rapoports report that many dual-career couples have chosen this life-style because they believe it offers significant advantages over the traditional model. These include increased family income, self-fulfillment and creative work involvement for the wife, and vicarious gratification for the husband through his wife's accomplishments. Despite special problems emanating from its deviance from and conflict with traditional family norms and structure, the dual-career pattern emerged as an important alternative model of family structure after 1960.

Since the early 1960s, then, the family has demonstrated that it is an institution characterized by considerable dynamism. The traditional nuclear family may have been the ideal toward which many Americans aspired, but the reality of increasing divorce, later marriage, and more families headed by women meant that living in a permanent nuclear family for most of one's life was no longer the norm. At the same time, emerging alternative family forms—single-parent and dual-career families, for example—created viable living situations for many Americans, although these newer forms of course were not without their own strains and problems. What is clear is that the institution of the family changed in this period. In the following section I trace the effects of those changes on socialization patterns and on women's role in the economy.

CHANGING FAMILY PATTERNS AND THEIR IMPLICATIONS

The changes, strains, and contradictions characterizing American family life after 1960 were, as I have argued, largely the product of extrafamilial socioeconomic and demographic changes. From a different perspective however, these changes in the family can be viewed as factors that of themselves produced or accelerated change both within and outside of family life. In the following section I explore the direct effects of the changes in the family on socialization practices and economic institutions. Their contribution to the development of the women's liberation movement will be explored in the following chapters.

Familial Change and Socialization

Since one of the major and most widely recognized functions of the nuclear family has been that of socializing the next generation, it would be surprising to find that changes in the family do not produce some alterations in the patterns and practices of socialization within the family sphere. The combination of such familial changes as declining fertility, rising divorce rates, decreasing satisfaction with the exclusive housewife-mother role, and increasing emphasis on the dominant ideology's approval of self-development and fulfillment of family members exerted considerable pressure on traditional socialization practices. The socialization of a young girl could no longer be based on the assumption that her adult role would include large numbers of offspring to rear, housewifery as the ultimate and only fulfillment, or even a permanent spouse on whom to depend. The traditional components inculcated into the female personality were obviously less functional in the new circumstances. In addition, the ideology of self-fulfillment may have encouraged women to seek new models of self-development to replace the increasingly less applicable traditional ones. Of course, to suggest that socialization processes and the definition of the feminine personality were under pressure to change is not to argue that such changes occurred immediately or were even consciously recognized by most of the population. Rather, my hypothesis is that the structural and ideological changes in the family helped to erode the legitimacy of the traditional goals that influenced female socialization, and also to authenticate the search for new directions of female definition and development.

The emergence of alternative family forms may also have contributed to the direct pressures for change in socialization practices. In female-headed families and in dual-career families women deviated from traditional female patterns of economic dependence on men and exclusive housewife roles. They thus served as alternative role models for their children and for others who came into contact with them. In addition, their circumstances made it unlikely that their interaction with their children would be identical to that of women who were full-time wives and housewives. Although this interaction could be expected to vary widely, depending heavily on individual patterns, women in dual-career families probably encouraged their daughters to take an interest in careers and female heads of families probably emphasized the need to be economically self-sufficient more often than was true of other mothers.

Even some women in traditional housewife-mother roles may have contributed to change in socialization patterns through their function as negative role models for girls. Women who were dissatisfied or frustrated with the role of exclusive housewife and/or felt themselves trapped in that role would undoubtedly communicate their unhappiness, explicitly or implicitly, to their children. Daughters of such women may have reacted to their mothers' signals by planning for career-oriented futures, and to avoid replicating their mothers' frustrations, they themselves may have exerted pressure on socialization practices. By rejecting their mothers' models of femininity and by demanding from schools, religious institutions, and other agencies of socialization the training to fulfill nontraditional goals, it is likely that at least some young women contributed to changing socialization patterns.

Another effect of familial change on socialization practices was to increase the demand for nonfamilial caretakers of young children. Although the hegemonic ideology asserted the essentiality of mothers' care for the healthy development of children, the rise of single-parent and dual-career families made it difficult for many mothers to provide exclusive care even for their very young children. The geographical mobility of American families made it unlikely that most mothers would be able to call on close relatives for help in providing care for children, and the number of private household workers who might have been able to fulfill these responsibilities was rapidly declining (Table 4.4). Thus the need for group care became apparent, and its advent created a situation whereby individual mothers no longer had complete control of their young childrens' socialization. The influence of professionals' and even of other parents' ideas of acceptable values in a group care setting may have contributed to change in socialization practices, as well as to the legitimation of the idea of collective patterns of child rearing.

Familial Change and the Economy

Strains and changes in family life may have had effects outside of the institution of the family and socialization practices. Economic institutions, although often perceived as completely separate from family life, were not exempt from pressures for change. Rising divorce rates and the increasing number of female-headed and dual-career families all implied a decrease in the number of family units for whom an adult woman was able to devote full-time attention to providing child care, coping with emergencies, organizing schedules, and maintaining the household. Women who did not have spouses or who lived in dual-career families had to cope with demands to fulfill many home-based responsibilities while at the same time carrying out occupational roles. Employers' requirement that they conform to rigid schedules was difficult, if not impossible, for many women in such circumstances. Pressures were thus placed on economic institutions to establish more flexible scheduling, allowing workers to choose the hours best suited to their personal needs. These same familial changes, and the decreased likelihood that women would devote themselves exclusively to domestic roles, generated increasing pressures on economic institutions to provide a wide variety of goods and services traditionally supplied by women in the home. Changes in the family thus created new demands on economic institutions and contributed to changes in patterns of work for employers and employees.

CONCLUSION

The position of women in the family has altered considerably since the early 1960s as the institution of the family itself has undergone substantial change. Moreover, the broader social changes attendant upon economic development have affected the family and made clear its interdependence with the rest of society. At the same time, the traditional role of women in the family sphere evidenced strains and contradictions as alterations in the family occurred, leading to changes in female personality development and women's position in the economy. As these changes interacted with alterations in the family and newly emergent family forms, pressure mounted for further change in the position of American women.

NOTES

1. Excellent critiques of this type of family theory may be found in Ann Oakley, *Woman's Work*, pp. 178-85, and in Arlene S. and Jerome H. Skolnick (eds.), *Family in Transition* (Boston: Little Brown, 1971), pp. 10-14.

2. Skolnick and Skolnick, *Family in Transition*, p. 8

3. For example, Benston, "Political Economy of Women's Liberation," and Eli Zaretsky, *Capitalism, the Family and Personal Life* (New York: Harper & Row, 1976).

4. Richard A. Easterlin, "The Economics and Sociology of Fertility: A Synthesis" (unpublished paper prepared for the Seminar on Early Industrialization, Shifts in Fertility and Changes in Family Structure, Princeton University, June 1972).

5. See, for example, Gary S. Becker, "An Economic Analysis of Fertility," in *Demographic and Economic Change in Developed Countries: A Conference of the Universities-National Bureau Committee for Economic Research* (Princeton: Princeton University, 1960), pp. 209-31.

6. See Sweet, *Women in the Labor Force*, and William G. Bowen and T. Aldrich Finegan, *The Economics of Labor Force Participation* (Princeton: Princeton University Press, 1969).

7. See Pascal K. Whelpton, Arthur A. Campbell, and John E. Patterson, *Fertility and Family Planning in the United States* (Princeton: Princeton University Press, 1966), and K. O. Mason, *Women's Labor Force Participation and Fertility* (Research Triangle: Research Triangle Press, 1974).

8. Goode, *World Revolution*, pp. 4-6.

9. Benston, "Political Economy of Women's Liberation."

10. I am not suggesting that all or even most women at this time were engaged in prestigious occupations. It is true, however, that a high proportion of women were employed in white-collar occupations that have traditionally been accorded a certain status in the occupational hierarchy. See Chapter 4 above.

11. Zaretsky, *Capitalism, the Family and Personal Life*.

12. *Ibid.*, p. 60.

13. For a particularly interesting discussion of the links between family life and economic institutions see Rosabeth Moss Kanter, *Work and the Family in the United States* (New York: Russell Sage Foundation, 1977).

14. Zaretsky, *Capitalism, the Family and Personal Life*, p. 55.

15. Arthur J. Norton and Paul C. Glick, "Marital Instability: Past, Present and Future," *Journal of Social Issues*, 32 (1976):12.

16. Ross and Sawhill, *Time of Transition*, p. 36.

17. *Ibid.*, pp. 57-60.

18. Norton and Glick, "Marital Instability," p. 12. Harris and Roper polls of 1970 and 1974 illustrate this change in attitudes: in 1970, 53% of those polled approved of divorce as a solution to unhappy marriage; by 1974, 60% approved. Louis Harris and Associates, *The 1970 Virginia Slims American Women's Opinion Poll*, 1970; The Roper Organization, *The Virginia Slims American Women's Opinion Poll, Vol. III*, 1974.

19. Carol A. Brown, Roslyn Feldberg, Elizabeth Fox, and Janet Kohen, "Divorce: Chance of a New Lifetime," *Journal of Social Issues*, 32 (1976):119-134.

20. Peter J. Stein, *Single* (Englewood Cliffs: Prentice-Hall, 1976). p. 108

21. Ross and Sawhill, *Time of Transition*, pp. 38-40.

22. F. Ivan Nye and Lois W. Hoffman (eds.), *The Employed Mother in America* (Chicago: Rand McNally, 1963), and Lois W. Hoffman, and F. Ivan Nye (eds.), *Working Mothers* (San Franscisco: Jossey Bass, 1974).

23. Lois W. Hoffman, "Parental Power Relations and the Division of Household Tasks," in Nye and Hoffman (eds.), *The Employed Mother*, pp. 215-31.

24. Stephen J. Bahr, "Effects on Power and Division of Labor in the Family," in Hoffman and Nye (eds.), *Working Mothers*, pp. 167-85.

25. F. Ivan Nye, "Marital Interaction," in Nye and Hoffman (eds.), *Employed Mother*, pp 263-81; F. Ivan Nye, "Husband and Wife Relationship," in Hoffman and Nye (eds.), *Working Mothers*, pp. 186-206.

26. I have excluded communes from this discussion because they became widespread on the American scene only in the late 1960s and early 1970s, that is, after the advent of the women's movement; they therefore could not have significantly influenced the early development of the movement. For an excellent discussion of communal experiments see Rosabeth Moss Kanter, *Commitment and Community: Communes and Utopias in Sociological Pespective* (Cambridge, Mass.: Harvard University Press, 1972).

27. Ross and Sawhill, *Time of Transition*.

28. *Ibid.*

29. *Ibid*, p. 6

30. *Ibid*, p. 5

31. In 1973 the median income of husband-wife families was $13,030, of families headed by males, $10,740, and of families headed by females, $5,800. See J. R. Chapman and M. Gates, *Women into Wives* (Beverly Hills: Sage, 1977), Statistical Appendix, p. 312.

32. In 1973, only 22% of court-ordered payments to AFDC families were met in full, and in 50% of all cases there was no compliance whatsoever. Ross and Sawhill, *Time of Transition*, p. 175-76.

33. Daniel P. Moynihan, *The Negro Family: The Case for National Action* (Washington, D.C.: U. S. Department of Labor, Office of Planning and Research, 1965), p. 5.

34. For example, see Lee Rainwater and William Yancey, *The Moynihan Report and the Politics of Controversy* (Cambridge, Mass.: MIT Press, 1967).

35. Andrew Billingsly, *Black Families in White America* (Englewood Cliffs: Prentice-Hall, 1969); Carol Stack, *All Our Kin: Strategies for Survival in a Black Community* (New York: Harper & Row, 1974); Robert Staples, "Toward a Sociology of the Black Family: A Theoretical and Methodological Assessment," *Journal of Marriage and the Family*, 33 (1971): 119-35.

36. Ross and Sawhill, "What Happens to Children in Female Headed Families," in *Time of Transition*, pp. 129-58.

37. I shall use the term *dual-career family* and the definition of these families provided in the early work of Rhona and Robert Rapoport. According to them, dual-career families are those two-worker families with children in which both adults are involved in careers that require a high degree of commitment and are characterized by continuous development (career ladders). Rhona and Robert Rapoport, "The Dual Career Family: A Variant Pattern and Social Change," *Human Relations*, Jan. 22, 1969, p. 3-30.

38. Margaret Paloma and T. Neal Garland, "The Myth of the Egalitarian Family: Familial Roles and the Professionally Employed Wife" (paper presented at the 65th Annual Meeting of the American Sociological Association, September 1970). See also T. Neal Garland, "The Better Half. The Male in the Dual Profession Family," in Safilios-Rothschild (ed.), *Toward a Sociology of Women*, pp. 199-215.

39. See two works by Rhona and Robert Rapoport: *Dual Career Families* (New York: Penguin, 1971), and *Dual Career Families Re-examined* (New York: Harper & Row, 1977).

40. Louis Coser, *Greedy Institutions* (New York: Free Press, 1974), Chapter 6.

41. Lynda Lytle Holmstrom, *The Two-Career Family* (Cambridge, Mass.: Schenkman, 1972), p. 95.

TABLES

Table 5.1

CRUDE BIRTH RATES, 1960-1975

Year	Whites	Negro and Other Races	Total
1960	22.7	32.1	23.7
1965	18.3	27.6	19.4
1970	17.4	25.1	18.4
1971	16.2	24.7	17.2
1972	14.6	22.9	15.6
1973	13.9	21.9	14.9
1974	14.0	21.9	14.9
1975	**	**	14.8

SOURCE: *Statistical Abstract of the U.S., 1977,* pp. 5-7.

**Data not available.

Table 5.2

AVERAGE DAILY TIME CONTRIBUTED BY HUSBANDS AND WIVES TO HOUSEHOLD WORK (HOURS)

No. of Children	Nonemployed Wife Households		Employed Wife Households	
	Wife	Husband	Wife	Husband
0	5.7	1.4	3.9	1.1
2	7.3	1.6	6.0	2.0
4	8.5	1.6	5.6	1.2
5+	9.2	1.8	*	*

SOURCE: J. Chapman and Margaret Gates (eds.), *Women Into Wives,* (Beverly Hills: Sage, 1977). p. 303 (Statistical Appendix), Data collected *1968-1971.* Sample size 1,318 Syracuse, Courtland County, N.Y.

*Time not computed since number of families in sample was too small (fewer than 4).

Table 5.3
A. MARITAL STATUS, 1960 AND 1975
(BY PERCENTAGES)

Marital Status	Males		Females	
	1960	*1975*	*1960*	*1975*
Single	25.3	20.8	19.0	14.6
Married	69.1	72.8	65.6	66.7
Widowed	3.7	2.7	12.8	13.4
Divorced	1.9	3.7	2.6	5.3

SOURCE: *Statistical Abstract of the U.S., 1976,* p. 37.

B. SINGLE (NEVER MARRIED) PERSONS AS A PERCENTAGE OF THE TOTAL POPULATION, BY AGE AND SEX, 1960 AND 1975

Age	1960		1975	
	Males	*Females*	*Males*	*Females*
18	94.6	75.6	96.8	83.7
19	87.1	59.7	89.3	71.4
20-24	53.1	28.4	59.9	40.3
25-29	20.8	10.5	22.3	13.8
30-34	11.9	6.9	11.1	7.5
All persons aged 18 and over	17.3	11.9	20.8	14.6

SOURCE: *Statistical Abstract of the U.S., 1976,* p. 38.

Table 5.3 (Continued)

C. FIRST MARRIAGES, DIVORCES, AND REMARRIAGES, 1960-1974

Period	First Marriages		Divorces		Remarriages	
	Thousands	Rate[1]	Thousands	Rate[2]	Thousands	Rate[3]
1960-1962	1,205	112	407	16	345	119
1963-1965	1,311	109	452	17	415	143
1966-1968	1,440	107	535	20	511	166
1969-1971	1,649	109	702	26	515	152
1972-1974	1,662	103	907	32	601	151

SOURCES: Glick and Norton, "Marital Instability," p. 6.

[1] Per 1,000 single women aged 14-44.

[2] Per 1,000 married women aged 14-44.

[3] Per 1,000 widowed and divorced women aged 14-54.

D. NUMBER OF DIVORCED PERSONS, BY RACE, 1960 AND 1972
(PER 1,000 MARRIED PERSONS, SPOUSE PRESENT)

Race	Males		Females	
	1960	1972	1960	1972
All races	28	38	42	66
Whites	27	37	38	61
Negro and other races	37	56	89	125

SOURCE: *Current Population Reports: Population Characteristics,* No. 242 (Washington, D.C.: Bureau of the Census, 1972), p. 20.

E. LIVING ARRANGEMENTS OF SINGLE PERSONS AGED 25-34, BY SEX, 1970 AND 1975

	Males		Females	
Status	*1970*	*1975*	*1970*	*1975*
Head of household	29.7	39.3	37.7	49.5
Head of primary family	3.9	3.3	10.0	14.6
Primary individual	25.7	36.0	27.7	34.9
Living alone	20.7	21.8	27.3	30.4
Not head of household	70.3	60.7	62.3	50.4
In families	58.3	48.2	51.0	40.5
Secondary individual	12.1	12.6	11.3	10.0

SOURCE: *Current Population Reports,* "Marital Status and Living Arrangements," No. 287, March, 1975, p. 4.

F. MEDIAN AGE AT FIRST MARRIAGE, BY SEX, 1960-1977

Year	*Males*	*Females*
1960	22.8	20.3
1968	22.8	20.6
1970	23.2	20.8
1975	23.5	21.1
1977	24.0	21.6

SOURCE: "Marital Status and Living Arrangements," No. 323, April, 1977, p.2.

Table 5.4

A. FEMALE-HEADED FAMILIES, BY RACE AND PRESENCE OF CHILDREN, 1960-1974
(IN THOUSANDS)

	All Races			Whites			Nonwhites		
	Total	With Members under 18		Total	With Members under 18		Total	With Members under 18	
Year	No.	No.	(%)	No.	No.	(%)	No.	No.	(%)
1960	4,492	2,542	56.6	3,543	1,834	51.8	949	708	74.6
1965	5,005	2,896	59.9	3,879	2,020	52.1	1,126	876	77.8
1970	5,580	3,374	60.5	4,185	2,263	54.1	1,395	1,111	79.6
1974	6,804	4,598	67.6	4,853	2,989	61.6	1,951	1,609	82.5

SOURCE: Heather L. Ross and Isabel V. Sawhill, *Time of Transition: The Growth of Families Headed by Women* (Washington, D.C.: The Urban Institute, 1975), p. 193.

B. POOR FAMILIES WITH CHILDREN UNDER 18,
BY SEX AND RACE OF HEAD, 1960-1972
(BY PERCENTAGES)

	Whites		Nonwhites	
Year	Female Head	Male Head	Female Head	Male Head
1960	24.5	75.5	34.9	65.1
1965	30.3	69.7	41.6	58.4
1970	40.1	59.9	62.3	37.7
1972	43.3	56.7	69.0	31.0

SOURCE: Jane R. Chapman and Margaret Gates, *Women into Wives,* (Beverly Hills: Sage, 1977), p. 306.

C. FAMILIES HEADED BY WOMEN AND MEN, 1960-1976

Year	Total No.	Male Head (%)	Female Head (%)
1960	45,062	90.0	10.0
1965	47,836	89.5	10.5
1970	51,227	89.1	10.9
1975	55,700	87.0	13.0
1976	56,244	86.7	13.3

SOURCES: *Women Who Head Families—A Socioeconomic Analysis,* 1977, p. 4; *Women Who Head Families—A Socioeconomic Analysis,* 1978, p. 83.

Chapter 6
Sources of
the Women's Movement

The rise in the 1960s of a social movement focused on the needs and concerns of women was predicted by virtually no one in the social science community. A few scholars had pointed to contradictions in the position of American women, and others had actually called for the establishment of a movement to alter that position, but no one expected the women's movement to develop when and as it did.[1] In the previous chapters we have explored in depth the structural changes associated with the process of economic development, which by the 1960s had altered the family lives, educational experiences, personality formation, and economic roles of many American women. But whereas these changes had occurred without conscious, collective effort on the part of women, the women's movement that emerged in the 1960s represented a set of conscious ideals and actions. The movement was both a response to and an effort to carry through and extend those structural changes that had already developed in the society. The structure and the ideology of the movement reflected and interpreted the ways in which women's lives had been altered. At the same time, the movement extended awareness of and gave collective meaning to those changes and pointed to directions for and means of future change.

This chapter is concerned with understanding the factors underlying the emergence of the women's movement after 1964. My hypothesis is that the changes in women's personality and economic and family position promoted the creation and shaped the nature of this new social movement. I shall highlight aspects of those changes—themselves the result of trends associated with economic development—that could be expected to stimulate the emergence of a women's movement. In addition, I shall also note those aspects of women's changing position that tended to retard the formation of a social movement organized by and dedicated to the liberation of women.

147

PERSONALITY CHANGE

I earlier noted Erikson's theory that the emergence of a new collective personality can result from structural changes in society's institutions. Following Freud, Erikson suggests that new social circumstances may trigger the development of personal characteristics that had been repressed during the process of socialization. Accordingly, in my view the changed circumstances associated with economic development were experienced by many American women after 1960, and contributed to the development of a new collective female personality. In turn the emergence of this new model of femininity promoted the creation of a social movement focused on further changing women's lives.

Among the changes in the female personality that occurred after 1960 and that contributed to the growth of this movement, one could include alteration in the traditional norm of passive femininity. The decline in submissiveness and passivity might be expected to increase the willingness of individual women to take an active role in examining and acting to change aspects of their lives with which they were dissatisfied. With increased achievement orientation and higher self-esteem, which I have hypothesized as consistent with women's new collective personality, there would presumably also be an increase in the confidence to act on one's own behalf. The growth of an independent identity among women might produce less reliance on others, particularly husbands, and increase the likelihood that women would make their own decisions about whether to support a women's movement.

Greater intellectual achievement and higher educational attainment might also be expected to promote the growth of a social movement by releasing creative abilities that some women could channel into activities directed toward changing women's lives. Finally, the exposure of younger women to mothers or adult female role models who reared their daughters or interacted with young women according to nontraditional conceptions of femininity could also have a positive effect. In this case, such experiences might render those younger women comfortable enough with the new collective personality to regard it as the legitimate model of femininity. These younger women then could be expected to press for society's acceptance of the new collective personality without feelings of guilt, anxiety, or ambivalence about the "rightness" of what they were doing. All these factors would tend to counter the inconsistency between traditional femininity and active involvement in a social movement dedicated to women's liberation.

At the same time, alterations in female personality and in ideas of "normal" femininity imply some negative consequences for the development of a broad women's movement. Major social changes do not affect all members of a society in the same way or even at the same time, and may in fact create serious friction among social groups. The embodiment of a new ideological definition of femininity in the personalities of some women in the society might serve to divide them sharply from women who had not experienced those changes and who retained a commitment to more traditional femininity. In addition, the new social personality, especially when evident among only a minority of women in the society, could easily be labeled as deviant or even neurotic. This consequence might not only discourage others from joining the movement or seriously considering its goals, but might also create confusion and insecurity among supporters of and participants in the movement itself.

In sum, I suggest that the emergence of a new collective female personality enhanced the likelihood that women would join together in a social movement that, among other goals, would press society to accept the legitimacy of the new female personality characteristics and also to accommodate socialization processes to the new model of femininity. Nevertheless, as noted above, the appearance of such differences in personality among American women might retard the development of a women's movement by tending to isolate activists, to leave them open to charges of deviance, and to discourage other women from resisting the repressive socialization processes to which they had been subjected.

FEMALE EMPLOYMENT

The growing number of women workers in the American economy also played a causal role in the emergence of the women's movement. As I noted, Marxist theory holds that the growth of a new and permanent group of workers creates the potential for the development of a social movement. Such a movement is possible because of the common circumstances in which the workers find themselves, their close proximity and ability to communicate easily with one another, the permanence of their new position, and their common sense of oppression or exploitation. Such objective circumstances create the potential for subjective feelings of group solidarity, and for the emergence of an alternative ideology necessary for the development of a movement for social change.

Although Marx was writing about the development of an urban and industrial proletariat, this same approach can be applied to the expansion of the female labor force. A growing number of employed women, according to this model, would be a prerequisite for ending women's isolation in domestic roles, for establishing and communication of group awareness, and for developing interest in broader economic and social issues outside of the family sphere. Marxist theory does not provide a predictive model that might allow us to understand in detail the transition from the growth in female employment to the emergence of a social movement. Theories of "critical mass," which suggest the number of participants must reach a certain point before a social movement can emerge, are vague in specifying exactly how large that "critical mass" must be in given circumstances. Marxist theory itself is vague about those circumstances, other than the growth in numbers, of communication, and of oppression or exploitation, that may affect the nature of the social movement that emerges, or indeed influence whether any movement develops at all. Nonetheless, it is possible to analyze those factors that would hypothetically advance or inhibit the emergence of a particular social movement and shape its development.

Several specific features of the recent alterations in women's economic position may have been advantageous to the development of a social movement among women. One important recent change is that the participation of women in the labor force reflects greater uninterrupted and full-time involvement. There is considerable evidence that women increasingly depend upon themselves for income and that therefore their involvement in the labor force is not a matter of choice any more than is that of the typical male worker. Rapidly rising divorce rates since 1960, the upsurge in the number of single women and persons living alone or with unrelated individuals, and the astounding growth in the number of families headed by females (Table 5.4) are all indications that millions of women must and do support themselves, and often their children as well.

Even among those women who are married and living with their husbands, the trends are clearly in the direction of two-earner families. Such demographic characteristics as the presence of young children or husbands earning relatively high incomes, which at the beginning of the period were typical primarily of women who were not in the labor force, have become increasingly typical of working women (Table 4.2) and no longer deter most women from long-term and uninterrupted work experiences. Finally, the recent period has been characterized by steady growth in the number of young women undertaking arduous and expensive professional training in fields such as medicine, dentistry, and law (Table 4.8), indicating strong commitment to demanding and serious careers. The increasing number of women who earn their own incomes, the rising labor force participation rates of married women, the growing number of women undertaking serious career preparation— all indicate that paid employment is an integral and important part of the adult roles of increasingly large numbers of American women.

I suggest that identification and solidarity with other workers, and especially other women workers, is more likely to develop in a situation where women workers view their employment as important and integral to their lives and where their commitment to and activity in the labor force is long and uninterrupted. With work as a central focus of women's adult lives, group awareness and communication are more likely to develop than under circumstances where employment was seen as a temporary phenomenon. The recent trends outlined above make the development of a women's social movement more likely than was true in an earlier period, when women were largely excluded from the labor force altogether or engaged in employment only late in life and/ or intermittently.

A second characteristic of female employment that might increase the likelihood of the emergence of a women's social movement is the disadvantaged and segregated position of American women in the labor force. The deprivation of women as a group of employed workers, as compared with male workers, has been documented at length in Tables 4.6 and 4.7. Working women have always earned less than their male counterparts, experienced higher unemployment rates, and been concentrated in the least prestigious occupations; moreover, these trends have not disappeared in the recent period, and at least one—the earnings gap between men and women workers—has even intensified. It is likely that women as a group would be aware of the conditions characteristic of their employment, especially since the segregation of occupations by sex would facilitate the recognition that their disadvantaged position was based on sex. The occupational concentration of women would also enhance the possibilities for communication and the development of group solidarity, as women found themselves in contact with other women workers in similar positions. Conversely, the small number of women employed in "men's" jobs might be drawn to one another by similar experiences and problems created by their unique status. Thus the special disadvantages and inferior status of women workers, coupled with their segregation in a relatively small number of occupations, might be expected to produce high levels of awareness of and dissatisfaction with their position in the labor force. Such circumstances would also seem likely to promote the development of a social movement focused on problems and experiences common to working women.

Another factor that might tend to enhance the level of solidarity necessary for the development of a movement of working women is the increasing similarity of the work experiences of black and white women. Just as sex has been a criterion by which the labor force has been segregated and divided, so too is there a history of discrimination against and occupational segregation of blacks in the American labor force. Recent trends indicate, however, that at least for women workers, black and white patterns are converging as more white women join the labor force and more black women move out of household service occupations and into clerical and other categories where white women are concentrated (Table 4.4). Such changes in both black and white work experiences may presage the possibility, perhaps for the first time in American history, that black and white women will join together in a broad social movement.

Finally, we should note the implications that the increasing levels of educational attainment among members of the female labor force have for the creation of a social movement. Although evidence with respect to the relationship between the development of social movements and levels of education is not conclusive, the social movements of the 1960s in the United States—civil rights, antiwar, and student rights and power—had a disproportionate number of educated individuals in their constituencies, and particularly in the rank of activist leaders.[2] The rising levels of educational attainment among women workers, and the particularly high rates of labor force participation among very highly educated women, indicate that if education leads to an increasing awareness of problems and inequalities in society, prompts articulate critiques of unsatisfactory aspects of society, and/or develops skills useful in organizing for social change, women workers as a group are increasingly likely to possess such characteristics.

In sum, the increasing participation of women in the labor force, the trend in favor of serious long-term work commitment, the concentration of women in sexually segregated occupations, and their disadvantaged position as a group when compared with that of men are all factors conducive to the development of dissatisfaction, awareness of common problems, and communication among women workers. Additionally, the lessening of racial divisions among women workers and the rising levels of education also might contribute to the emergence of a movement for social change that at least partly focuses on the nature and special problems of women as workers in the American economy.

However, some aspects of the alterations in the economic position of women might hypothetically work in precisely the opposite direction, and serve as obstacles to the potential development of a women's movement. One such inhibiting factor is that, despite its size, the recent expansion of the female labor force has not been rapid enough. Even now, only about half of all women in the United States are in the labor force. Thus the potential differences in outlook, experience, and interests between women workers and nonworking women may seriously inhibit the development of a women's movement embracing both constituencies. Indeed, nonworking women might perceive the employment of other women as a threat to their own status as homemakers and/or to their husband's jobs, particularly in periods of high unemployment. Such a situation might sap much of the strength of a social movement that focuses much of its attention on women's problems as workers.

Divisions within the female labor force itself may also serve as potential obstacles to the development of the solidarity, group awareness, and communication necessary to the building of a social movement. Although racial differences in labor force participation and experience have lessened in the past decade and a half, it is nonetheless true that black women continue in a disadvantaged economic position not only with respect to male workers but also in comparison with white working women (Tables 4.6 and 4.7). Other differences in labor force participation rates and/or occupational or wage positions among different ethnic and minority-group women could also have disruptive effects on the development of a women's movement. The history of American labor is also a history of the obstacles to working-class solidarity and organization emanating from racial and ethnic divisions among the workers themselves.[3] It is not implausible to suggest a similar disruptive effect among women workers.

The hierarchical division of labor that is characteristic of modern economic production also creates powerful internal divisions within the working class. Even though women remain largely concentrated in

153

similar occupations and can therefore be expected to be located at roughly similar levels in the work hierarchy, differences still remain. Some Marxists have argued that such hierarchical differences are created by the capitalist class precisely to inhibit class solidarity. Whatever the source, such differentiation exists and grows more exaggerated with the process of economic development.[4] Thus, to take an extreme example, the differences between women assembly line workers and women teachers may be perceived by those women as more permanent and important than any common experiences or unity they might have as working women. Similarly, legal secretaries might not believe that they have enough in common with corporation secretarial pool typists or bank tellers to warrant communication or group solidarity, even though all three occupations are classified as clerical.

Still more characteristics of women workers may be detrimental to the creation of a women's movement. Disparities in levels of education, regional differences, and the different viewpoints of women who work to support themselves and/or their families and women who can rely on others (especially husbands) for the bulk of family income may contribute to divisions among working women. How these differences may show themselves is still unclear. Perhaps, for example, the reliance on a husband for part of total family income may free women from fear of the risks associated with agitation in favor of sexual equality at work, and they may be more aware of and willing to act against discrimination in hiring, pay, or promotion. On the other hand, relying on others for support may make some women more complacent about low wages or unequal promotion opportunities, and therefore less willing to act in solidarity with other women workers. Regardless of the specific direction these differences take, such divisions within the ranks of working women can be expected to decrease the likelihood that a strong and united movement dedicated to the problems of working women will emerge. Similarly, the differences noted above between working and nonworking women reduce the possibility that links could be forged between a working women's movement and a wider women's movement.

In sum, I have argued that the changing economic position of women has the potential to create circumstances conducive to the emergence of a social movement. Whether a social movement is in fact created in such a situation depends of course upon a number of variables, such as opportunities for communication, development of feelings of solidarity among workers that are able to overcome ethnic, geographical, religious, or educational differences, awareness of the common sources of perceived problems, and belief that positive changes can be accomplished through united struggle. It appears however that the changes in women's economic position after 1960 would be generally supportive of, if not decisive for, the development of a modern women's movement.

CHANGES IN THE FAMILY

Changes in the American family after 1960 would contribute in many ways to the growth of the women's liberation movement, although there would also seem to be some countervailing tendencies. Among the many changes occurring at this time, the decline in fertility seems least ambiguous in its effects on the development of a women's movement. Clearly, a drop in the birth rate would be a necessary, if not a sufficient, condition for the development of a movement dedicated to changing women's traditional roles. With shrinking family functions and fewer family members for whom to perform these functions, it became unnecessary for many women to fulfill the role of full-time and exclusive domesticity in the traditional fashion. Time at home of course could always be filled by increasing the standards of housekeeping, but it was difficult to equate the importance of such activities with that of infant care or children's education. Thus the decline in the birth rate and the increase in female longevity reduced the period of childbearing and child care to a relatively small portion of a woman's life, at once creating a void in the housekeeping role and pushing women toward alternative pursuits. These factors also made participation possible for women already pulled toward nondomestic roles and activities associated with new definitions of femininity.

The increase in divorce rates and in female-headed families also had an important part in the challenge to women's traditional home-bound role. Even for those women who did not experience divorce themselves, the example of friends and relatives involved in divorces or separations may have raised the possibility of similar marital disruption, moving some women to break with traditional roles and begin to learn to support themselves economically and to develop the social and psychological skills necessary for an independent adult life. The strong American belief in achievement and self-fulfillment would certainly encourage such women to search for alternative roles.

155

In sum, familial change triggered participation of women in non-familial interests and activities, which gave them experience and knowl-edge of the wider society outside of their relatively protected home roles. For many women, these experiences were dependent on their own personal resources as individuals, rather than on their derivative status as wives or mothers. Thus changes in the family—associated with higher divorce rates, lower birth rates, and increased female participa-tion in extrafamilial spheres—would tend to enhance the creation of a social movement whose ideology stressed the need for women to create meaningful roles for themselves outside of exclusive housewifery and motherhood. Women who were experiencing these changes could be expected to be sympathetic to a movement that articulated their experiences and their needs for new roles.

Yet even the changes in the family outlined above, although they created real pressures for change in women's overall domestic roles and in nonfamilial spheres of activity, did not necessarily demand the emergence of a women's movement. The factor of crucial importance was the multitude of problems and obstacles blocking the paths of individual women who attempted to define alternative roles or defini-tions for themselves as women. The hegemony of traditional concep-tions of femininity and women's roles meant that women who deviated even slightly from these norms were met with hostility and discrimina-tion from such varied sources as employers and fellow workers, educa-tional institutions, religious authorities, and family members—parents, spouses, and even children. There was an obvious need for a supportive group that could legitimate their "deviance" and deal with their anxie-ties and fears on that account, and at the same time actively fight against discrimination and social hostility. Family change not only reduced women's home-bound isolation, but also created a group of women—workers, divorcees, female heads of families, women whose children were grown, educated women, and girls or young women eager to avoid the domestic frustrations of their mothers—who would be likely to recognize and act on their need for alternative female role definitions. The insurmountable problems of creating such a role alone in the face of social hostility made the emergence of a collective move-ment possible.

The role of the family and its strains in contributing to the creation of a social movement should not obscure the fact that the family was also the source of tendencies working to impede the development and growth of a women's movement. For example, the structure of the housewife role, that is, the separation of home and work, of public lives and private realms in American society relegated the housewife role and the women who filled it to a relatively isolated existence. The social interaction of women, which was limited primarily to their children and other housewives, could be expected to do little toward generating interest in or skills applicable to nonfamilial problems or situations.[5] Thus housewifery was conducive to a world view that would likely extend only minimally beyond the home itself, or beyond the immediate needs of individual family members. This was reinforced by the traditional division of labor between the sexes in the nuclear family, which reserved all extrafamilial concerns and/or responsibilities to the male (the instrumental role). Finally, housewives' isolation in and concentration on their families, and their reluctance to engage in pursuits outside that protected realm, were probably further reinforced by the low self-esteem and lack of confidence that the role of "just a housewife" confers on women.

These effects of the housewife role, which the majority of American women fulfilled in 1960, would seem likely to retard the development of a women's movement in several ways. The orientation of housewives to their homes and individual family members might serve as an obstacle to their awareness of the development of a new movement, or to factual accounts of such a movement's goals, demands, or tactics. Even if knowledge of or interest in the movement were to develop, many housewives' ability to participate would be severely limited by their burdens of child care and domestic maintenance. The complete economic dependence of housewives on their husbands and the lack of self-confidence engendered by their role would militate against their active participation in a social movement, particularly as such behavior would be regarded as decidedly "deviant" according to social definitions of femininity. Social action by housewives might be condoned if perceived as necessary to the family's well-being or survival, but it would probably be severely sanctioned in the context of a movement that could be viewed as a threat to the traditional family. Finally, the ideology of housewifery emphasizes self-sacrificing service to others' (family members') needs. A social movement that explored and attempted to fulfill the needs of women themselves might seem to many housewives too contradictory and threatening to the set of beliefs and attitudes that were inculcated in them through the process of socialization and on which they had heretofore based their lives. Thus both the ideology and structure of the housewife role in the traditional nuclear family would inhibit the emergence of a women's movement.

Ironically, obstacles to the growth of a women's movement existed even within those family structures that differed from the traditional nuclear family. As we noted above, factors associated with rising divorce rates gave momentum to the development of a women's movement; yet the problems and strains associated with separation and divorce may also have had some retarding effects. Especially for women whose experience was limited to housewifery, the demands for independence, economic self-sufficiency, and single-parent status that were triggered by divorce or separation may have been overwhelming. Inexperienced and unable to cope with the prospect of independence, many women may have attempted to retreat as quickly as possible to housewife status by remarrying. Evidence of extremely high and rising rates of remarriage after 1960 make this hypothesis all the more plausible. Rising divorce rates may also have created the fear of divorce and its problems in many currently married women, dissuading them from any attempts to alter relationships or roles within their marriages. In other words, the experience or fear of divorce in a society characterized by high rates of marital instability may have contributed to a conservative stance among some women and to their rejection of a social movement concerned with altering women's roles. The belief that the problems of women's roles and the inequality of marital relationships were at least less difficult to bear than the strains associated with divorce or changing roles may have produced a tendency to accept traditional housewife and marital roles, even while rising divorce rates and an emergent women's movement testified to the widespread inadequacy of those very roles and relationships.

Even when women rejected exclusive domesticity, some aspects of their experiences were probably inimical to the growth of a women's movement. Most important in this regard may have been the negative experiences of some women who left full-time housewifery to join the labor force. As noted above, to the extent that women experienced discrimination, or were confined to trivial, low-paid, boring, or dead-end jobs, they found little satisfaction in their work experience. The double burden of household work and employment that many working women had to bear, and the extra expenses for child care and/or domestic maintenance that female employment often entailed may have increased negative attitudes toward employment. Accordingly,

these strains may have discouraged both working women and housewives from supporting a social movement that would seek women's
liberation from exclusive housewifery. Until the alternative to such
domesticity became more appealing, even those who believed that
women must move beyond exclusive housewifery may have rejected a
movement for social change.

Among women who enjoyed their work and supported the women's
movement, there may have been other barriers to actual participation in
the movement. The incomes of some women were too low to permit
them to hire others to help with household tasks, and the burden of
their responsibilities for both work and home may have made it impossible for them to spend time in organizational or political activities.
Even among women whose salaries allowed them to be relieved of many
domestic tasks, active participation in the women's movement may
have been difficult. I have noted that one of the "dilemmas" of women
in dual-career families is that of an overload of responsibilities. The
additional demands of participation in a political movement may have
produced untenable strains in their fulfillment of other roles, at home
and at work, which they deemed to have priority. Thus obstacles to
the development of a women's movement may have been present even
among women who through divorce or labor force participation had
deviated from traditional definitions of femininity, as well as among
those women who continued to fulfill more traditional roles.

A final area of ambiguity with respect to support or rejection of a
social movement among women lies in the realm of ideology. The belief in personal fulfillment and achievement has been cited previously as
a force that contributed positively to the rise of a social movement
dedicated to changing women's roles. However, that ideology has a
decidedly individualistic focus. The emphasis on the individual's dis-
covery of his/her own needs and development of his/her own unique
potential may have militated against a collective search for social
change. A social movement of course involves collective action, which
many women may have avoided or rejected in their personal quest for
change or "liberation." The very ideology of achievement that helped
to stimulate women to look beyond exclusive domesticity for fulfillment, may have served as an obstacle to women's willingness to engage
in that search through a collective movement.

Many changes in society preceded the development of the women's
movement in the mid-1960s. Strains in the hegemonic ideology concerning women, and structural changes in American society—dramatic

alterations in women's labor force status, in the processes of personality development among young women, in the nature of the American family—had their source in the long-term process of economic development. Changes in these aspects of life were mutually reinforcing, as women's actual experiences as students, wives, mothers, and workers all underwent significant alteration. I have hypothesized that these changes produced strains and pressures that, despite obstacles, ultimately promoted the development of a new social movement seeking further change in all aspects of women's lives.

NOTES

1. Keniston, *The Uncommitted*; Friedan, *Feminine Mystique*.
2. Richard Flacks, *Youth and Social Change* (Chicago: Markham, 1971).
3. Anderson, *Toward a New Sociology*, pp. 121-26.
4. Harry Braverman, *Labor and Monopoly Capital: The Degradation of Work in the Twentieth Century* (New York: Monthly Review Press, 1974).
5. In their study of working-class housewives, Rainwater and his colleagues note those women's social isolation, fatalism, and low self-esteem; similarly, Friedan, found that the middle-class women in her sample were isolated from and afraid of non-family-oriented situations. Lee Rainwater, Richard Coleman, and Gerald Handel, *Workingman's Wife: Her Personality, World and Life Style* (New York: Oceana, 1959); Freidan, *Feminine Mystique*. See also Oakley, *Sociology of Housework*.

Chapter 7
The Women's Movement

With emergence of the women's movement in the 1960s, American women for the first time in more than forty years organized themselves on a national scale into a political movement focused on their own needs. My hypothesis is that structural changes in women's lives that accompanied the long-term process of economic development were central to the growth and organization of this new social movement, which carried the seeds of a distinctive women's consciousness.

But how did women organize themselves? Why did some women in the early 1960s develop the group consciousness necessary for the development of a social movement dedicated to changing women's status in American society? How were they able to resist the traditional hegemony that ascribed women to inferior status in society, and how did they begin to view themselves and other women in a different way? How did the structure of the movement and the characteristics of the participants change over time? These are the questions that this chapter addresses in examining the origins, development, and limits of the women's movement.

GROWTH OF CONSCIOUSNESS

The first evidence of a new women's social movement[1] was the organizing convention of a group that took the name, National Organization of Women. The formal announcement of this group's incorporation was made public in October 1966, and its founding statement articulated its purpose:

> to take action to bring women into full participation in the mainstream of American society *now*, exercising all the privileges and responsibilities thereof in truly equal partnership with men.[2]

At the same time, but with a less formalized structure and without national publicity or knowledge, a women's "liberation" movement was developing within the ranks of a variety of civil rights, student, and leftist groups. These women's groups, often first constituted as women's caucuses within a parent organization, gradually developed autonomy and independence, and were later joined by many young femininists who had no previous ties to other activist organizations. By 1968 these groups were receiving national recognition as a burgeoning women's liberation movement.[3] Despite their many similarities, women's "rights" groups, the most important of which was NOW, and the loosely structured women's "liberation" movement were two very separate and sometimes hostile entities, which only in retrospect can be viewed as part of a wider women's movement emerging at that time. For this reason I shall analyze separately the origins and development of each set of groups prior to 1970.

NOW

Who were the activists sparking the organization of NOW, and to what can we attribute their unique collective consciousness in the early 1960s? The three hundred men and women who were charter members of NOW in 1966 were similar to one another in both social background and social status. Most were highly educated, came from middle-class backgrounds, and held prestigious occupations. A majority of the members of the first executive board were professionals, working for government agencies, labor unions, or in the communications industry. Betty Friedan, author of the widely read *Feminine Mystique*, was undoubtedly the driving force behind the decision to form an organization, and was subsequently elected as its first president. The social status and position of the women involved were important factors in the process of developing a collective consciousness.[4]

In previous chapters I hypothesized that structural change has an important influence on the social personality that is characteristic of a society and on its alterations. Erikson's theory suggests that major structural change often precipitates the development of or search for a new collective personality on the part of certain individuals or groups in society.[5] The social position of the women founders of NOW indicates the importance of structural change, for they differed from most American women in their high levels of educational attainment, their involvement in demanding careers, and, owing to their affluence, their relative freedom from the burdens of domesticity. Their involvement in political activity outside of their families, and their assertion of their rights as women is evidence of their deviance from the pattern of passiveness, low achievement, and exclusive domesticity that was characteristic of the traditionally defined collective feminine personality. Rather, they asserted a new feminine personality type characterized by high aspirations, strong identity formation, and self-assertive activity. These were necessary to sustain their achievement patterns and their deviance from more conventional definitions of femininity.

In their common position as highly educated, occupationally successful, and/or politically active women, the founders of NOW experienced a unique set of strains and contradictions. One such contradiction is what sociologists call "poorly crystallized status," which refers to a situation in which an individual is accorded high social status for some attributes of his/her personality or position, but low social status for other attributes.[6] The high social status and relative affluence of NOW women, their high educational attainment, and especially their professional success, was in marked contrast to the low status to which they were socially ascribed as women. For the women among NOW's founders who were not in the labor force, such as Friedan, the contradiction was sharp between their high educational attainment and their low status not merely as women but especially as housewives. In the case of employed activist women, additional strains were produced by the myriad problems surrounding their attempts to combine political activism with professional careers and family responsibilities, and by the problems attendant upon their being one of the few women in prestigious occupations.[7] These common strains and problems may have contributed to the further growth of a new social personality, as women developed characteristics necessary to cope with new sorts of stress. Thus the early founders of NOW experienced in common profound contradictions emanating from poorly crystallized status, from their expression of "deviant" personality traits, and from special problems attendant upon new (especially high status occupational) roles. These shared characteristics created the potential for bonds among individuals disproportionately affected by structural changes in women's social definition and roles.

The rise of a collective consciousness, and the development of a social movement, however, do not necessarily follow from the appearance in a few scattered individuals of a new personality type, shared problems, or the willingness to resist a repressive traditional model of personality. The translation of these individual characteristics into a collective consciousness and social movement requires contact among such people. In retrospect, several seemingly unconnected public events in the early 1960s can be seen to have provided that contact and to have facilitated the growth of networks among women of similar social positions who were experiencing similar strains and who were willing to resist traditional definitions of feminity and female roles and also express new ones.

One important event was the publication in 1963 of Friedan's *The Feminine Mystique*, with its scathing attack on the inferior status of women in American society, its insistence that women's problems were social rather than personal, and its passionate call for social change. Friedan focused primarily on the problems of educated middle-class women, and the book was widely read and discussed among such women. Most important, it indicated that women's problems were shared, and at the same time suggested that something could be done about them.

A second public event that contributed to the growth of common beliefs and contacts among women was the passage of the Civil Rights Act of 1964, which prohibited discrimination in employment in the United States. Also included in the act was a provision against discrimination based on sex, and a special government agency, the Equal Economic Opportunities Commission, was mandated to enforce it.[8] This legislation raised public awareness of discrimination against women, and the establishment of the EEOC legitimated the fight against economic discrimination.

Action at the executive level of govenment was also important. As early as 1961, President John F. Kennedy established a Presidential Commission on the Status of Women. During the next few years, numerous state-level commissions brought together individuals (primarily women) and funded their investigations into women's status in American society. This government action, too, helped to legitimate the idea that the problems of American women deserved recognition and study. Moreover, it sparked investigations focused on examining and solving the problems relating to women's status.

Finally, in the early 1960s, widespread public sympathy for the civil rights struggle among American blacks had an important influence on the women who were to found NOW. On the one hand the civil rights movement raised to prominence the ideas that all Americans were guaranteed equal opportunity and that equality was denied to some groups. On the other hand, the movement provided the model of an oppressed group of individuals taking direct action to ensure their rights as Americans. Many whites, especially the educated and members of the middle class, gained political experience by working directly or indirectly in support of this movement.

All these events strengthened women's collective consciousness, and, perhaps more important, provided the first contacts among the women who were to found a new social movement. Indeed, it was at a June 1966 meeting in Washington of commissions on the status of women that the initial call for NOW's founding convention was issued after discussions among assembled representatives and observers. Jo Freeman states that the founding of NOW was at least partially stimulated by the urgings of some individuals within the EEOC, who asserted that discrimination against women would be taken a great deal more seriously "if there were some sort of N.A.A.C.P. [National Association for the Advancement of Colored People] for women to put pressure on the government."[9] The NOW founding convention was held on October 29, 1966.

Thus in the early 1960s the convergence of several factors sparked the development of a collective women's consciousness and the emergence of a new social movement out of the personality changes and feelings of strain and dissatisfaction with the position of women in American society that were experienced by scattered individuals. The women who organized NOW were clearly "deviant" in their collective personality, in their ideological commitment to change in women's position, and in their willingness to act collectively to achieve that change. By 1966 they had begun to act as a group in accordance with their common perception of themselves and other women as autonomous individuals capable of expressing a collective personality and of taking on roles different from those traditionally accorded to women by society.

Women's Liberation Groups

The development of the other major group of women activists in the mid-1960s was also marked by the convergence of structural, personality, ideological, and organizational factors. But the specific nature of these factors was somewhat different than that outlined for NOW. This second set of activist women, who came to be known as women's liberationists, differed from NOW activists in significant ways: they were considerably younger than NOW's founders; they generally had not established either families or occupational commitments; many were involved in graduate education; and they had been actively involved in one or more social protest movements in the early and middle 1960s.[10]

Analysis of their social origins and their motivations for forming a women's movement is hampered by the diffuse nature of their movement. Women's liberation groups, as I shall discuss in detail later, tended to be small, private, and loosely connected, with no requirements as to dues, attendance, or membership cards to distinguish those who "belonged." In addition, movement in and out of groups was constant, which makes data collection difficult, as did the distrust with which women's liberationists often greeted media and academic outsiders who wanted to "study" them.[11] Nonetheless, information based on other protest movements and on women's own accounts of their experiences in the movement provide an outline of the sources of this sector of the overall women's movement.

The single most important unifying factor among women in the diverse women's liberation groups that began to emerge in late 1967 was their previous direct participation in social protest activities—against the war in Vietnam, and for civil rights, student power, and participatory democracy in the United States—earlier in the decade. The literature on the activists in these movements between 1962 and 1967 offers some information about the origins of activism among these largely college-educated young people. Richard Flacks and others have shown that the affluent, secular, and politically liberal parents of many of these activists tended to encourage moral and political idealism in their children.[12] For example, activists' parents, significantly more often than the parents of nonactivists, encouraged their children to think seriously about intellectual and political issues, to express their moral outrage at injustice, and to be willing to act on the basis of their beliefs.[13] At least partly as a result of this socialization process, young activists shared a common vision of a more free and egalitarian society and believed that they were uniquely suited to give reality to that vision. Both male and female activists were clearly nonconformist with respect to the wider youth subculture of the later 1950s and early 1960s out of which they emerged. The "deviance" of women activists was even more pronounced, however, as they were breaking not only with the general cultural expectations regarding youth, but also with those deemed appropriate to femininity.

In looking to understand the development of activism among middle-class college women in the early 1960s, the special role of mothers in their daughters' socialization merits consideration. My hypothesis is that nonsexist upbringing and nontraditional adult role models were important in the development of a new collective female personality on the part of younger activist women. Information indicates that the mothers of activists were employed in significantly higher numbers than were the mothers of nonactivists, and that they enjoyed their largely white-collar occupations.[14] There is some evidence, then, that socialization by mothers who in the early 1960s undertook nontraditional female roles by joining the labor force may have been an important factor in producing daughters who viewed women as active, competent, and "feminine" outside of the limits of traditional definitions of femininity.[15] Many of the activists' mothers who were not employed may have fitted Friedan's description of affluent, educated women experiencing frustration and dissatisfaction with their constricted domestic roles. Their daughters' reaction may have been to avoid such futures for themselves by actively participating in political movements focused on social change, which viewed the rejection of "adult," family-oriented lives. Young activist women clearly deviated from traditional stereotypes of femininity in their active participation in movements for social change, and it is likely that their mothers' own moderate deviance from or frustration with adult models of exclusively domestic femininity were important sources of their daughters' nonconformity.

In addition to parental influence, structural changes in society have also been hypothesized as important causal factors in the emergence of an activist or "protest-prone" personality.[16] The changes cited most often in the literature include: rising affluence, which freed some young people from worry about their future livelihood and allowed them the "luxury" of worrying about oppression and the lack of democracy in American society; rising levels of educational attainment, which produced not only "critical intellect" (an intellectual stance that questions existing norms and practices) but also the ability to articulate criticism in increasingly effective ways; and growth in the size of universities and colleges, which put masses of students together on campuses and outside of the influence of other sectors of the population. Increasing educational attainment tended to prepare students for occupations, primarily the professions, that require individuals who could think for themselves, be innovative, and work creatively. This potential for innovation was applied by many students to political and moral issues in American life. Finally, the increasing size of universities brought with it bureaucratization, to which students objected and from which they felt alienated because of the contrast between their democratic home lives and the inflexible organization of academic bureaucracies.[17] These structural changes imply the decreasing functionality of the traditional collective personality characteristic of young people, and created pressure for social and personal change.

As we have seen, activism in a variety of social movements in the early 1960s sprang from new social circumstances and strains that deeply affected some young people. Young women who responded to these pressures by becoming actively involved in movements for social change shared similar social backgrounds, socialization experiences, ideological commitments to social change, and were acquainted with one another through the informal networks provided by the New Left and other movements. The focus of their belief in social change and their willingness to participate in political activity in the early 1960s however, was limited to such issues as student power, free universities, black civil rights, or, for fewer, the establishment of socialism. A distinctive women's consciousness was lacking until the years 1964-1967, when it emerged largely as a function of the common experiences of women as participants in earlier protest movements.

The first indication of this growing consciousness came in 1964-1965, when women in two of the most influential activist groups, the Student Nonviolent Coordinating Committee (SNCC) and the Students for a Democratic Society (SDS), independently attempted to raise objections to women's roles within these organizations.[18] Women within the New Left and civil rights movements, they argued, were treated as inferior, were relegated to such "women's" tasks as typing or cooking, were displayed as sexually attractive companions to male leaders, and were not taken seriously as political actors in the struggle for social change. Similar arguments were made with increasing frequency after 1964, and were prominent at the 1967 National Conference for a New Politics, which aimed to bring together all left and protest groups. But such attempts to redefine and assert the importance of women's roles within protest organizations were consistently met with ridicule and rejection throughout the mid-1960s.[19]

An important factor contributing to the growth of a collective women's consciousness, therefore, was dissatisfaction with women's roles in the social protest movements of the early and middle 1960s. The contradiction between the goals of the movements, which centered on freedom and equality, and the unequal and exploited position of women within those movements generated collective outrage. The networks available within the protest movement made communication of their dissatisfaction relatively easy for female activists, and their frustration was fed by the constant rejection of their demands for equality on the part of male (and some female) activists.

The growing belief among many activist women that they were being oppressed was reinforced by the growth of a new social movement among blacks, the black power movement, which was based on a model that emphasized ideological in addition to economic oppression of social groups. As Juliet Mitchell notes, the black power movement attempted to expose and change the social and cultural sources of stereotyping and prejudice that often generated feelings of self-hatred and inferiority among blacks.[20] Black power was a separatist social movement based on a critique of cultural and psychological deprivation, and dedicated to building a new collective consciousness and an alternative ideology of pride and self-confidence among blacks. Women activists perceived similarities between the black position and their own in the ideological relegation of women to inferior status as compared with men, and in the resultant feelings of low self-esteem and self-hatred characteristic of many women. The legitimacy of a model of separatism and of consciousness building to counter an oppressive ideology was extremely influential in activist women's decision to form a women's liberation movement.

Finally, as Jo Freeman points out, the development of a new social movement focused on women's liberation was encouraged by the decline of the New Left, by the virtual elimination of white participation in the black movement, and by the rise of draft resistance as the only growing political movement after 1967. Freeman argues that women's participation in the antidraft movement was unsatisfactory, since "this movement more than any other exemplified the social inequities of the sexes. Men could resist the draft. Women could only counsel resistance."[21] Thus there was no readily available outlet for the political energies and desire for social change that characterized many of the women who had been active in earlier social protest movements. The convergence of their rising collective consciousness, the decline of other protest movements, and the legitimacy afforded to separatist movements by the black power movement catalyzed in the emergence of a separate women's liberation movement in 1968. This movement at once sought to develop its own understanding of women's oppression and to spread to others a collective consciousness of the need for social change in women's position in American society.

The rise of a women's movement in the mid-1960s thus had two major focuses: the older, professional married women of NOW, and the younger student activists in the social protest movements of the early 1960s who created the women's liberation movement. When viewed together, the activists in NOW and the women's liberation movement appear remarkably similar in their social background characteristics, and therefore in their susceptibility to the effects of structural changes in women's position in American society. Both groups were largely from middle- or upper-middle-class families, both had been exposed to or were then attaining high levels of education, with the possibility of participating in professional careers, and both exhibited new collective female personalities characterized by aspirations for self-determination, achievement, and new female roles. Indeed, it is not impossible that some women who were active in the women's liberation movement had mothers who were participants in NOW. Both groups were deeply affected by the structural changes in women's education, personality development, family life, and economic position that had occurred prior to and were continuing into the 1960s. In addition, the climate of social protest in the 1960s, and especially the model of the black struggle for civil rights and self-esteem, deeply affected women activists in both groups and was important, in different ways, to the growth of a collective consciousness among both NOW members and women's liberationists.

Despite these strong similarities, however, differences in age, personal and cultural style, experiences, communication and friendship networks, and, to a certain extent, self-definition as politically "liberal" or "radical" created two separate branches of the women's movement in the 1960s. Each group was to be important in creating and sustaining a social movement that advanced new definitions, personalities, and roles for women in American society.

ORGANIZATION OF THE MOVEMENT

The organizational structures evolved by the new women's movement were closely related to and influenced by the specific nature of each group's origins. NOW constituted itself as a national organization, with a formal constitution and elected officers with specified duties. Freeman correctly notes that in these early years NOW "functioned only within the limits of traditional pressure group activity."[22] The focus of NOW's activities was to press for government legislation on behalf of women, and in particular, to monitor the EEOC's efforts to combat economic discrimination against women. The organization continued to grow steadily in the years immediately following 1966, although it suffered from internal tensions.[23] In 1967, women who were opposed to NOW's stand in favor of the repeal of all abortion laws withdrew from the organization and formed the Women's Equity Action League. The following year saw the departure of women who disagreed with NOW's inclusion of men and with what they perceived as the "elitist" nature of NOW's organizational structure.

The year 1970 was a major watershed for NOW as an organization and for the women's movement as a whole. In August, NOW sponsored a highly successful Women's Strike for Equality, the largest demonstration concerning women ever held in the United States. The strike was particularly important for the women's movement because it involved close cooperation between NOW and many other women's groups, all of which supported the action, and also because NOW's local chapters expanded rapidly in the aftermath of the massive publicity given to the strike. NOW itself grew and altered considerably after 1970, broadening its focus, granting more autonomy to local chapters, and reducing the hierarchical nature of its organizational structure. In addition, the composition of NOW's membership gradually changed, with increasing numbers of younger women, nonprofessionals, and women who had previously been active in the women's liberation movement joining the organization.[24] As a result, NOW and women's liberation groups increasingly overlapped in membership, ideology, and action after 1970.

In contrast to the formal structure of NOW in its early years, the organizational structure of the many women's liberation groups which emerged after 1967 was amorphous. This loose organizational structure was consciously advocated by women involved in the early movement, who wanted to avoid the hierarchical model of the 1960s protest movements and organizations, and at the same time pursue a more personal, participatory, and intimate political style. The intense commitment to equality and to the full participation of all members in all decisions characteristic of women's liberation was at once the legacy of women's discrimination within earlier movements and the fruition of a new political emphasis on the personal and the emotional. Thus a loosely integrated series of small groups of anywhere from seven to twenty women—what Freeman refers to as "a diffuse social system with a common culture"[25]—was formed across the country.

The small group structure not only facilitated maximum participation by all members, but was also consistent with the movement's emphasis on the exploration of members' psychological and personal oppression as women. Such discussion was possible only in the context of small groups in which bonds of personal trust and intimacy had developed. In a pamphlet exploring the small group concept, Pamela Allen commented on the assumptions behind this type of structure:

> Women are oppressed by society and by individual men, and are beginning to rise against that oppression . . . . For this to be successful we must develop an ideology and learn to think autonomously. The group experience has helped me to synthesize and deepen my emotional and intellectual understanding of the predicament of being female in this society and the concerns with which we must deal in building a women's movement.[26]

Thus activist women who desired to create a separate movement for social change evolved the all-woman small group or consciousness-raising structure in order to advance the process of building the movement, to provide themselves with personal support groups to help withstand society's negative sanctioning, and to allow them to construct a new ideology out of their understanding of their own cultural and psychological oppression as women.

The name eventually given to the small groups emerging all over the United States in the late 1960s was women's liberation. At first these scattered groups were united only by friendship networks and by a fledgling newsletter called the "Voice of the Women's Liberation Movement," which had a circulation of a little over two thousand in 1968.[27] The goal of these groups was to develop collective consciousness and a new ideology by conducting discussions in small groups and/or by engaging in "actions" that attempted to make public an alternative view of women by exposing the social and cultural sources of women's oppression. The first, and probably most widely publicized, of these actions was the demonstration at the 1968 Miss America Contest, where, according to inaccurate media accounts, women burned their bras.[28] Thus in the first few years of its existence, the women's liberation movement eschewed all formal organizational structure, with the exception of a few national gatherings called to exchange ideas. Women's liberation groups formed and dissolved regularly, although the absolute number of such groups mushroomed before 1970, as did the number of periodicals and newsletters that articulated the growing collective consciousness and ideology. Groups remained small and autonomous, emphasizing egalitarian practice within the group and focusing on their goal of raising consciousness in keeping with the slogan, "the personal is the political."

By 1970, however, many small women's liberation groups experienced growing dissatisfaction with their previously coveted autonomy, and in many cities women's centers or women's unions emerged as umbrella groups to coordinate and/or coalesce the scattered movement. The focus of attention within the movement itself began to shift toward the development of an overall political strategy to change women's lives as well as their consciousness. Significant effort was made to apply pressure to social institutions for change benefiting women, and experiments with alternative institutions that could serve as models for society were encouraged. These changes in the women's liberation sector of the overall movement, which occurred at roughly the same time as did the alterations in NOW, were symbolized by the massive participation of women's liberation groups in the August 1970 Women's Strike, which was largely organized by NOW. Although differences remained after this point between the two major types of groups, the entire women's movement was increasingly characterized on the one hand by local autonomy and personal consciousness raising and on the other by attention to institutional change and the development of long-term policies and coordination of strategy. As Freeman states, "The Women's Liberation Movement may have had two distinct origins, but like the branches of two neighboring trees, its progeny have spread over both trunks so thickly that one cannot easily detect the roots of specific leaves."[29]

PROGRESS AND PROBLEMS

After 1970 the women's movement continued to expand its numbers of both supporters and activists. Maren Carden estimates that by 1973 the total number of active participants in the movement was between 80,000 and 100,000.[30] There is also evidence of growing sympathy and support for the movement in the population at large. A series of polls conducted by Harris Associates between 1970 and 1974 indicates an increase in the percentage of women who favored "efforts to strengthen or change women's status in society" (40 percent in 1970, 57 percent in 1974).[31] However it became increasingly clear that some women refused to support, and indeed were strongly hostile to the women's movement.

By the middle of the decade, a number of scholarly studies offered analyses of the factors important in distinguishing between women who participate in or support the women's movement and those who do not.[32] Most of these studies are not fully representative of activists in the movement because they limited their samples to groups of undergraduate and/or graduate university students. Nonetheless, since the women's movement was rapidly expanding among this sector of the population, and since most of these studies took care to compare activists (defined by their attendance at women's liberation movement meetings) with matched samples of nonactivist students, this research is valuable in illuminating the composition of an important group of women's movement activists after 1970.

The picture that emerges from a review of these studies is one revealing strong similarities to the characteristics of activists in the early years of the women's movement. A disproportionate number of the college women who were active in the movement after 1970 were raised in affluent homes by politically liberal and religiously secular parents. Their mothers were more likely to have had labor force experience than were the mothers of nonactivist women. Student activists in the women's movement were more likely than nonactivists to exhibit strong aspirations for achievement—often focused on professional careers—high levels of personal independence, and self-definitions as political "radicals" rather than as liberals or conservatives. This evidence implies that student activists in the early 1970s were drawn from the same social backgrounds and evidenced the same personal characteristics as had earlier women's movement activists.

Research based on interviews with activist and nonactivist college women reveal important differences in their views of the issues raised by the women's movement and of the movement itself.[33] Women activists supported changes in a wide variety of traditional aspects of women's lives, including work roles, definitions of femininity, sex role expectations, abortion laws, and family roles. In contrast, nonactivist women only supported the legalization of abortion and better career opportunities for women; proposed change in sex roles, family organization or definitions of femininity failed to elicit their approval. In addition, non-activist respondants expressed negative feelings about the "militant" tactics of the movement and voiced fears that the movement would "destroy the family and make women just like men." Nonactivists only rarely reported feeling "personally oppressed by the stereotype of femininity" and did not feel that they had ever been discriminated against because of their sex. Activists, in contrast, consistently stated that they had been personally harmed by the traditional treatment of and attitudes toward women in American society. This research indicates that many college women in the early seventies were sympathetic to only a very narrow range of changes sought by the women's movement, and expressed fear of, and in some cases hostility to, a movement that advocated widespread changes in women's lives.

Despite the movement's growth and evidence of spreading support among both students and non-students after 1970, many women continued to resist the movement's attempts to recruit them or to gain their support. In the population as a whole, Harris and Roper polls indicate that opposition to the women's movement and/or to the issues for which it stands is strongly associated with a number of variables, with older women, less educated women, and women with relatively low family incomes most likely to take the opposing side. In addition, nonsupporters are more likely to reside in rural rather than urban areas, to be married rather than single or divorced, and to live in the South or Midwest rather than the East or West. In addition, Susan Welch reported that opponents are more likely to attend church regularly, to be full-time housewives, and to describe themselves as politically conservative.[34]

In response to the movement's problems in attracting support among certain groups of women, activists in the 1970s attempted to overcome the class, ethnic, and regional underrepresentation that had characterized much of the movement's history. It was obvious that some groups of women, such as those who define themselves as politically conservative, would not be willing to support the movement as long as it continued to press for increased equality and for change in the position of women, and the movement made no attempt to include such women. With respect to other groups that expressed only limited support for the movement, however, activists attempted to surmount what they perceived as undesirable and less permanent obstacles to the spread of women's collective consciousness. The underrepresentation of low-income, poorly educated women (often labeled "working class" in the sociological literature) is an example of a limitation that was troublesome to many movement activists, and some groups have attempted to understand and correct it.

The reluctance of many working-class women to support the women's movement is accounted for by the interaction of several variables. Unlike the well-educated and affluent women who organized the movement, working-class women in the 1960s were less affected by women's changing economic, educational, and familial status. For example, working-class and poor women have a significantly longer history of labor force participation than do middle-class women and thus are more likely to have been employed prior to the changes in the 1960s. In addition, their labor force experience has more often involved unskilled occupations than is true of their middle-class sisters. Such employment is most often undertaken because their husbands cannot provide adequate family incomes. The new opportunities opening up to women in the 1960s most often required high levels of technical skill or education, to which working-class women rarely had access. While middle-class women often viewed employment as a positive opportunity for growth or development, work was viewed and experienced by many working-class women as an unwanted burden. A movement dedicated to increased female labor force participation and represented by many women with lucrative and rewarding careers may have been perceived as closed to working-class women, or as irrelevant or even contrary to their needs.

Another source of the barriers between the movement and working-class women concerns personality change. The changes in personality that we have examined are more likely to be characteristic of middle-class rather than poor or working-class women. Several studies of working-class wives report the presence of low self-esteem and fatalism, strong traditional family orientation, and little concern with or knowledge of extrafamilial matters.[35] Such women are significantly less likely to participate in any kind of organization or activity than are more educated or middle-class women. Furthermore, these characteristics are quite different from the achievement-oriented, autonomous, self-defining personality type that developed in the 1960s among the founders and supporters of the women's movement. Working-class women and women's movement activists, because they evidence such divergent personalities and world views, may have unwittingly offended one another and thus widened the gap that different social backgrounds and labor force experiences had already created.

Finally, working-class women bear larger numbers of children than do women in high socioeconomic strata, and many studies report that they view their family relationships as the center of their lives.[36] The effects of declining fertility on women's attitudes toward themselves and their role in the family had less impact on working-class and poor women, whose birth rates, although slowly dropping during our period, remained significantly higher than those of other women. Working-class women thus have continued to evidence traditional attitudes to their roles and relationships within the family. To the extent that the women's movement is associated with nontraditional family behavior and attitudes it may have appeared and may continue to seem threatening to these more traditional conceptions of femininity and family. Middle-class and working-class women have thus been divided from one another by the differential class impact of structural change, which affected the attitudes and behavior of the former group far more than it did the latter in the 1960s and 70s.

Age as well as income and educational differences divide women in their response to the women's movement. Studies indicate that older women, regardless of class, are another group to which only a limited collective women's consciousness has spread. The differential impact of structural changes after 1960 on women is again important in explaining the hesitation of these women to support the women's movement. Changes in women's fertility, education, and labor force participation after 1960, which significantly affected younger women who had not yet established families or reared their children, had less impact on older women who had already formulated their life patterns. Women who had reached maturity by the early sixties had typically been socialized to accept and had set their goals on full-time domesticity. Thus a "generation gap" appeared, for behavior and attitudes about such issues as labor force participation, familial orientation, fertility, and domesticity were often correlated with age. Support for the women's movement and its proposals for change was less often characteristic of older women than of their daughters.

Reinforcing these differences was the actual age composition of the women's movement in the 1960s. The movement, especially the women's liberation sector, was disproportionately composed of women in their twenties and early thirties, many of whom had had no experience of full-time domesticity. These circumstances contributed to the impression that older women, especially full-time housewives, were not welcome in the movement. Divisions between the groups were intensified by the movement's encouragement of labor force participation which must have seemed irrelevant to women who had never worked and who did not anticipate joining the labor force. Indeed, some of these women may have seen the movement's emphasis on the importance of women's equal economic competition with men as a potential threat to the family income provided by their husbands. Also, the movement's emphasis on change in women's exclusively domestic role may have been interpreted as criticism of the roles and norms by which older women had lived and had given meaning to their lives. For these reasons, the women's movement has been relatively unsuccessful in obtaining support or recruits from among older women in general, and particularly from those who have lived their lives in a domestic pattern and who may feel either too old or simply uninterested in making any changes.

There has also been much concern in the women's movement over the failure of a collective women's consciousness to spread widely among minority women in the United States. The nonrepresentation of older minority women, of minority women who have always been full-time housewives, and of low-income minority women is of course at least partly explained by the factors discussed above. However, the failure of minority women to participate in the women's movement in large numbers has other sources as well. The case of black women is of particular interest, since one of the first statements of women's liberation was made by a black woman in a civil rights organization (SNCC) at the beginning of the sixties. Nevertheless, the participation of blacks in the women's movement has been minimal, in part because the women's movement was organized at a time when black political organizations were strong and visible in the United States. The political energies of many black women in the areas of equal rights and social change thus focused primarily on the oppressed position of black people in the society. Many black women believed that the struggles for change in the position of women and blacks could not occur simultaneously, and that they were forced to make a choice between the two movements.[37] And in a society in which minorities are denied basic rights and are involved in struggles against discrimination, minority women were pulled more strongly toward participation in ethnic movements. Unlike other groups of women who are underrepresented as activists in the women's movement, however, minority women appear to be supportive of and sympathetic to the women's movement and to the changes it advocates. For example, the Roper polls report that in 1974, 67 percent of the black women responding, as compared with 55 percent of the white respondents, favored efforts to strengthen or change women's status in society.[38] Minority women's perception of their own oppression may produce strong sympathy for other movements for social change, even when they themselves are not active participants in those movements.

Attempts in the late 1970s to obtain ratification of the Equal Rights Amendment (ERA) by the required thirty-eight states demonstrated other divisions between supporters and opponents of the women's movement. Ratification became a central concern of the movement during this period. In an article analyzing opinion on ERA in Illinois, Joan Huber and her colleagues indicate that demographic characteristics are associated with different attitudes toward the amendment. The proportion of ERA supporters among women who were highly educated, non-Protestant, or divorced at least once was significantly higher than the proportion of supporters among the female population as a whole.[39] While these personal and demographic characteristics differentiated supporters from nonsupporters in Illinois, even stronger differences were found between the two groups with respect to their assessments of the consequences of the ERA. Women who thought that the ERA would improve women's job opportunities favored it, while those who believed that it would negatively affect men's job opportunities or make divorce easier opposed ratification. Huber et al. conclude that women's concerns about jobs, the health of the economy, and divorce are crucial to their attitudes not only toward the amendment but also toward the women's movement as a whole.

Despite the barriers to organizing or gaining support from certain groups of American women, there are indications that in the most recent period the women's movement has made gains in spreading a

women's collective consciousness to previously opposing or nonpartici-
pant groups. Barbara Deckard cites, for example, the founding of the
Coalition of Labor Union Women (CLUW) and cases of successful
organizing in urban working-class neighborhoods, the formation of
Older Women's Liberation (OWL), and the creation of the National
Black Feminist Organization (NBFO) as indications of the growing
heterogeneity of the women's movement.[40] CLUW has been especially
successful in involving working-class women in the women's movement,
and the creation of NBFO has made clear the willingness of some black
women to work within the women's and black movements simultaneously. Another largely black group, the Welfare Rights Organization,
has developed strong ties between the women's movement and low-
income women not in the labor force. Thus the women's movement,
despite remaining difficulties with the underrepresentation of some
groups of women, has become both larger and more diverse in the
decade of the seventies.

This diversity is reflected in the wide range of projects in which the
movement has been involved in the seventies. In addition to projects
emphasized in the sixties, such as consciousness-raising groups, struggles
against economic discrimination, and challenges to sexist agencies of
socialization, the movement has initiated other activities that have had
a wide impact on all sectors of American society. A mass circulation
magazine (*Ms.*) that has acquired a large national audience has emerged,
women's studies programs have been developed at many colleges and
universities, and strong women's caucuses have been organized in professional organizations and political parties. In addition, many more
women have run for and been elected to political office in the seventies;
thousands of women, representing a wide cross-section of the population in age, religion, ethnic origin, and political persuasion, showed
their support for the women's movement at the National Women's
Conference in Texas in the fall of 1977; and over 100,000 persons
marched in Washington, D.C., in July 1978 in support of the ratification of the ERA.

The women's movement has institutionalized the struggle for change
in women's position in American society, and is nationally recognized
as the formulator of an alternative ideology that challenges traditional
hegemonic conceptions of male and female personality, of the family,
and of women's economic and political role in society.

NOTES

1. I have adopted Herbert Blumer's definition of a social movement as "a collective enterprise seeking to establish a new order of life." Blumer, "Social Movements," in Alfred McClung Lee (ed.), *Principles of Sociology* (New York: Barnes and Noble, 1946), pp. 199-22.

2. Quoted in Judith Hole and Ellen Levine (eds.), *Rebirth of Feminism* (New York: Quadrangle, 1971), p. 85.

3. The date 1968 is selected as important because in that year there occurred the first national gathering of the small independent groups that considered themselves part of a new feminist social movement. See Jo Freeman, *The Politics of Women's Liberation* (New York: David McKay, 1975), p. 106-7.

4. I omit from this discussion the men who were part of NOW when it was founded, since they were few in number and information on them is almost non-existent.

5. See above, Chapters 3 and 6.

6. Gerhard Lenski, "Status Crystallization: A Non-Vertical Dimension of Social Status," *American Sociological Review*, 19 (1954):405-13.

7. Maren Lockwood Carden, *The New Feminist Movement* (New York: Russell Sage Foundation (1974), p. 24.

8. "Many observers felt that the 'sex' amendment was a calculated political maneuver designed . . . to bring so much controversy to the bill as to kill it entirely." Hole and Levine, *Rebirth of Feminism*, p. 30.

9. Freeman, *Politics of Women's Liberation*, p. 54.

10. Carden, *New Feminist Movement*, pp. 59-71.

11. For discussion of the relationship between the women's movement and the media, see Freeman, *Politics of Women's Liberation*, pp. 111-14 and Hole and Levine, *Rebirth of Feminism*, pp. 266-70.

12. Kenneth Keniston and Michael Lerner, "Selected References on Student Protest," American Academy of Political and Social Science, *Annals*, 395 (1971):184-95; Richard Flacks, "The Liberated Generation: An Exploration of the Roots of Student Protest" *Journal of Social Issues*, 23 (1967):52-75.

13. *Ibid.*

14. *Ibid.*

15. Ruth Hartley, "Children's Concepts of Male and Female Roles," *Merrill-Palmer Quarterly*, 6 (1960):84-91.

16. Kenneth Keniston, *Young Radicals* (New York: Harcourt, Brace and World, 1968).

17. Flacks, *Youth and Social Change*.

18. Sara Evans, "The Origins of the Women's Liberation Movement," *Radical America*, 9 (1975):1-12.

19. Freeman, *Politics of Women's Liberation*, pp. 56-62; Hole and Levine, *Rebirth of Feminism*, pp. 109-14.

20. Mitchell, *Woman's Estate*, pp. 22-24.

21. Freeman, *Politics of Women's Liberation*, p. 59. It should be noted that many women who founded and/or participated in the new women's movement also strongly supported and even participated in the anti-war movement that mushroomed during this same period.

22. *Ibid.*, p. 73.

23. Carden, *New Feminist Movement*, p. 194. Carden provides data on NOW membership and also discusses at length the internal problems of the organization.

24. Freeman, *Politics of Women's Liberation*, pp. 84-87.

25. *Ibid.*, p. 104.

26. Pamela Allen, *Free Space: A Perspective on the Small Group in Women's Liberation* (New York: Times Change Press, 1970), pp. 4-5.

27. Carden estimates that by 1972, 61 periodicals were circulating within the women's movement. She states that by 1969 there were active women's liberation groups in at least 40 American cities. By 1970, New York City alone had approximately 50 functioning groups. Carden, *New Feminist Movement*, pp. 64-69, 78-81.

28. Burning of bras never actually occurred at this demonstration; the widely believed and repeated story is an all too typical example of media distortion of the movement. Hole and Levine, *Rebirth of Feminism* pp. 229-30.

29. Freeman, *Politics of Women's Liberation*, p. 147.

30. Carden, *New Feminist Movement*, p. 140.

31. Harris, *Poll*, 1970, 1972, 1974.

32. See, for example: Jean Goldschmidt, Mary Gergen, Karen Quigley, Kenneth Gergen, "The Women's Liberation Movement: Attitudes and Action," *Journal of Personality*, 42 (1974):601-16; Joan D. Mandle, "Attitudes Toward the Women's Liberation Movement and their Correlates: A Case Study of Undergraduate Women" (Ph.D. diss., Bryn Mawr College, 1974); Carolyn Stoloff, "Who Joins Women's Liberation?" *Psychiatry*, 36 (1973):325-40; Judith and Leonard Worell, "Support and Opposition to the Women's Liberation Movement: Some Personality and Parental Correlates," *Journal of Research in Personality*, 11 (1977): 10-20.

33. See Joan D. Mandle, "Undergraduate Activists in the Women's Movement and their Public: Attitudes Towards Marriage and the Family" *Sociological Focus*, 8 (1975):257-69; Mandle, "Normative Change and the Women's Liberation Movement" (unpublished paper, November 1976).

34. Harris, *Poll*, 1970, 1972, Roper, *Poll*, 1974; Susan Welch, "Support Among Women for the Issues of the Women's Movement," *Sociological Quarterly*, 16 (1975):216-27.

35. Rainwater et al., *Workingman's Wife*; Mirra Komarovsky, *Blue Collar Marriage* (New York: Random House, 1962); Oakley, *Sociology of Housework*.

36. Lee Rainwater and Karol Weinstein, *And the Poor Get Children* (Chicago: Quadrangle, 1960).

37. Frances Beale, "Double Jeopardy: To Be Black and Female," in D. Babcox and M. Belkin (eds), *Liberation Now: Writings from the Women's Liberation Movement* (New York: Dell 1971), pp. 185-96. Beale was one of the first to argue that black women should participate in both black and women's movements.

38. Roper, *Poll*, 1974, p. 3.

39. Joan Huber, Cynthia Rexroat, and Glenna Spitze, "A Crucible of Opinion on Women's Status: ERA in Illinois," *Social Forces*, 57 (1978):forthcoming.

40. Barbara Deckard, *The Women's Movement* (New York: Harper & Row, 1975), pp. 344-65.

Chapter 8
A New Ideology

The process of economic development was crucial in setting in motion alterations in women's personality and psychological development, and in producing changes in their labor force experience and family roles. These material changes also contributed to the emergence of a social movement dedicated to the continuation and extension of changes in women's lives. The impact of the women's movement has been particularly significant in the realm of ideas. For the unique contribution of a social movement is often the development of an alternative set of ideas and values that challenges and attempts to undermine the current ideological hegemony. The women's movement formulated such a new ideology, and by struggling to gain acceptance for it, movement activists contributed to the process of social change.

THE ROLE OF IDEOLOGY

The role of ideology has been an important focus in theories of social change. Simone de Beauvoir, a French existentialist philosopher, addressed this issue in her classic work, *The Second Sex*, which offers a cogent analysis of women's position in society.[1] De Beauvoir's view of women's oppression and change is primarily concerned with the area of ideas, ideology, consciousness, and individual choice. Her primary assumption, influenced by her adherence to existentialist philosophy, is that women are an oppressed group, the "second sex," because they are not autonomous, self-defining individuals. De Beauvoir believes that individual self-identity and freedom are achieved through conflict. Each individual, a Subject, can achieve identity only in being opposed, by setting itself up as the essential. This entails defining all others as the inessential, the Object. In order to be truly human, then, each individual must actively consider itself the Subject, claim its own importance, and resist the passive acceptance of others' definition of it as Object. De Beauvoir argues that only when two individuals or groups interact, each making reciprocal claims of its own importance and self-definition, are the requirements for mutual respect and autonomy fulfilled. The relegation of females as a group to an inferior status, according to de Beauvoir, is rooted in their passive response to definition by males. Males define themselves as Subject and similarly define women as Object, that is, "the inessential, the incidental. Thus humanity is male, and man defines woman not in herself but relative to him."[2] Female oppression is rooted in the female sex's inability or unwillingness to engage in the process of self-definition. Instead, women depend on and accept men's definition of them as the Other. Since no reciprocal claims of subjectivity are made between men and women, there exists no basis for mutual respect or equality. Women's oppression, according to de Beauvoir, is at base rooted in men's and women's ideas about themselves in relation to others, with women submitting to men's definition of them, indeed, defining themselves, as the Other. They do not control or rebel against the ideology that defines them as inferior, and thus they view themselves and behave as the second sex.

Since in de Beauvoir's view ideas and consciousness are the sources of women's oppression, the social change she advocates not surprisingly involves the alteration of those ideological constraints. She argues that women's oppression will only end when they consciously assert their human potential by claiming themselves as Subject and asserting their right to autonomous self-definition. The key to changing women's inferior status, then, is the creation of a new set of beliefs that will influence their view both of themselves and of the wider reality of which they are a part. In de Beauvoir's terms, this new ideology must replace the hegemonic view that relegates women to passive "objects" in the eyes of men, other women, and themselves.

The new ideological hegemony can only be created by the active and self-conscious choice of women themselves, according to de Beauvoir. Thus her work points to the importance of subjective consciousness—one's view of oneself and of one's place in reality—as a crucial element in the process of social change. Women, argues de Beauvoir, must collectively develop an alternative ideology as the basis for their freedom and liberation from "secondary" or inferior status. Although she emphasizes the importance for women's liberation of changing ideas, of creating a new consciousness, and of ending women's isolation from one another, her discussion fails to address in detail the role of a social movement in the formulation and acceptance of the group's alternative ideology.

Thus there is a need for a theoretical framework that explores the relationship between social movements and ideological change. Marxist theory, in part, provides such a link. Specifically, Antonio Gramsci, an Italian Marxist, has undertaken a sophisticated exploration of the creation and importance of a new ideological hegemony in the process of social change.[3] Gramsci argues that radical social change requires not only the presence of structural (primarily economic) changes, but also the development of a revolutionary consciousness among the members of society. In the creation of this consciousness, the projection of an alternative ideology—a new hegemony—is absolutely crucial. Revolutionary social change, according to Gramsci, is possible only when the ideas associated with members of the ruling class are replaced by a new view of reality. The role of a social movement involves, among other things, the articulation of and the attempt to gain acceptance for a new world view. Through its presentation of a vision of the new organization and functioning of society, the social movement seeks to convince society's members that change is not only possible but also desirable. Thus the creation and content of an alternative ideology are crucial components of the process of social change and are uniquely contributed by the rise of social movements.

THE WOMEN'S MOVEMENT AND THE NEW HEGEMONY

Women's consciousness, which emerged in the middle 1960s along with the women's movement, constituted an embryonic ideological hegemony. The ideas formulated by the women's movement merged in an ideology that was in contradiction and represented a challenge to the dominant world view, particularly with respect to traditional women's roles. This alternative ideology reflected the structural sources of the women's movement in its focus on issues of personality and socialization, women's economic position, and the family. An underlying unity existed within this developing and often diffuse ideology in the shared desire for change in women's position and for the destruction of traditional ideas of female inferiority, passivity, and domesticity.

Nonetheless, within the movement the expressions and interpretations of this ideology were diverse. Some women activists emphasized the importance of confronting and attempting to change the institutions and structure of society, while others rejected the possibility of accomplishing such change and emphasized the creation of alternative, often separate, institutions that would function on their own. For example, while some women challenged the organization of the medical profession and sought to alter it, other women activists concentrated on the goal of establishing alternative women's health centers and clinics.[4] Other differences concerned the extent of change thought necessary to "liberate" women. Some groups emphasized the importance of consolidating changes that had already begun in various spheres of women's lives. They proposed ideas that would help to alleviate women's special problems and assist in integrating them into the mainstream of society. Other groups within the movement proposed a future in which both men's and women's lives would be altered and improved by radical transformations in the society. Despite these differences, however, the women's movement as a whole projected a vision of changes in women's personality, family, and work roles that challenged the dominant hegemony.

Personality

A major concern of activists in the women's movement of the sixties and seventies was the strength of the traditional ideology, and of the socialization practices based upon it, in repressing women's potential for self-development and actualization.[5] Therefore one set of goals of the women's movement centered on the acceptance of a new collective female personality and the eradication of sexist socialization patterns. Projected models of personality envisioned women as self-sufficient, active, and competent individuals, in contrast to the traditional ideology's assumptions of female passivity, dependency, incompetence. Despite agreement on this general model, there were differences in the emphases and even in the content of the proposals made by women's movement activists in searching for alternative to the dominant ideology.

One sector of the women's movement emphasized the goal of altering female socialization patterns to make them similar to those of males. In this way, it was thought, the "negative" characteristics of traditional femininity would be eliminated, and the new collective female personality would incorporate such desirable, traditionally "masculine," characteristics as achievement orientation, independence, intellectual attainment, and emotional control. Women's movement activists advocated changes in socialization patterns that would make the socialization experience of young girls as similar as possible to that of their brothers.

Others in the women's movement articulated a vision of even more radical change in the personality development of both men and women. This position challenged not only female socialization patterns but also those of males, and it envisioned an androgynous personality type. As defined by Sandra Bem, a feminist psychologist who has made important contributions to research on this subject, the concept of androgyny implies that

> it is possible for an individual to be both masculine and feminine, both instrumental and expressive, both agentic and communal, depending on the situational appropriateness of these various modalities; and even for an individual to blend these complementary modalities in a single act, for example to fire an employee if the circumstances warrant it, but to do so with sensitivity to the human emotions that such an act invariably produces.[6]

Bem considers the androgynous personality type to be a model of healthy personality development both for women and for men. Such a personality would incorporate a balance of traditionally segregated "masculine" and "feminine" characteristics, and as noted above, it would be flexible enough on the one hand to engage in competent, independent, and achievement-oriented behavior, and on the other hand, to express nurturant and emotionally responsive behavior and attitudes.

Bem and others have argued that the benefits of androgyny over traditionally sex-typed personalities are enormous,[7] claiming that androgynous personality development would eliminate the severe repression required for the creation of traditional masculinity or femininity. The model of androgynous development would eliminate the rigid set of sex-specific social norms into which an individual must be socialized, and would allow greater freedom and choice to the individual because of its tolerance of flexibility and of wide-ranging characteristics in the individual personality.

Another set of social and personal benefits claimed for androgynous development concerns the elimination of negative characteristics associated with traditional masculinity and femininity. If women were encouraged to develop personality characteristics that included competence and independence as well as nurturance and emotionality, low self-esteem and feelings of inferiority would be reduced or eliminated as a characteristically "female" syndrome, and would be replaced by individual fulfillment and self-actualization. At the same time, advocates of androgyny also point to its potential for eliminating negative personality characteristics associated with traditional masculinity.[8] Such characteristics as extreme aggressiveness, lack of emotional expressiveness, and the need for superiority over women might be less typical of men as a group if boys were encouraged to be warm and gentle as well as tough and competent during the process of androgynous socialization. Thus the result of androgynous socialization, it is claimed, would be the development of individuals who, with wide variation, would incorporate the most positive aspects of both traditional masculinity and traditional femininity.

Like other activists in the women's movement, proponents of androgyny attempted to gain legitimacy for their model of personality development in the population as a whole and especially among agents of socialization, such as schools, media representatives, and publishers. But there have been sharp disagreements between the advocates of androgyny and those women activists whose emphasis has been centered on ideas of altering femininity by incorporating traditionally masculine characteristics. Proponents of androgyny criticize the latter groups by arguing that their model of personality development would merely replicate in women those negative characteristics presently associated with masculinity. In addition, they claim that such a model does not contribute to the reduction of repression or rigidity in the creation of personality, but merely makes the content of repression uniform across the sexes. For women to substitute traditionally masculine characteristics for traditionally feminine ones, they argue, would not benefit women, men, or society.

On the other hand, skeptics of the model of androgyny have questioned the feasibility of an androgynous personality type. Would it be possible, they ask, for adult men and women who have been socialized by traditional norms and practices to make the transition to androgyny, even if they desired to do so? The conservative power of personality structures developed in early childhood would make such drastic changes difficult for most women and men. Critics of androgyny note in addition that without alterations in the personalities of adults, it is impossible to expect parents and other socializers to succeed in raising the next generation according to androgynous principles and norms. Even with the best of intentions, adult socializers would find it difficult to transmit a set of norms or to tolerate personality characteristics that diverge so sharply from those by which they themselves were raised and which they exhibit as adults. Finally, opponents of an androgynous model of personality suggest that it is premature to claim that society or individuals would benefit from androgyny as the collective social personality, since there are relatively few androgynous personality types in society whose experiences might be studied.

Despite their differences and the weaknesses exposed by their disagreements, both groups of women's movement activists have projected significant new ideas about male and female personality development and have proposed models that challenge traditional socialization patterns. In this way, the women's movement has helped to stimulate discussion, both within and outside of academia, of personality development and of various models of healthy personalities for adults and children.[9] In seeking to legitimate an alternative ideology, the women's movement has challenged and exposed the limits of the traditional ideological hegemony and of the patterns of female personality development that have been dominant in American society.

Work Roles

New ideas with respect to women's economic role in society were also developed by the women's movement. In previous chapters we have discussed the importance of economic change and increased female labor force participation in creating the women's liberation movement and in contributing to the development of women's collective consciousness. The women's movement challenged traditional conceptions of the unreliability and inferiority of women as workers, and of the general incompatibility of femininity with paid labor.[10] As was the case with respect to the ideology of personality development, activists within the movement agreed on the need for change but projected different models of women's economic roles and economic change. Some groups proposed the integration of women into the economic system on an equal par with male workers; others envisioned a more radical transformation of the economic system.

The ideological position of the majority of women's movement activists emphasized the goal of the egalitarian integration of women into the labor force. In order to gain legitimacy for this idea, activists stressed the ubiquity of traditional ideologies of women and work, which view the world of work as masculine—that is, a place for those with male characteristics—and as a sphere that was inimical not only to femininity but also to domesticity and motherhood. This ideological hegemony contributed to men's discrimination against women in the labor force and to women's hesitation to plan or train for serious job or career commitments. In addition, it was claimed that this dominant ideology resulted in the waste of talent and skills in the society, and in personal costs for women who were discouraged from developing their potential talents.

In challenging the hegemony of traditional ideas of women and work, one sector of women's movement activists envisioned changes that they believed would ensure the economic equality of men and women in the labor force. They argued, for example, that women should be offered opportunities for education and training similar to those offered to men. They called for government legislation to encourage women's participation in the labor force and to prohibit discrimination against those who were employed. It was hoped that such laws would not only make discrimination illegal but also encourage the development of egalitarian attitudes among women and men. In addition, feminists pointed to the need for changes in early socialization patterns, which traditionally discouraged women from viewing work as an important and integral element in their lives, and which encouraged boys to view work as their exclusive province and responsibility. Only with similarity in the socialization experiences of boys and girls could such traditional attitudes be replaced with new ideas of economic equality between the sexes.

Another alternative to the traditional ideas of women and work was proposed by a small but vocal sector of the women's movement. Their model not only envisioned the elimination of women's traditional labor force experience of exploitation and inferiority, but also advocated changes in the position of men in the labor force and in the functioning of the economic system itself. They criticized the economic system in the United States for its inflexibility, its authoritarian and hierarchical structure, and its exploitative organization, as well as for its special discrimination against women. The alternative ideology they proposed advocated an egalitarian economic structure that would be flexible and responsive to human needs.

Some of the changes called for by this new model of work involved only minor alterations in economic institutions, but others constituted radical challenges to the society. With respect to the former, it was suggested, for example, the acceptance of greater flexibility on the part of employers with respect to daily schedules, sick leaves, or leaves of absence would improve the responsiveness of economic institutions to human needs. These changes were initially envisioned because of the special problems encountered by women in coordinating the demands made on them by work responsibilities on the one hand and home-family duties on the other. However, the demand was later expanded to a broader challenge to the ideological hegemony that maintained that workers should be available at their employer's behest and that work responsibilites should be given priority over all other needs or duties. Thus women's movement activists proposed an ideological alternative which emphasized the right of all workers to arrange their work lives flexibly and in accordance with a wide variety of non-work-related "needs," ranging from the enjoyment gained from increased free time to learn, study, or play, to the desire to care for a child or an ill or old relative or friend.

Some feminists projected an ideology which would legitimate the reduction or even the elimination of the authoritarian and hierarchical organization of economic institutions. Often it was women's experiences in the democratically structured small groups of the women's liberation movement that created intense opposition to authoritarian structures and contributed to the vision of alternative modes of production. The ideological alternative most often projected was a model of cooperation and sharing. Some activists believed that democracy could be incorporated into the economic structure of American society by allowing workers to participate more fully in decision-making processes at their work places. Other activists in the women's movement believed that a more radical vision of the socialist organization of work and economic institutions was necessary to ensure their responsiveness to human needs. Socialist feminists in addition affirmed the responsibility of the society to provide meaningful work for all its members, without discrimination against women or other groups.[11]

Conflict within the movement over the nature of the required economic changes was intense. Feminist socialists, for example, argued that without an ideology centered on the radical transformation of the economic system, women would merely find themselves working at the same alienating, dehumanizing, menial jobs in which men traditionally had been employed. They argued that because women were relatively new entrants into the labor force and because they were supported by a broad social movement, they were uniquely positioned to press for changes in traditional hierarchical and authoritarian practices in economic institutions. Finally, these activists noted that for the women's movement even to achieve the minimal goals of the egalitarian integration of women into the labor force, traditional ideologies and practices would have to be altered dramatically. These changes, the argument went, could best be accomplished by the projection of a new radical ideology that challenged a broad range of the oppressive aspects of traditional capitalist society, and that offered to both male and female workers the vision of improved and more gratifying work experiences.

Socialist feminists have in turn been sharply criticized by other groups of activists, who claim that the goal of women's economic equality would be lost in an ideology that emphasizes a wide range of economic changes. In addition, many activists in the women's movement reject the model of a cooperative or socialist organization of the economy, and thus object to goals that go beyond the integration of women into the capitalist economic structure. Finally, many groups in the women's movement believe that to press for the radical economic changes advocated by other feminists could increase opposition to the women's movement among those people who might agree with the goal of economic equality for men and women, but who would disagree with other changes in the economy.

Despite these differing emphases and models of change, a new ideology of women's role in the economy has been projected since the early 1960s by activists in the women's movement. This ideology has challenged the traditional hegemonic view which asserts the masculinity of work and women's exclusion from or inferior status within the economic system. It has strongly advocated women's participation and equality within the economy as beneficial to women themselves and to society as a whole, and has pressed for the acceptance of a new ideological hegemony.

Family

I have discussed the changes in the family in America that contributed to the development of a women's movement after 1960. Although at that time the traditional nuclear family was no longer the only model of family life in American society, the dominant traditional attitudes still idealized the nuclear family as the only "normal" type, criticizing women who were not full-time homemakers, lauding childbirth as the apex of a woman's accomplishment, and stigmatizing divorced and single-parent families. The women's movement formulated numerous counters to this traditional hegemony. The unifying theme of the new ideology was that exclusive domesticity and the ascription of women to motherhood and familial roles at once blocked the development of women's full potential, created personal unhappiness and frustration, and deprived the society of a wide range of individual contributions. More specifically, the new ideology proposed alternative ways of thinking about childbearing, marital relationships, and the structure of the family itself.[12]

One aspect of the new ideology of the family concerns family size. The traditional hegemony has attempted to specify acceptable or proper family size, but it has vacillated over time between advocating large numbers of children and suggesting that it is "better" to limit the number of children to two or three.[13] Activists in the women's movement have challenged this normative structure with an alternative ideology that advocates parents' freedom to choose for themselves the number of offspring they will have. In addition, activists stress that there cannot be real freedom of choice in reproductive behavior as long as childlessness is viewed as incompatible with femininity and womanhood. Thus they have argued that the range of acceptable alternatives should include voluntary childlessness, and they have pointed to the benefits of childlessness by underscoring the psychological, material, and physical burdens associated with childbearing and child rearing. This is of course in sharp contrast to the traditional assertion that all women want to be, should be, and will be made happy by being mothers.

In an attempt to increase freedom in fertility decisions, activists in the women's movement have advocated widespread sex education, the availability of contraceptive devices, and access to abortion. They also view fertility freedom as tied to ideological changes in socialization patterns and in women's economic role. For example, they point out that traditional socialization practices encourage high levels of fertility by teaching girls that their femininity depends on motherhood and domesticity and by implying that reproduction is also evidence of a man's claim to masculinity.[14] Such pronatalist teachings interfere with reproductive freedom as young people mature into adulthood. In addition, many activists in the women's movement argue that reproductive choice is closely related to women's ability to take advantage of attractive employment opportunities. If women are ascribed to domestic and familial roles and excluded from alternative spheres, they are unable to exercise real freedom of choice about whether and/or how many children they wish to bear. Thus, according to women activists, commitment to freedom in making reproductive decisions is linked to ideological changes concerning childbearing itself, and also to those concerning personality development and women's economic role.

The women's movement has also contributed to a new ideology concerning relationships between men and women, both within and outside of marriage. In general, activists have advanced new ways of thinking about male-female relationships based on equality and mutuality rather than on traditional male superiority and female inferiority. In doing so, some activists have been sharply critical of marriage as an institution, claiming that it fosters inequality between spouses. As an alternative, they have projected the vision of nonmarital, long-term unions between men and women who establish "living-together" relationships. Such nonmarital unions, it is argued, would have all the advantages of traditional marriage, but not its inherent tendencies toward inequality.

A small group of women's movement activists has espoused the idea of ending all relationships between the sexes, arguing that these inevitably exploit and oppress women. Members of this group often advocate celibacy or lesbian relationships as alternatives to traditional female inequality both within and outside of marriage.[15] The movement's ideological commitment to sexual choice and its inclusion of women and groups who make explicit their lesbianism has promoted a new legitimacy and openness about homosexuality in the society as a whole. Although there has been significant resistance to the ideology that advocates equality for avowed homosexuals (both male and female), homosexuals and their supporters have actively pressed for those rights and have more recently established a social movement of their own on a national scale.

Finally, other activists in the women's movement have argued for ideas which stress the modification rather than the elimination of marriage in order to achieve equality between men and women. One proposal suggests the incorporation of marital "contracts" into the marriage ceremony, which would make explicit the egalitarian responsibilities, privileges, and duties within marriage, and thus counter any tendencies toward inequality. Activists have also challenged laws concerning marriage, which they perceive as the embodiment of traditional ideologies, and they have proposed new laws that would encourage freedom of choice, equality, and mutuality within the relationship.

Activists in the women's movement who have been concerned with gaining support for a new ideology advocating egalitarian relationships between the sexes have also recognized the need for challenging traditional views in other areas of women's lives. For example, they have pointed out that adults who have been socialized in accordance with the traditional norms that maintain that girls and women are inferior to boys and men would be likely to develop nonegalitarian relationships and to be unable to attain the goal of mutuality envisioned by the ideology of the women's movement. Similarly, the traditional ideas that stress the exclusion of women from the labor force make it likely that women are often completely dependent economically on men; mutuality and equality would be difficult to attain under such circumstances, even with the best of intentions between partners. Thus the women's movement has stressed the interdependence of systems of belief, in this case pointing to the links between the vision of equality and mutuality in personal relationships between men and women on the one hand, and visions of nonsexist socialization and equal economic participation and status on the other.

Along with new views of childbearing and of relationships between the sexes, the women's movement has also advanced new ideas concerning child care and domestic maintenance. The diverse elements of the movement united in challenging the traditional assumptions that domestic maintenance and child care are inherently fulfilling to all women, and that they are fully the responsibility of and can be adequately carried out only by mothers.[16] As an alternative model, some activists proposed the equal sharing of all domestic responsibilities by the man and woman involved in a living unit. Such sharing is usually viewed as a means of breaking down the sexist division of household tasks, which traditionally differentiate between "male" categories (taking out garbage, caring for the lawn, making repairs, and teaching athletics to sons) and "female" categories (washing, caring for babies and the emotional needs of older children, cooking, and cleaning).

Other women's movement activists sought legitimacy for ideas advocating the development of large-scale support services, such as laundries, child care and after school activity centers, and restaurants. Such social services, it was argued, would relieve both men and women of much of the responsibility for domestic care, thus rendering the remaining tasks less burdensome and more likely to be shared. These activists argued that many household tasks would be done more efficiently if production were rationalized in this way. Another advantage of the idea of increased reliance on social services might be that negative attitudes toward household chores would be destroyed more rapidly, as these tasks would be partially transformed into "real," that is, paid, work.[17]

Activists also stressed that ideological changes affecting the care of children and the home would contribute to the elimination of sexist socialization patterns and ideas. The traditional ideology of femininity and masculinity, inculcated into children by parents, was reinforced by the parents' division of labor in the home, according to which women were exclusively responsible for child care and domestic maintenance. The new ideology of sharing would provide children with models of both men and women assuming responsibility for home and child care. Activists argued further that both female and male children would benefit psychologically by the increased contact with their fathers that such a sharing arrangement would encourage. Finally, acceptance of the new pattern of home and child care was thought to encourage women's participation in the labor force. An ideology which challenged women's traditionally exclusive responsibility for home care would also serve to weaken ideas legitimating women's exclusion from the labor force. Alternatively, as women engaged equally in employment, they would have less time and less inclination to accept full responsibility for domesticity, and men would have less excuse for avoiding that responsibility. The acceptance of a nonsexist ideology concerning changes in home roles would at once reinforce and also be made more likely by the society's acceptance of ideas of equal personal relationships between the sexes, equal responsibility for family income, and nonsexist personality development and socialization.

Perhaps most basic to the vision of change in the family projected by the new consciousness of the women's movement was its advocacy of changes in the nuclear family itself. The traditional ideology of the family assumed not only that the nuclear family was the only "normal" and efficient family form consistent with the needs of American society, but also that the stability of society itself rested on the maintenance of an unchanging nuclear family structure. This ideology also asserted that the family in general, and mothers in particular, were the sole reliable sources of emotional warmth and comfort available in a modern society such as that of the United States.

The women's movement however challenged this traditional view, pointing out its weaknesses and raising the possibility of alternative familial forms. The new ideology projected by the women's movement as a whole contained internal differences, but, in contrast to the traditional belief in the need for stability, it emphasized tolerance for changes in family structure and functioning and an openness to wide experimentation. The new vision articulated by the movement promoted the values of mutuality and of maximum equality and individual freedom in family relationships. To achieve these goals, some groups of activists believed that changes only in the functioning of the nuclear family, particularly in terms of role allocation, would be adequate. Other activists, however, advocated major changes in its structure as well as in its functioning.

The need for reallocation of roles within the nuclear family was recognized by women's movement activists who believed that the goals of mutuality and equality within the family sphere could be achieved within traditional nuclear family forms. They envisioned a nuclear family in which both spouses shared equally in obtaining family income, raising children, and caring for the home. They claimed that the problems associated with traditionally organized nuclear families, such as the isolation of women in the home, the economic burden on men as sole supporters, the inequality between spouses, and the sexist socialization of children, would be reduced and ultimately eliminated by the reorganization of the nuclear family envisioned by this new ideology. Indeed, activists with an ideological commitment to altering the functioning but not the structure of the traditional nuclear family point to the resemblance between their ideal model and the actual organization of some dual-career families in which, they claim, inequality and sexism have been reduced.[18]

Those activists who envisioned more radical changes in the traditional family based many of their proposals upon the belief that the structure of the nuclear family—not merely women's ascriptive roles within it—is a major obstacle to the goals of freedom and equality within the family. Thus they advocated social acceptance for such nontraditional family forms as the single-parent family. Others projected models of voluntary

childlessness, of living with men outside of marriage, or of avoiding relationships with men altogether as means of overcoming the inequality
that they perceived as inherent in the nuclear family structure.

Still other activists in the women's movement envisioned an egalitarian family which would include children, relationships with men,
and even marriage, and which would replace the traditional nuclear
family form with a communal structure. Advocates of communal living patterns claim many advantages for this model of family life.[19] In
such a family, they argue, there would be full sharing and equality
among members of the commune, regardless of sex. In addition, the
isolation of the nuclear family structure would be completely eliminated, the dependency of spouses on one another spread to other adult
members of the commune, and the burden of home and child care
lightened by its division among several adults. Moreover, children
would benefit by supportive and warm relationships with adults other
than their biological parents. Perhaps the most unique aspect of the
communal model would be its ability to maintain its commitment to
nonsexist behavioral patterns. Because each member of the communal
family would have the right and obligation to monitor the behavior and
attitudes of other members, the tendency for single individuals or
dyadic couples to fail to fulfill real sharing or to slip into patterns of
sexism or inequality would be minimized. Family life would not be
private and unobserved in a commune, and therefore even latent tendencies toward sexism might be challenged. Finally, for the sector of
the women's movement committed to socialist ideology, a communal
living situation could provide a model of a cooperative and egalitarian
family even in the context of the inequality and exploitation characteristic of capitalism. As an alternative, the model of communal living
most directly challenged the traditional norms and values attached to
the dominant nuclear family structure.

Disagreements concerning which model of the family could best
achieve the goals of challenging the traditional ideology and establishing
a vision of familial equality have characterized the women's movement
since its inception. Advocates of models of radical change in the structure of the nuclear family argue that the retention of that form will
merely continue the unequal and oppressive features of traditional
families. They argue that only a radical break with the hegemonic ideological commitment to the nuclear family form can ensure that the
present generation of adults will achieve equality in family relationships
and that the next generation will be socialized in a nonsexist manner.

Acceptance of the model of a private and isolated nuclear family, they claim, will produce resistance to equality and will fail to destroy the pockets of sexism that exist even among couples who seem to articulate nonsexist ideas and who seem to practice mutuality and equality.[20]

For their part, advocates of models of less drastic change in the family point to problems which characterize single-parents families, cite evidence of the inequality and sexism which often pervade the relationships of unmarried couples living together, and argue that most Americans want to marry and live in nuclear families. These activists also claim that the commune is not a viable alternative family form. They point to historical examples to show that communal experiments have been characterized by instability and problems of internal authoritarianism and inequality, and that in practice, they have failed to achieve the high ideals with which they are associated ideologically.[21] In addition, critics maintain that communes would be an unacceptable alternative to the majority of Americans who value the privacy of the nuclear organization of the family. Finally, some activists suggest that members of society have been discouraged from the effort to make their own nuclear families more egalitarian because of the movement's ideological emphasis on the inherent sexism of the nuclear family form.

Despite these internal disagreements, however, the women's movement's projection of an alternative ideology of the family has challenged the dominant ideological hegemony, exposed the weaknesses of the traditional nuclear family, and encouraged tolerance for the development of a variety of alternative family organizations and structures.

CONCLUSION

This chapter has explored the alternative ideology developed by the women's movement as a challenge to traditional concepts of women and their roles. The importance of an alternative world view for the process of social change rests on its promotion of a new consciousness and its attempt to erode the legitimacy of traditional concepts. The emergent ideological hegemony of the women's movement provided a new vision of women's personality development, of their roles as workers, and of their home and family lives. Differences within the movement are apparent, but taken together, these ideas provide a shared challenge to the dominant traditional view of women and of their place in society.

NOTES

1. Simone de Beauvoir, *The Second Sex* (New York: Knopf, 1952).

2. *Ibid.*, p. *xvii.*

3. Antonio Gramsci, *The Modern Prince and Other Writings* (New York: International Publishers, 1957).

4. Mitchell, *Woman's Estate.* Mitchell includes an interesting discussion of "politicos" and "feminists," some of whose differences are similar to those we have elaborated.

5. Critiques of traditional personality development and socialization from a feminist perspective are voluminous. Among the most interesting are: Judith M. Bardwick and Elizabeth Douvan, "Ambivalence: The Socialization of Women," in Vivian Gornick and Barbara Moran (eds.), *Woman in Sexist Society* (New York: Basic Books, 1971), pp. 147-59; Sandra L. and Daryl J. Bem, "Training the Woman to Know Her Place: The Power of a Non-Conscious Ideology," in M. H. Garskoff (ed.), *Roles Women Play: Readings Toward Women's Liberation* (Belmont: Brooks/Cole, 1971), pp. 84-96; Caroline Bird, "The Androgynous Life," in Mary Lou Thompson (ed.), *Voices of the New Feminism* (Boston: Beacon, 1970), pp. 178-98; Dana Densmore, "On The Temptation to be a Beautiful Object," in Safilios-Rothschild (ed.), *Toward a Sociology of Women*, pp. 96-100; Jo Freeman, "The Building of the Guilded Cage," in Anne Koedt, Ellen Levine, Anita Rapone (eds.), *Radical Feminism* (New York: Quadrangle, 1973), pp. 127-50; Walter R. Gove and Jeanette F. Tudor, "Adult Sex Roles and Mental Illness," in Joan Huber (ed.), *Changing Women in a Changing Society* (Chicago: University of Chicago Press, 1973), pp. 50-73; Naomi Weisstein, " 'Kinde, Kuche, Kirche' as Scientific Law: Psychology Constructs the Female," in Robin Morgan (ed.), *Sisterhood is Powerful* (New York: Random House, 1970), pp. 205-19.

6. Sandra L. Bem, "Probing the Promise of Androgyny," in Alexandra G. Kaplan and Joan P. Bean (eds.), *Beyond Sex Role Stereotypes: Readings Toward a Psychology of Androgyny* (Boston: Little, Brown, 1976), pp. 47-62.

7. In addition to Bem, see Alice Rossi, "Equality between the Sexes: An Immodest Proposal," in Robert Jay Lifton (ed.), *The Woman in America* (Boston: Houghton Mifflin, 1964), pp. 98-143, and Alexandra S. Kaplan and Joan P. Bean (eds.), *Beyond Sex Role Stereotypes.*

8. Warren Farrell, *The Liberated Man: Beyond Masculinity; Freeing Men and Their Relationships with Women* (New York: Random House, 1974).

9. Maccoby (ed.), *Development of Sex Differences*; Maccoby and Jacklin, *Psychology of Sex Differences.*

10. Articles from the wide-ranging literature produced by the women's movement on women and work include: Judith Ann, "The Secretarial Proletariat," in Morgan (ed.), *Sisterhood Is Powerful*, pp. 86-100; Margaret Benston, "Political Economy of Women's Liberation"; Cynthia Fuchs Epstein, "Positive Effects of the Multiple Negative: Explaining the Success of Black Professional Women," in Huber (ed.), *Changing Women in a Changing Society*, pp. 150-73; Hannah Papenek, "Men, Women and Work: Reflections on the Two-Person Career" in *ibid.*, pp. 90-110; Alice Rossi, "Women in Science: Why So Few?" in Safilios-Rothschild (ed.), *Toward a Sociology of Women*, pp. 141-53; Marilyn Saltzman-Webb, "Women as Secretary, Sexpot, Spender, Sow, Civic Actor, Sickie," in Garskoff (ed.), *Roles Women Play*, pp. 7-24; Roslyn Willet, "Working in a Man's World: The Woman Executive," in Gornick and Moran (eds.), *Woman in Sexist Society*, pp. 367-83.

11. "Socialist Feminism: Papers from the New American Movement" (Conference on Feminism and Socialism, Durham, N.C., November 1972); See also, Koedt et al., *Radical Feminism.*

12. The following are selections from women's movement literature that critique the dominant ideology relating to the family and propose alternative models: Jessie Bernard, "The Paradox of the Happy Marriage," in Gornick and Moran (eds.), *Woman in Sexist Society*, pp. 85-98; Laura Berquist, "How Come a Nice Girl Like You Isn't Married," in Safilios-Rothschild (ed.), *Toward a Sociology of Women*, pp. 107-11; Gael Greene, "A Vote Against Motherhood:

A Wife Challenges the Importance of Childbearing" in *ibid.*, pp. 112-15; Cicely Hamilton, "Marriage as a Trade," in Nancy Reeves (ed.), *Womankind: Beyond the Stereotypes* (New York: Aldine, 1971), pp. 204-11; Leo Kanowitz, "Married Women and the Law of Support," in *ibid.*, pp. 221-225; Laurel Limpus, "Sexual Repression and the Family" in *ibid.*, pp. 353-63; Pat Mainardi, "The Politics of Housework," in Morgan (ed.), *Sisterhood is Powerful*, pp. 447-54; Judy Syfers, "Why I Want a Wife," in Koedt et al. (eds.), *Radical Feminism*, pp. 60-63.

13.   Linda Gordon, *Women's Body, Woman's Right: A Social History of Birth Control in America* (New York: Grossman, 1976).

14.   Judith Blake, *Coercive Pronatalism and American Population Policy, Preliminary Papers: Results in Current Research in Demography* (Berkeley: University of California Press, 1972).

15.   Sidney Abbott and Barbara Love, "Is Women's Liberation a Lesbian Plot?" in Gornick and Moran (eds.), *Woman in Sexist Society*, pp. 601-21.

16.   Carole Joffe, *Friendly Intruders: Childcare Professionals and Family Life* (Berkeley: University of California Press, 1977).

17.   Margaret Benston, "Political Economy of Women's Liberation."

18.   Rhona Rapoport and Robert Rapoport, "Changes in the 70s," in *Dual Career Families Re-Examined*, pp. 324-58.

19.   Kanter, *Commitment and Community*.

20.   Holmstrom, *Two-Career Family*; Paloma and Garland, "Myth of the Egalitarian Family."

21.   Kanter, *Commitment and Community*; Rosabeth Moss Kanter (ed.), *Communes: Creating and Managing the Collective Life* (New York: Harper & Row, 1973).

Chapter 9
Conclusion

In concluding this study of women and social change, I want to return to the basic polarities raised in the first chapter: change and stability; material and ideological forces; and macro and micro levels of analysis. I have found that an emphasis on the processes of change best clarifies the profound experiences of women in the last decade and a half. However, this study of women has also suggested that a focus on change must be informed by an understanding of the forces of stability that resist social alteration. With respect to the primacy of ideas or material forces in causing change, I have argued that the latter are the major originating factors. However, material forces can help to generate an ideological challenge to the dominant hegemony, which in turn becomes an important source of change in its own right. Finally the importance of economic development for changes in women's lives led to an emphasis on macro analyses of institutions and social structure. Nonetheless, a complete understanding of women and change has required micro analyses of personality development, personal relationships, and intimate family interaction as well.

CHANGE AND STABILITY

Economic development created pressures for change in women's collective personality in the 1960s. These material pressures were reinforced by the impulse for personality change associated with the alternative ideology articulated by the women's movement. At the same time, however, important aspects of the human personality and the process of socialization militated against any change in the collective female personality.

Material changes, such as declining birth rates and increased female educational attainment and labor force participation, contributed to the emergence of a new collective personality among certain groups of American women in the beginning of the 1960s. The women's movement was largely initiated by these women, many of whom already exhibited the new personality type. Through the movement, they articulated an ideology designed to legitimate this personality and convey it to others. The ideal they envisioned was one of women characterized by independence, competence, and high self-esteem. Some activists even contemplated the complete replacement of traditional masculinity and femininity with androgyny.

However, the emergence of this new collective personality among large numbers of women and the widespread acceptance of the movement's vision of personality change were constrained by forces of stability. One obstacle to change lay in what Freudian theory refers to as the inherent nature of the human personality. Freud argued that behavioral patterns and attitudes inculcated into young children by their parents are extraordinarily resistant to subsequent alteration. Thus, even among those adults who desired to reject traditional femininity and adopt completely new personality aspects, change was often difficult. And even as those adults, as agents of socialization, endeavored to teach nonsexist patterns, they often unconsciously transmitted to their children the traditional goals, values, attitudes, or personality characteristics that they thought they had rejected and abandoned.

Another obstacle to rapid or widespread change in the collective social personality concerns the tensions generated in situations where individuals with different personality types engage in intimate interaction. The family is just such a setting, and pain and disruption were inevitable where parents and children or husbands and wives differed on the model of the collective personality to which they adhered or aspired. For example, daughters with aspirations for independence may have clashed with parents' more traditional ideas of femininity, or husbands may have objected to their wives' newly developed competence or self-confidence. The problems so created could well have been so painful for some people as to induce longings for stability and/or resistance to the model of personality change envisioned by the women's movement.

Change in the personalities of many women and men has surely occurred since the early 1960s. Throughout the society, people have also become aware of an alternative ideology that emphasizes the benefits of new models of personality development and nonsexist socialization. However, the extent and rate of acceptance of a new collective personality for women or men has been slowed by factors that make such changes painful, personally threatening, and sometimes simply impossible.

Even in periods of rapid social change, forces of stability make themselves felt and affect the potential for and the limits of change. The dramatic alterations in women's economic role in American society that have occurred since the 1960s are associated with the rapid economic development and expansion that characterized the postwar period. At the same time, however, other factors have continued to limit the full and equal participation of women in the labor force and the kinds of changes possible in the economic system.

Structural changes in the economy in the form of rising female labor force participation rates contributed to the development of the women's movement, which itself created pressure for further change by its advocacy of new ideas about women and work. The movement sought to legitimate women's labor force participation, to gain equality for women workers, and to marshal support for increasing the responsiveness of economic institutions to human and social needs. For some activists, these changes were tied to the projection of a socialist reorganization of the economy.

Despite the many real far-reaching changes in women's economic position, numerous forces have worked to offset the strong pressures for change, including the traditional burdens of childbearing, and child rearing, which have limited women's ability to participate fully in the economy. Conservative ideas about women's domestic responsibilities and the "masculinity" of work, and the lack of adequate social services that could perform some of women's traditional home roles confined the extent of change that was feasible in their economic roles. Sex-typed occupations, in addition to subtle and not so subtle dicrimination by employers, also constrained and discouraged women's serious commitment to work and careers. Finally, some business firms have continued to enforce hierarchical and alienating forms of labor even in the face of efforts associated with the women's movement to alter the nature of the work experience. Thus, although dramatic changes have been made in women's participation in the labor force and in ideas about women and work, powerful forces have constrained their full and equal participation and have weakened the attempts to initiate more radical changes in the nature of work for both women and men.

A similar interaction between the forces of change and stability can be demonstrated in the area of women's home roles. Economic development has stimulated pervasive changes in all aspects of the family, including the decline in fertility, in the number of full-time housewives, and in the proportion of stable marriages. These material changes, along with others mentioned earlier, contributed to the emergence of the women's movement. Women in the movement who were dissatisfied with the traditional familial patterns of inequality responded to the many changes through which the family was going by calling for further alterations in order to achieve goals of sharing, equality, and freedom in family life. Some even advocated the complete abolition of marriage and of the family.

Alongside these pressures for change, however, were resistant tendencies in the structure of the family and in the traditional ideological hegemony. The dependency of women, which is built into the structure of the traditional nuclear family, is one such influence. For women to make the decision to reject their exclusive family roles was often difficult because they had never had to assume complete economic responsibility for themselves. There was a psychological dimension to this problem as well. As de Beauvoir points out, women's identity has been so closely tied to their social definition as wives and mothers that to choose a nondomestic orientation would require an existential leap.[1] The pain and difficulty of asserting one's own identity, as de Beauvoir notes, have made the retention of the old definition extraordinarily tempting.

A second obstacle to change in the family emanates from the traditional ideological hegemony, which threatens that any change in women's role will destroy not only the family but also the society. Such ideas compromised many people's willingness to weigh seriously the alternative ideas projected by the women's movement or to experiment with changes in their own families. Finally, the widespread cultural suspicion of any change advocated by a social movement was directed toward the movement's proposals for alterations in the family and imposed a severe limit on changes in this direction. In American society, with its highly valued individualism, groups of people in favor of change are often objects of distrust and derision, and a movement's alternative ideology is frequently suspect. Especially when members of a society do not participate in a social movement, they may feel that changes are being "forced" on them, and they therefore resist not only the changes but also the movement's claim to legitimacy. Especially in its early years, the women's movement was plagued by such reactions from both men and women, which seriously restricted its ability to bring about the changes it advocated.

Thus the interaction of factors creating change and those attempting to maintain stability are a constant feature of society. Emphasis on one to the exclusion of the other is not appropriate for a complete social analysis. Although many sources of resistance have slowed or reduced the extent of changes in women's roles since the sixties, there is nonetheless convincing evidence of widespread social change. The process of economic development and the material changes it involved have altered women's lives and also helped to generate a social movement that challenged the dominant ideological hegemony.

IDEOLOGY AND MATERIAL FORCES

Just as I have emphasized change but also sought to elucidate the forces of stability, so too I have argued for the primacy of material sources of social change while also pointing to the contribution of ideology. What light does this study shed on the interaction and limits of material and ideological forces of change?

Technological, material changes stimulate myriad alterations in social institutions and in the roles, personal lives, and social positions of society's members. Once set in motion, these material forces exert continued pressure for further changes in the society in two ways. First, they generate tensions and contradictions because of the unevenness with which they affect various institutions and different aspects of individuals' lives; these tensions constitute independent pressures for change, as members of society attempt to resolve them. Second, material changes may trigger the emergence of a social movement, which may in turn alter society's norms, values, and ways of thinking by its challenge to the dominant ideology and its articulation of an alternative world view. Although material forces are the major long-term source of social change, they generate pressures for change in the realm of ideas as well, which can both reinforce and extend the process of social change.

Many examples of the continued pressure for change exerted by the contradictions and inconsistencies associated with prior technological changes can be found in the experience of women after 1960. One such example concerns women's increasing labor force participation and the rise in divorce rates with which it was associated. These dramatic changes in women's lives also brought new social problems, as large numbers of divorced women, many with young children, confronted the low pay, high levels of unemployment, and slow advancement characteristic of women's overall labor force position. In addition, tensions and crises were created as employed mothers were unable to find or pay for adequate alternative care for their children.[2] Thus a contradiction emerged between the rapid changes occurring in some aspects of women's lives—divorce and employment—and the lack of change in other important areas—social provision of adequate child care and equality between the sexes in the labor force. The unevenness of change caused social and personal problems for large numbers of individuals, and the existence of these new problems in turn created pressure for change, as individuals tried to find solutions for themselves and others.

A second way in which material changes in society can exert continued pressure for broad social change is through their contribution to the creation of self-conscious social movements. Unlike material forces, which most often function without the conscious guidance or often even the awareness of the members of the society, the pressures for change generated by a social movement are widely apparent. The rise of a movement often signals the development of a well-formulated ideology that presents to society an alternative set of norms, values, and ideas. In a modern society, the ability of social movements to project their ideas and visions of change is enormous because the all-pervasive media network can transmit these ideas—even if it disapproves of them— to a large proportion of the population through newspapers, magazines, and especially television. Thus it often seems as if the social movement and its ideological challenges are the sole sources of change. Less frequently recognized by supporters and opponents of the movement are the material alterations that gave birth to the movement itself and that often continue to exert pressure for change independent of the conscious action of movement participants. However, the importance of material changes that generated and continue to reinforce the ideological challenge posed by the movement does not diminish the importance of that alternative ideology as a force for change in its own right.

Alterations in women's lives since the early 1960s have resulted from the interaction and reinforcement of material changes and the women's movement's articulation of a new ideology. In fact, their interaction in any given change that has occurred in women's position in society is so complex that their individual contributions are impossible to disentangle. However, the limits of each contribution by itself, without the reinforcement of the other, can be seen more easily.

Ideological pressures for social change can be extraordinarily important in reinforcing and furthering material changes. On the one hand, without the introduction of alternative ideologies, traditional ideas and beliefs constitute potent counter influences that may alter the nature of or undermine material changes. In a previous section I mentioned the retarding effects on change in women's lives resulting from traditional views of the family and of women's homebound roles. However, challenges to that hegemony, posed by an alternative ideology, may serve to lessen its negative impact on change. Furthermore, strong ideological challenges to traditional belief systems can exert an independent positive force for social change. By projecting an attractive vision of the future, a new ideology may motivate individuals to accept and/or to press for the realization of that future. By appealing to the imagination, alternative ideologies may trigger hopes and dreams that are normally repressed in the routine of coping with daily life. In the case of the women's movement, the projected benefits of an androgynous collective personality, for example, may bring to consciousness some desires and characteristics that were repressed in childhood as inappropriate to traditional masculinity or femininity. Similarly, the movement's model of creative and non-alienating work roles might stimulate the desire for craftsmanship and control over the process of production presently denied by the hierarchical and bureaucratized organization of work. Both the desire to achieve a different and better future and the release of longings that have been repressed may be stimulated by the articulation of an alternative ideology.

The new belief system formulated by a social movement may also play an intermediary role in social change by strengthening those material changes that are weak or those that tend to be transient in nature. The changes in women's lives resulting from declining fertility rates is an appropriate example of this. Demographers agree that birth rates tend to move in cyclical patterns. Thus the increased possibilities for women's liberation triggered by declining birth rates in the early 1960s could later be threatened by an upward movement in the birth rate. However, changes in ideology that legitimate egalitarian social roles for women might mean that a commitment to women's liberation would continue even if material pressure in the form of low birth rates ends.

The same argument can be made with respect to women's role in economic change. I have suggested that increases in female labor force participation rates in the last two decades have been closely associated with pressures for change in women's secondary status in society. Both the supply of and demand for labor in a capitalist society, however, are subject to cyclical trends. Thus, a continued increase in or even the stabilization of female employment cannot be assured. A decline in woman's labor force participation could represent a threat to the gains women have made in obtaining equality. If however, a new ideology of equality for women were legitimated and accepted by the society, it might serve to offset pressures to abandon the struggle for women's liberation.

Thus an alternative ideology can exert pressure for change independent of the continuation of the material factors from which it originally emerged. Without the reinforcement of new beliefs, material changes, although potent, are less likely to create and sustain change and less likely to produce the kinds of changes that are most fulfilling to society's members. With the projection of a future vision on the part of a social movement, however, individuals can consciously attempt to influence and alter society according to patterns that they believe would be beneficial. The women's movement, which was stimulated by material changes in the society, articulated the vision of an egalitarian and free society that would allow the full development of human potential among men and women. The vision of this future constituted an independent and reinforcing source of social change.

Just as material changes alone have limitations with respect to the extent and nature of the social changes they can produce, so too a new ideology must be continually reinforced by material alterations if it is to be maximally effective in creating pressure for change. The acceptance of a new set of beliefs can sometimes mask the retention of traditional institutions, social structures, or relationships. Harriet Holter argues that as the ideology of equality between men and women has been popularly embraced, inequality merely went underground, manifesting itself in personal and psychological relationships.[3] Holter also suggests that the superficial acceptance of a new ideological hegemony on the part of social elites or governments may be an attempt to give the impression of rapid social change while preserving stability. For example, their adoption of the idea of equality between the sexes may be an attempt to mask their failure to supply the significant social resources required to attain that goal.

This process of course may not be purposely deceitful. Komarovsky's interviews with male college seniors testifies to the ability of individuals to give lip service to new ideas while at the same time unknowingly retaining traditional ones.[4] Her subjects largely maintained that they accepted the equality of women and men and expected that their wives would be engaged in careers. At the same time, however, most of these same young men strongly believed that children should be reared by their own mothers, that day care centers could not be adequate substitutes for maternal care, and that they would not be willing to compromise their careers by promoting their wives' careers or taking responsibility for rearing their children. Clearly their ideas about child care and women's roles contradict their beliefs in egalitarian marital relationships. Thus, although there may be widespread verbal support for alternative ideas and seeming acceptance of a new hegemony, in fact the structure of the society or various aspects of personal relationships may have altered very little, and older ideas may remain latent. The ease with which new beliefs are accepted may divert attention from the material changes that are necessary for substantive social change to be achieved. Social movements, as primary carriers of new ideologies, must recognize the danger of relying on ideas as a source of social change without the continued reinforcement of material and structural changes.

Widespread changes in women's economic and family roles and in their personal lives and identities since the early 1960s have been both the involuntary result of economic development and also the conscious product of a social movement. The interaction and reinforcement of these forces has made change rapid, dramatic, and visible to, if not approved by, most members of American society. Much of the material impetus for change preceded and contributed to the emergence of the women's movement and its projection of an egalitarian, nonsexist society. It is likely, however, that only the continued struggle by participants in that movement can achieve the fulfillment of their vision of a good society.

MACRO AND MICRO ANALYSES

The various aspects of women's lives explored in this study reflect the importance of both macro and micro levels of analysis. An overview of society or an institution may be obtained by examining phenomena on a macro level. The process of economic development, for example, is a concept that encompasses change in the society as a whole. At the same time, however, change on the macro level of the society represents the clustering of individual decisions and reflects factors that can be best explained by reference to the individuals' desire for or resistance to change.

With respect to women's personality development and socialization, the macro level analysis employs the concept of a collective social personality, that is, a set of personality characteristics that are shared by members of the society. An examination of traditional personality characteristics of adult women in American society reveals similarities in their shared passivity, low self-esteem, dependence, and low achievement orientation. The period after 1960 was characterized by the emergence of a new collective personality with new definitions of femininity. This change in social definition of the collective female personality was an important source of the rise of the women's movement, which then reinforced and attempted to gain legitimacy for and adoption of the new model of female personality development.

Micro analysis of personality and change emphasizes the nature of socialization and personality development on an individual level, offering a discussion of the intimate interactions that mold individual members of the society. Freudian theory clarifies the powerful role of parents, for example, in repressing in daughters those personality attributes that do not conform to society's acceptable model of femininity. The physical power of a child's parents and their ability to withdraw the love on which their child is almost completely dependent renders them extraordinarily influential in this socialization process. Later in her personal development, a girl receives negative sanctions for "nonfeminine" behavior from other agencies of socialization—peer groups, teachers, models from literature, movies, and television—to which she looks for identity and social definition. Thus on a personal level, a girl experiences different individuals and groups who attempt to induce or coerce her to internalize and conform to the culturally accepted collective model of femininity.

Challenges to or changes in traditional conceptions of the collective social personality are also experienced on the individual level. Personal relationships between male and female activists in the New Left in the early 1960s provided an important motivation for individual women to form a separate group dedicated to new models of femininity and personal development. In another example, the personal anger and tension generated in a woman who was treated both as a competent professional and as a woman with secondary status may have been important in her decision to become an active supporter of NOW and to seek legitimation for new definitions of femininity. Thus a micro understanding of individual sources of personality development and of individual motivations to seek actively an alternative identity, and a macro analysis of the characteristics of the traditional collective female personality and the emergence of a new model of femininity together are necessary for a comprehensive examination of this important aspect of women's lives.

With respect to the economy, the macro analysis emphasizes the crucial part played by economic development in altering women's economic role in society. Women's labor force participation rates have risen slowly in the past and more rapidly since 1960, as the economy demanded more labor and as women more frequently were able and willing to supply themselves as workers. The supply and demand factors associated with the movement of women into paid employment indicate the existence of widespread changes in the economic structure of society. These changes contributed to the emergence of the women's movement, which in turn exerted its own pressure for change in the economy in general and in women's economic position in particular. On the macro level, the movement sought to legitimate the ideas of female labor force participation, of economic equality for women, and of a more responsive and democratic organization of the economy.

These major trends and pressures for change were also experienced on the micro level. Increases in female labor force participation rates represent the individual decisions of women to seek paid work. A woman is influenced in her decision to seek employment by a number of factors, including the number and ages of her children, how much money she can earn, her husband's attitude (if she is married), the availability and extent of other sources of income, and the availability of suitable work.[5] Similarly, an analysis of micro-level experiences can offer insights into the formation of attitudes, for example, toward the women's movement. Personal experiences at work may be central to a woman's decision to support or even become active in such a social movement. The belief that she is denied a promotion or paid less than a male colleague because of her sex may trigger investigation of and commitment to the alternative ideology advanced by the women's movement.

Finally, the macro analysis of the family in this book stresses the defining characteristics of and the changes central to this social institution. Changes in the institution of the family that are associated with long-term economic development can be expressed on the macro level as, for example, an increase in the divorce rate, a decline in the birth rate, or a rise in female-headed families or communal living arrangements. My analysis emphasizes the breakdown of the traditional nuclear family and the emergence of other family forms. Changes in family structure contributed to the rise of the women's movement and to the formulation of its alternative view of the family. This ideological challenge to traditional ideas reinforced and legitimated experimentation with and tolerance of changing familial norms and structures.

The family, which can be analyzed as a social institution on a macro level, is of course experienced by each of us in the most intimate and personal terms. For example, since birth rates reflect the clustering of individual decisions with respect to fertility, an analysis of the components of that decision on an individual level provide important insights. Similarly, while the individual decision to divorce a spouse contributes to general trends, it may be experienced by an individual woman as personal pain, anxiety or hope. Her personal decision is influenced by factors specific to her, such as the ages and number of her children, her ability to earn income, the importance to her of religious sanctions, or her own idea of the ideal amount of love and respect in a marital relationship. Finally, intimate family experiences may also be reflected in individual attitudes toward the alternative ideology formulated by the women's movement. A girl's experience of her mother's abuse or belittling at the hands of her father, for example, may increase the attractiveness to her of the movement's model of competent and independent women or of the movement's ideology of egalitarian marriage and mutual respect between husbands and wives. A daughter's personal family experience, then, may contribute to her later commitment to or activism in the creation of social change on the macro level of the society as a whole.

The changes in women's lives that led to the emergence of the women's movement in the 1960s were most often experienced as individual changes or as personal strains. At the same time, however, those changes in personality and economic and family roles were part of widespread alterations associated with long-term economic development. The women's movement itself, on a macro level, was an important new source of pressure for social change in women's lives and in the society as a whole. Most often, however, commitment to the movement and to its vision of a truly liberated and egalitarian society was experienced on an intimate and personal level as a way of creating a better and more meaningful life for women and men in the society they share.

NOTES

1. De Beauvoir, *The Second Sex*.
2. Ross and Sawhill, *Time of Transition*.
3. Harriet Holter, *Sex Roles and Social Structure* (Oslo: Universitetsforlaget, 1970).
4. Mirra Komarovsky, "Images of Femininity and Masculinity: Beliefs, Norms, and Preferences," in Komarovsky, *Dilemmas of Masculinity: A Study of College Youth* (New York: W. W. Norton, 1976), pp. 10-44.
5. Nye and Hoffman, *Employed Mother*, pp. 18-39.

Selected Bibliography

THEORY AND SOCIAL CHANGE

Allport, Gordon W. *The Nature of Prejudice.* New York: Doubleday, 1954.

Anderson, C. Arnold, and Bowman, Mary Jean (eds.). *Education and Economic Development.* Chicago: Aldine, 1965.

Anderson, Charles H. *Toward a New Sociology.* Homewood: Dorsey Press, 1975.

Barber, Bernard, and Inkeles, Alex. *Stability and Social Change.* Boston: Little, Brown, 1971.

Barnes, Henry Elmer. *An Introduction to the History of Sociology.* Chicago: University of Chicago Press, 1948.

Blumer, Herbert. "Social Movements." In Alfred McClung Lee (ed.), *Principles of Sociology* (New York: Barnes and Noble, 1946), pp. 199-222.

Bosserup, Esther. *Women's Role in Economic Development.* New York: St. Martin's Press, 1970.

Bottomore, Tom. *Marxist Sociology.* London: Macmillan, 1975.

Braverman, Harry. *Labor and Monopoly Capital: The Degradation of Work in the Twentieth Century.* New York: Monthly Review Press, 1974.

Dahrendorf, R. "Out of Utopia: Toward a Reorientation of Sociological Analysis." *American Journal of Sociology,* 64 (1958):115-27.

Domhoff, G. William. *Who Rules America.* Englewood Cliffs: Prentice-Hall, 1967.

Easterlin, Richard A. "Economic Growth: An Overview." In *The International Encyclopedia of the Social Sciences* (New York: Macmillan, 1968), 4:395-408.

Eisenstadt, S. N. *Revolution and the Transformation of Societies.* New York: Free Press, 1978.

Flacks, Richard. "The Liberated Generation: An Exploration of the Roots of Student Protest." *Journal of Social Issues,* 23 (1967):52-75.

————. *Youth and Social Change.* Chicago: Markham, 1971.

Gerth, H., and Mills, C. W. *From Max Weber: Essays in Sociology.* New York: Oxford University Press, 1958.

Gouldner, Alvin. *The Coming Crisis of Western Sociology.* New York: Basic Books, 1970.

Gramsci, Antonio. *The Modern Prince and Other Writings.* New York: International Publishers, 1957.

Keniston, Kenneth. *The Uncommitted.* New York: Delta, 1960.

————. *Young Radicals.* New York: Harcourt, 1968.

Kuznets, Simon. *Population, Capital and Growth.* New York: W. W. Norton, 1973.

Lenski, Gerhard. "Status Crystallization: A Non-vertical Dimension of Social Status." *American Sociological Review,* 19 (1954):405-13.

Martindale, Don. *The Nature and Types of Sociological Theory.* Boston: Houghton Mifflin, 1960.

Marx, Karl. *Capital: A Critique of Political Economy.* New York: International Publishers, 1973.

————, and Engels, Frederick. *The Communist Manifesto.* New York: International Publishers, 1948.

Mills, C. Wright. *The Sociological Imagination.* New York: Oxford University Press, 1959.

Moore, W. E. *Social Change.* 2d ed. Englewood Cliffs: Prentice-Hall, 1974.

Nisbet, Robert A. *The Sociological Tradition.* New York: Basic Books, 1966.

Ogburn, William F. *Social Change with Respect to Culture and Original Nature*. New York: Viking Press, 1950.
Parsons, Talcott. *The Social System*. Glencoe: Free Press, 1951.
―――― (ed.). *The Theory of Social and Economic Organization*. Glencoe: Free Press, 1957.
――――. *Societies: Evolutionary and Comparative Perspectives*. Englewood Cliffs: Prentice-Hall, 1966.
Russell, Bertrand. *A History of Western Philosophy*. New York: Simon & Schuster, 1945.
Sicherman, Barbara. "American History: A Review Essay." *Signs*, 1 (1975):461-86.
Slater, Philip. *The Pursuit of Loneliness*. Boston: Beacon Press, 1970.
Smelser, Neil. *Social Change in the Industrial Revolution: An Application of Theory to the British Cotton Industry*. Chicago: University of Chicago Press, 1959.
Tucker, Robert C. (ed.). *Marx-Engels Reader*. New York: W. W. Norton, 1972.
Weber, Max. *The Protestant Ethic and the Spirit of Capitalism*. Ed., Talcott Parsons. New York: Charles Scribner's Sons, 1958.

WOMEN AND MEN

Bebel, August. *Women Under Socialism*. New York: Schocken, 1971.
Bird, Caroline. *Born Female*. New York: David McKay, 1968.
Cade, Toni (ed.). *The Black Woman*. New York: Signet, 1970.
Cohart, Mary (ed.). *Unsung Champions of Women*. Albuquerque: University of New Mexico Press, 1975.
de Beauvoir, Simone. *The Second Sex*. New York: Knoof, 1952.
Farrell, Warren. *The Liberated Man: Beyond Masculinity; Freeing Men and Their Relationships with Women*. New York: Random House, 1974.
Filene, Peter. *Him/Her/Self*. New York: Harcourt Brace Jovanovich, 1975.
Freeman, Jo (ed.). *Women: A Feminist Perspective*. Palo Alto: Mayfield Publishers, 1975.
Freidl, Ernestine. *Women and Men: An Anthropologist's View*. New York: Holt, Rinehart and Winston, 1975.
Friedan, Betty. *The Feminine Mystique*. New York: W. W. Norton, 1963.
Gornick, Vivian, and Moran, Barbara (eds.). *Woman in Sexist Society*. New York: Basic Books, 1971.
Harris, Louis. *The Virginia Slims American Women's Opinion Poll*. 1970; 1972; 1974.
Holter, Harriet. *Sex Roles and Social Structure*. Oslo: Universitetsforlaget, 1970.
Huber, Joan (ed.). *Changing Women in a Changing Society*. Chicago: University of Chicago Press, 1973.
Kanowitz, L. *Women and the Law*. Albuquerque: University of New Mexico Press, 1969.
Lader, Lawrence. *Abortion II*. Boston: Beacon, 1974.
Ladner, Joyce. *Tomorrow's Tomorrow*. New York: Anchor, 1971.
Lifton, Robert Jay (ed.). *The Woman in America*. Boston: Houghton Mifflin, 1964.
Malbin, Nona Glazer, and Wachrer, Helen Youngelson (eds.). *Woman in a Man-Made World*. New York: Rand McNally, 1973.
Mead, Margaret. "Adolescence in Primitive and Modern Society." in V. F. Calverton and S. D. Schmalhausen (eds.), *The New Generation* (New York: Macauley, 1930), pp. 169-88.
――――. *Sex and Temperament in Three Primitive Cultures*. New York: Morrow, 1963.
Millet, Kate. *Sexual Politics*. New York: Doubleday, 1970.
Mitchell, Juliet. *Woman's Estate*. New York: Pantheon, 1971.
Oakley, Ann. *Sex, Gender and Society*. New York: Harper & Row, 1972.
Pleck, Joseph H., and Sawyer, Jack (eds.). *Men and Masculinity*. Englewood Cliffs: Prentice-Hall, 1974.
Reeves, Nancy (ed.). *Womankind: Beyond the Stereotypes*. New York: Aldine, 1971.

Rossi, Alice, and Calderwood, Ann (eds.). *Academic Women on the Move.* New York: Russell Sage Foundation, 1973.
—————. (ed.). *Essays on Sex Equality: John Stuart Mill and Harriet Taylor Mill.* Chicago: University of Chicago Press, 1970.
—————. (ed.). *The Feminist Papers from Adams to de Beauvoir.* New York: Bantam Books, 1974.
Roszak, Betty and Theodore (eds.). *Masculine/Feminine: Readings in Sexual Mythology and the Liberation of Women.* New York: Harper & Row, 1969.
Safilios-Rothschild, Constantina (ed.). *Toward a Sociology of Women.* Lexington: Xerox, 1972.
Walter, Barbara. "The Cult of True Womanhood, 1820-1860." *American Quarterly,* 18 (1966): 151-74.
Wollstonecraft, Mary. *A Vindication of the Rights of Women.* New York: W. W. Norton, 1967.

PERSONALITY

Aberle, David F., and Naegele, Kaspar D. "Middle Class Fathers' Occupational Role and Attitudes towards Children." *American Journal of Orthopsychiatry,* 22 (1952):366-78.
Broverman, Inge; Vogel, Susan; Broverman, Donald; Clarkson, Frank; and Rosencrantz, Paul. "Sex Role Stereotypes: A Current Appraisal." *Journal of Social Issues,* 28 (1972): 59-78.
—————. et al. "Sex Role Stereotypes and Clinical Judgments of Mental Health." *Journal of Consulting and Clinical Psychology,* 34 (1970):1-7.
Brown, Roger. *Social Psychology.* New York: Free Press, 1965.
Chesler, Phyllis. *Women and Madness.* New York: Avon, 1972.
Coleman, James. *The Adolescent Society.* New York: Free Press, 1961.
Courtney, Alice E., and Whipple, Thomas W. "Women in T.V. Commercials." *Journal of Communication,* 24, no. 2 (1974):110-18.
Endelman, Robert (ed.). *Personality and Social Life.* New York: Random House, 1967.
Erikson, Erik. *Childhood and Society.* 2d ed. New York: W. W. Norton, 1963.
—————. *Identity, Youth and Crisis.* New York: W. W. Norton, 1968.
—————. *Young Man Luther: A Study in Psychoanalysis and History.* New York: W. W. Norton, 1972.
Freud, Sigmund. *Civilization and its Discontents.* New York: W. W. Norton, 1961.
—————. *New Introductory Lectures on Psychoanalysis.* New York: W. W. Norton, 1965.
—————. *Standard Edition of the Complete Psychological Works of Sigmund Freud.* London: Hogarth Press, 1964.
Gardner, Jo Ann. "Sesame Street and Sex Role Stereotypes." *Women,* 1 (1970):10-14.
Goldberg, Phillip. "Are Women Prejudiced Against Women?" *Transaction,* 5 (1968):28-30.
Goodenough, Elizabeth. "Interest in Persons as an Aspect of Sex Differences in the Early Years." *Genetic Psychology Monographs,* 55 (1957):287-323.
Johnson, Miriam M. "Sex Role Learning in the Nuclear Family." *Child Development,* 34 (1963):319-33.
Kaplan, Alexandra G., and Bean, Joan P. (eds.). *Beyond Sex Role Stereotypes: Readings Toward a Psychology of Androgyny.* Boston: Little, Brown, 1976.
Komarovsky, Mirra. "Images of Femininity and Masculinity: Beliefs, Norms, and Preferences." In *Dilemmas of Masculinity: A Study of College Youth* (New York: W. W. Norton, 1976), pp. 10-44.
LaBarre, Weston. "The Cultural Basis of Emotions and Gestures." In Gerald Starr (ed.), *Social Structure and Personality* (Boston: Little, Brown, 1974), pp. 74-80.
Lakoff, Robin. *Language and Woman's Place.* New York: Harper & Row, 1975.

Levinson, Richard. "From Olive Oyl to Sweet Polly Purebred: Sex Role Stereotypes and Televised Cartoons." *Journal of Popular Culture*, 9 (1975):561-72.
Lewis, Michael. "Parents and Children: Sex Role Development." *School Review*, 80 (1972): 228-40.
Maccoby, Eleanor E. (ed.). *The Development of Sex Differences*. Stanford: Stanford University Press, 1966.
_____, and Jacklin, Carol N. (eds.). *The Psychology of Sex Differences*. Stanford: Stanford University Press, 1974.
Marcuse, Herbert. *Eros and Civilization: A Philosophic Inquiry into Freud*. Boston: Beacon, 1955.
Maslow, Abraham. *Motivation and Personality*. New York: Harper & Row, 1954.
Mednick, M.T.S.; Tangri, S. S.; and Hoffman, L. W. (eds.). *Women and Achievement*. New York: Wiley, 1975.
Mitchell, Juliet. *Psychoanalysis and Feminism*. New York: Pantheon, 1974.
Money, John, and Ekhardt, Anke. *Man and Woman, Boy and Girl*. Baltimore; Johns Hopkins University Press, 1972.
Nakamura, C. Y., and Rogers, M. M. "Parents Expectations of Autonomous Behavior and Children's Autonomy." *Developmental Psychology*, 1 (1969):613-17.
Nash, Sharon C. "The Relationship among Sex-Role Stereotyping, Sex Role Preference, and Sex Differences in Spatial Visualization." *Sex Roles*, 1 (1975):15-32.
Riesman, David. *The Lonely Crowd: A Study of the Changing American Character*. New Haven: Yale University Press, 1950.
Rosenberg, Florence, and Simmons, Roberta. "Sex Differences in Self-Concept at Adolescence." *Sex Roles*, 1 (1975):147-59.
Shaw, M. C., and McCuen, J. T. "The Onset of Academic Underachievement in Bright Children." *Journal of Educational Psychology*, 51 (1960):103-8.
Thorne, Barrie, and Henley, Nancy (eds.). *Language and Sex: Difference and Dominance*. Rowley: Newbury House, 1975.
Vaughter, Reesa M. "Psychology: Review Essay." *Signs*, 2 (1976)120-46.
Weitzman, Lenore, et al. "Sex Role Socialization in Picture Books for Pre-School Children." *American Journal of Sociology*, 77, no. 6 (1972):125-50.
Wrong, Dennis. "The Oversocialized Conception of Man in Modern Sociology." *American Sociological Review*, 26 (1961):183-93.

ECONOMY AND EDUCATION

Bowen, William G., and Finegan, T. Aldrich. *The Economics of Labor Force Participation*. Princeton: Princeton University Press, 1969.
Blaxall, Martha, and Reagan, Barbara (eds.). *Women and the Workplace: The Implications of Occupational Segregation*. Chicago: University of Chicago Press, 1976.
Bowles, Samuel, and Gintis, Herbert. *Schooling in Capitalist America*. New York: Basic Books, 1976.
Cain, Glen. *Married Women in the Labor Force: An Economic Analysis*. Chicago: University of Chicago Press, 1966.
Chapman, Jane Roberts (ed.). *Economic Independence for Women: The Foundation for Equal Rights*. Beverly Hills: Sage, 1976.
Clark, Alice. *The Working Life of Women in the Seventeenth Century*. New York: E. P. Dutton, 1919.
Douvan, Elizabeth, and Kay, Carol. "Motivational Factors in College Entrance." In Nevitt Sanford, (ed.), *The American College* (New York: Wiley, 1962), pp. 199-224.
Epstein, Cynthia F. *Woman's Place: Options and Limits in Professional Careers*. Berkeley: University of California Press, 1970.
Frazier, Nancy, and Sadlek, Myra. *Sexism in School and Society*. New York: Harper & Row, 1973.

Fuchs, Victor. "Differences in Hourly Earnings between Men and Women." *Monthly Labor Review*, 94, no. 5 (1971):9-15.

Gilman, Charlotte Perkins. *Women and Economics: A Study of the Economic Relation between Men and Women as a Factor in Social Evolution*. Boston: Maynard Press, 1900.

Gordon, David M. *Theories of Poverty and Underemployment*. Lexington: D.C. Heath, 1972.

Halsey, A. H., et al. (eds.). *Education, Economy and Society: A Reader in the Sociology of Education*. New York: Free Press, 1961.

Howe, Louise. *Pink Collar Workers*. New York: Putnam, 1977.

Kahne, Hilda, and Kohen, Andrew I. "Review Essay: Economic Perspectives on the Roles of Women in the American Economy." *Journal of Economic Literature*, 13 (1975): 1249-92.

Kanter, Rosabeth Moss. *Men and Women of the Corporation*. New York: Basic Books, 1974.

Kreps, Juanita. *Sex in the Marketplace*. Baltimore: Johns Hopkins University Press, 1971.

——— (ed.). *Women and the American Economy*. Englewood Cliffs: Prentice-Hall, 1976.

Lipman-Blumen, Jean. "Role De-Differentiation as a System Response to Crisis: Occupational and Political Roles of Women." *Sociological Inquiry*, 43 (1973):105-29.

Mason, K. O. *Women's Labor Force Participation and Fertility*. Research Triangle: Research Triangle Press, 1974.

Oppenheimer, Valerie Kincade. *The Female Labor Force in the United States: Demographic and Economic Factors Governing its Growth and Changing Composition. Population Monograph No. 5*. Berkeley: University of California Institute of International Studies, 1970.

Pinchbeck, Ivy. *Women Workers and the Industrial Revolution, 1750-1850*. London: George Routledge and Sons, Ltd., 1930.

Roby, Pamela. "Structural and Internalized Barriers to Women in Higher Education." In Safilios-Rothschild, (ed.), *Toward a Sociology of Women*, pp. 121-140.

Rossi, Alice. "Job Discrimination and What Women Can Do About It." *Atlantic*, 225 (March 1970):99.

Smuts, Robert W. *Women and Work in America*. New York: Columbia University Press, 1959.

Suter, Larry E., and Miller, Herman P. "Income Differences between Men and Career Women." *American Journal of Sociology*, 78 (1973):962-74.

Sweet, James A. *Women in the Labor Force*. New York: Seminar Press, 1973.

U.S. Department of Labor. *Women Workers Today*. Washington, D.C.: Women's Bureau, 1976.

Women's Bureau. *1965 Handbook on Women Workers. Bulletin No. 290*. Washington, D.C.: U.S. Department of Labor, *1965*.

FAMILY

Aries, Philippe. *Centuries of Childhood: A Social History of Family Life*. New York: Random House, 1962.

Banks, J.A. and Olive. *Feminism and Family Planning*. New York: Schocken, 1964.

Becker, Gary S. "An Economic Analysis of Fertility." In *Demographic and Economic Change in Developed Countries: A Conference of the Universities-National Bureau Committee for Economic Research* (Princeton: Princeton University Press, 1960), pp. 209-31.

Bernard, Jessie. *The Future of Motherhood*. New York: Penguin, 1974.

Bettleheim, Bruno. *Children of the Dream*. New York: Macmillan, 1969.

Billingsly, Andrew. *Black Families in White America*. Englewood Cliffs: Prentice-Hall, 1969.

Blake, Judith. *Coercive Pronatalism and American Population Policy, Preliminary Papers: Results in Current Research in Demography* (Berkeley: University of California Press, 1972).

Brown, Carol A.; Feldberg, Roslyn; Fox, Elizabeth; and Kohen, Janet. "Divorce: Chance of a New Lifetime." *Journal of Social Issues*, 32 (1976):119-34.

Chapman, J. R., and Gates, M. *Women into Wives*. Beverly Hills: Sage, 1977.

Dinitz, Simon; Dyney, Russell; and Clarke, Alfred. "Preferences for Male or Female Children: Traditional or Affectional." *Marriage and Family Living*, 16 (1954):128-30.

Easterlin, Richard A. "The Economics and Sociology of Fertility: A Synthesis." Unpublished paper prepared for the Seminar on Early Industrialization, Shifts in Fertility and Changes in Family Structure, Princeton University, June 1972.

Engels, Frederick. *The Origin of the Family, Private Property and the State.* New York: International Publishers, 1973.

Glick, Paul C. *American Families.* New York: Wiley, 1957.

Goode, William. *World Revolution of Family Patterns.* New York: Free Press, 1963.

Gordon, Linda. *Woman's Body, Woman's Right: A Social History of Birth Control in America.* New York: Grossman, 1976.

Hayghe, Howard. *Families and the Rise of Working Wives.* U S. Department of Labor, Special Force Report No. 189. Washington, D.C., 1976.

Hoffman, Lois W., and Nye, F. Ivan (eds.). *Working Mothers.* San Francisco: Jossey Bass, 1974.

Holmstrom, Lynda Lytle. *The Two-Career Family.* Cambridge: Schenkman, 1972.

Joffe, Carol. *Friendly Intruders: Childcare Professionals and Family Life.* Berkeley: University of California Press, 1977.

Kanter, Rosabeth Moss. *Commitment and Community: Communes and Utopias in Sociological Perspective.* Cambridge, Mass.: Harvard University Press, 1972.

————. *Work and the Family in the United States.* New York: Russell Sage Foundation, 1977.

Komarovsky, Mirra. *Blue Collar Marriage.* New York: Random House, 1962.

Lopata, Helena Z. *Occupation: Housewife.* New York: Oxford University Press, 1971.

Moore, Barrington, Jr. "Thoughts on the Future of the Family." In *Political Power and Social Theory: Six Studies* Cambridge, Mass.: Harvard University Press, 1958.

Moynihan, Daniel P. *The Negro Family: The Case for National Action.* Washington, D. C.: U.S. Department of Labor, Office of Planning and Research, 1965.

Norton, Arthur J., and Glick, Paul C. "Marital Instability: Past, Present and Future." *Journal of Social Issues*, 32 (1976):5-20.

Nye, F. Ivan, and Hoffman, Lois W. (eds.). *The Employed Mother in America.* Chicago: Rand McNally, 1963.

Oakley, Ann. *The Sociology of Housework.* New York: Pantheon, 1974.

————. *Woman's Work: The Housewife, Past and Present.* New York: Random House, 1976.

Paloma, Margaret, and Garland, T. Neal. "The Myth of the Egalitarian Family: Familial Roles and the Professionally Employed Wife." Paper presented at the 65th Annual Meeting of the American Sociological Association, September 1970.

Parsons, Talcott, and Bales, Robert F. *Family, Socialization and Interaction Process.* Glencoe: Free Press, 1955.

Rainwater, Lee, and Weinstein, Karol. *And the Poor Get Children.* Chicago: Quadrangle, 1960.

————, and Yancey, William. *The Moynihan Report and the Politics of Controversy.* Cambridge, Mass.: MIT Press, 1967.

————; Coleman, Richard; and Handel, Gerald. *Workingman's Wife: Her Personality, World and Life Style.* New York: Oceana, 1959.

Rapoport, Rhona and Robert. *Dual Career Families Re-Examined.* New York: Harper & Row, 1977.

Ross, Heather L., and Sawhill, Isabel V. *Time of Transition: The Growth of Families Headed by Women.* Washington, D.C.: The Urban Institute, 1975.

Rubin, Lillian. *Worlds of Pain: Life in the Working Class Family.* New York: Basic Books, 1977.

Shorter, Edward. *The Making of the Modern Family.* New York: Basic Books, 1975.

Skolnick, Arlene. *The Intimate Environment.* Boston: Little, Brown, 1973.

Skolnick, Arlene and Jerome (eds.). *Family in Transition.* Boston: Little Brown, 1971.

Stack, Carol. *All Our Kin: Strategies for Survival in a Black Community.* New York: Harper & Row, 1974.

Staples, Robert. "Toward a Sociology of the Black Family: A Theoretical and Methodological Assessment." *Journal of Marriage and the Family*, 33 (1971):119-35.

Stein, Peter J. *Single*. Englewood Cliffs: Prentice-Hall, 1976.
Talmon, Yonina. *Family and Community in the Kibbutz*. Cambridge, Mass.: Harvard University Press, 1972.
Whelpton, Pascal K.; Campbell, Arthur A.; and Patterson John E. *Fertility and Family Planning in the United States* Princeton: Princeton University Press, 1966.
Young, Michael, and Willmott, Peter. *The Symmetrical Family*. New York: Penguin, 1977.
Zaretsky, Eli. *Capitalism, the Family and Personal Life*. New York: Harper & Row, 1976.

WOMEN'S MOVEMENT

Allen, Pamela. *Free Space: A Perspective on the Small Group in Women's Liberation*. New York: Times Change Press, 1970.
Altbach, Edith H. (ed.). *From Feminism to Liberation*. Cambridge: Schenkman, 1971.
Beale, Frances. "Double Jeopardy: To Be Black and Female." In D. Babcox and M. Belkin (eds.), *Liberation Now: Writings from the Women's Liberation Movement* (New York: Dell, 1971), pp 185-196.
Benston, Margaret. "The Political Economy of Women's Liberation." *Monthly Review*, 21 (1969):13-27.
Carden, Maren Lockwood. *The New Feminist Movement*. New York: Russell Sage Foundation, 1974.
Deckard, Barbara. *The Women's Movement*. New York: Harper & Row, 1975.
Evans, Sara. "The Origins of the Women's Liberation Movement." *Radical America*, 9 (1975): 1-12.
Freeman, Jo. *The Politics of Women's Liberation*. New York: David McKay, 1975.
Garskoff, M. H. (ed.). *Roles Women Play: Readings Toward Women's Liberation*. Belmont: Brooks/Coles, 1971.
Goldschmidt, Jean; Gergen, Mary; Quigley, Karen; and Gergen, Kenneth. "The Women's Liberation Movement: Attitudes and Action." *Journal of Personality*, 42 (1974): 601-16.
Hole, Judith, and Levine, Ellen (eds.). *Rebirth of Feminism*. New York: Quadrangle, 1971.
Huber, Joan; Rexroat, Cynthia; and Spitze, Glenna. "A Crucible of Opinion on Women's Status: ERA in Illinois." *Social Forces*, 57 (1978):forthcoming.
Koedt, Anne; Levine, Ellen; and Rapone, Anita (eds.). *Radical Feminism*. New York: Quadrangle, 1973.
Kraditor, Aileen S. *The Ideas of the Woman Suffrage Movement, 1890-1920*. New York: Columbia University Press, 1965.
Mandle, Joan D. "Attitudes Toward the Women's Liberation Movement and their Correlates: A Case Study of Undergraduate Women." Ph.D. diss., Bryn Mawr College, 1974.
_____. "Undergraduate Activists in the Women's Movement and their Public Attitudes Towards Marriage and the Family." *Sociological Focus*, 8 (1975):257-69.
_____. "Women's Liberation: Humanizing Rather than Polarizing." American Academy of Political and Social Sciences, *Annals*, 397 (1971):118-28.
Morgan, Robin (ed.). *Sisterhood is Powerful*. New York: Random House, 1970.
O'Neill, William L. *Everyone was Brave*. Chicago: Quadrangle, 1969.
_____. *The Woman Movement: Feminism in the United States and England*. Chicago: Quadrangle, 1969.
Rowbotham, Sheila. *Women, Resistance and Revolution*. New York: Vintage, 1974.
Stoloff, Carolyn. "Who Joins Women's Liberation?" *Psychiatry*, 36 (1973):325-40.
Thompson, Mary Lou (ed.). *Voices of the New Feminism*. Boston: Beacon, 1970.
Welch, Susan. "Support Among Women for the Issues of the Women's Movement." *Sociological Quarterly*, 16 (1975):216-27.
Worell, Judith and Leonard. "Support and Opposition to the Women's Liberation Movement: Some Personality and Parental Correlates." *Journal of Research in Personality*, 11 (1977):10-20.

Indexes

AUTHOR INDEX

SUBJECT INDEX